DAY TRIPS
TO
JEWISH HISTORY

Libi Astaire

ASTER PRESS

First Published 2013
Revised 2020
Copyright: ©2013, 2020 Libi Astaire

Cover photos:
London's Great Synagogue: Drawing and engraving by Augustus
Pugin and Thomas Rowlandson; aquatint by Thomas Sunderland;
The Microcosm of London, Volume 3, by Rudolph Ackermann, 1809.
Close up of a Book/Challah: © Cottonbro/pexels.com
Girona Street/Kuzmir Headstones/Tiveria Street Sign: © Libi
Astaire

ISBN: 978-0-9885809-2-3

Published and distributed by:
Aster Press
Kansas-Jerusalem
asterpressbooks@gmail.com

Many of the essays in this book first appeared in *Mishpacha Magazine*, www.mishpacha.com, in a modified form. They reflect my interest, both as a journalist and a writer of historical novels, in some of the lesser-known byways of Jewish history and life.

Contents

THE EXPULSION FROM SPAIN
AND THE *ANUSIM*

In the Footsteps of the Ramban:
A Visit to Jewish Catalonia

Spain is a country that is rich in Jewish history. Yet there is only one region that had the distinction of having within its borders a city crowned with the title A Mother City in Israel: Catalonia.

The Catalans call it *rauxa*. Normally a down-to-earth, hard-working people who take pride in their *seny* (common sense), every once in a while they get what's called a *cop de rauxa* — a spontaneous burst of creative inspiration that hurtles them out of their ordinary lives and into the unexpected and the unknown.

I don't think that *rauxa* is on the world's list of highly contagious diseases, but perhaps it should be. For how else can I explain what happened during the summer of 2007, when I was looking for a simple, no-nonsense round-trip flight from Tel Aviv to Kansas City, Missouri that had decent connections and a reasonable price — and instead found myself mesmerized by an itinerary that offered a free stopover in what is the heart of *rauxa* country: Barcelona.

I think I can say with full honesty that before that moment it had never ever occurred to me to go to Barcelona. Yet once I saw the word, something clicked in my mind and wouldn't stop clicking. Barcelona is the capital of Catalonia, an autonomous region located in the northeastern corner of Spain. Thanks to my love of old maps of the Holy Land, I knew that Catalonia was the home of the famous Jewish mapmaker Avraham Cresques, whose fourteenth-century masterpiece, the *Catalan Atlas*, is one of the most spectacular maps of the world created during the Middle Ages. However, Catalonia has another and greater distinction, for it is home to a city that was once so full of Torah learning and so steeped with holiness that it was crowned with the title of "A Mother City in Israel," the highest praise that the Jewish people can bestow upon a place outside of the Land of Israel. In short, Catalonia is the home of Girona.

For those who know and love medieval Jewish history, the name Girona sends shivers down the spine. This is the city where Rabbeinu Yonah, author of *Sha'arei Teshuvah* (*The Gates of Repentance*), lived and taught Torah. It is the city where such luminaries as Rabbi Azriel, Rabbi Ezra ben Shlomo, and Rabbi Yaakov ben Sheshet established one of Spain's most important schools of *Kabbalah*. And last, but certainly not least, it is the city of the Ramban (Nachmanides), who lived there almost all his life, serving as the leader of Girona's Jewish community, as well as leader of all of Spanish Jewry, until he was forced to flee, at an advanced age, from his beloved birthplace.

What was it about the city of Girona that it merited all this glory, and would it still be possible to catch a glimpse of its former greatness? Would it be possible, I wondered, to walk in the footsteps of the Ramban, Rabbeinu Yonah, and all the other illustrious Torah sages who had called Girona home? Or had everything been destroyed after the Expulsion of the Jews from Spain in 1492?

After a little research, it seemed that it was possible. According to most sources, Girona, which is only about an hour's drive north of Barcelona, has one of the best-preserved Jewish Quarters in Spain. Yet still I resisted. Common sense told me that Catalonia, a region where kosher food is scarce and English is barely spoken, is not exactly a first-choice destination for the Torah-observant traveler. However, it was a photograph of a narrow passageway in Girona's Jewish Quarter that proved to be the nemesis of my saner self. Its steep stone steps winding upward seemed to beckon me to follow them back to a purer, more intensely spiritual time. Before I knew it, the deed had been done. I was booked on the flight to Barcelona.

Glimpses of a Golden Age

Legend has it that Jews established trading posts in Spain as early as the time of King Solomon, but solid data about Jewish communities only begins to appear in the third century. By the tenth century, Jews were actively engaged in economic and political life throughout the Iberian Peninsula, including in Catalonia. Whereas other parts of Spain experienced Golden Ages as early as the eleventh and twelfth centuries—and Catalonia and neighboring Aragon became united during this period—Catalonia's moment of glory reached its zenith during the thirteenth century. During the long reign of King Jaume I, known as the Conqueror, Barcelona was transformed into a major port city and Catalan ships ruled the profitable waters of the Mediterranean Sea.

The fortunes of Catalan Jews rose along with the fortunes of their fellow countrymen. Jaume I highly valued his Jewish merchants, who set up lucrative trading networks in both the Muslim countries of northern Africa and the Christian countries of southern Europe, filling the king's coffers in the process. Jews could also be found at the king's court, where they served as financial advisors, court secretaries, and doctors. He also offered protection to all the Jews who settled in his territory, a policy that was continued by his successors, and the map of Catalonia became dotted with dozens of Jewish communities. In practical terms, this protection meant that the Jews were "owned" by the crown. They paid taxes only to the king, and their fellow countrymen were not allowed to physically harm them, since they belonged to the king. However, Catalan towns were not entirely without power and they exercised this power in the end of the thirteenth century by forcing the Jews, whom they often eyed with jealousy and suspicion, to live in their own area of town, which was called a *juderia*.

Yet despite the ghettoization and other restrictions that limited their contact with non-Jews, and the high taxation, the 1200s and early 1300s were relatively good times for Catalan Jews. They were free to practice their religion and they were self-governed by a council called an *aljama*, which was comprised of distinguished members of their own community. They were able to build synagogues, *yeshivos* (Torah academies), Talmud Torah schools for the children, *mikva'os* (ritual baths), and shelters for the poor. Even the decree issued by the fourth Lateran Council, which stated that Jews must wear distinctive dress, was largely ignored in Catalonia— at a price, of course, since the Jews had to purchase their exemption.

Although not all of Catalonia's Jews were wealthy merchants— in fact most of them were artisans and simple craftsmen—there must have been more than a few. This is the period, after all, that saw the creation of Catalan illuminated masterpieces such as the

Golden Haggadah, the *Barcelona Haggadah*, and the *Sarajevo Haggadah*, all of which were probably created in Barcelona in the first half of the fourteenth century. However, the Jewish community's riches were not limited to only material goods. The thirteenth and fourteenth centuries were also the Golden Age of Torah scholarship in Catalonia, and it was during this period that the Ramban and Rabbeinu Yonah flourished in Girona, while their student Rabbi Shlomo ben Aderet, known as the Rashba, was a leader in Barcelona.

And what is left of all this life? What could I expect to see in modern-day Catalonia? I knew better than to ask about the whereabouts of the famous Passover *haggados*, which left Spain's shores in 1492, if not before. Both the *Golden Haggadah* and the *Barcelona Haggadah* are now sitting in the British Museum in London, while the *Sarajevo Haggadah* is in Sarajevo, where it is on display at the National Museum of Bosnia and Herzegovina.But what about the buildings? Would it be possible to sit in the yeshivah where the Ramban expounded upon the Torah and pray in the synagogue where Rabbeinu Yonah stood before his Maker? Now that I was in Girona, it was time to find out.

El Call

By the time I unpacked and dug out my digital camera, it was already early evening—which turned out to be a perfect time for a first visit to Girona's historic district. The heat of the day had passed and the fading sunlight was casting a gentle glow upon the brightly painted houses that stand guard upon the banks of the Onyar River.

Once, these houses stood flush against the wall that protected the medieval city from invaders, but as the city began to expand and new neighborhoods were built, the wall came down. On this day in early summer, the only "invaders" traversing the river were a mother duck and her ducklings, who lazily paddled through the water—and, of course, the tourists, who, like me, were crossing the bridges connecting the old city to the new, in search of Girona's medieval quarter.

Strategically placed street signs pointed the way to El Call, the name most commonly used today to designate the Jewish Quarters found in Catalan towns. It was the word "call" that provided me with my first encounter with Catalonia's sometimes ambivalent feelings about its Jewish past. Why, I wondered, was this particular word used in Catalonia, and not the more common *juderia*, which is used throughout the rest of Spain? And what does the word "call" mean, anyway?

Ask a non-Jew in Girona—and since there aren't any Jews living in Girona today non-Jews are the only ones you can ask—and they will immediately reply that it comes from the Latin word *callis*, which means a narrow street. A tour guide or guidebook will fill in a little more information. Because the Jews had to live within a contained area, as their population grew they had to find creative ways to house the new members of their community. One solution was to cover sections of the street and build houses on top of the covered passageway. Another solution was to build out into the street as far as possible, which added space to the homes, but turned the streets into cramped alleyways.

If you happen to ask the question while visiting a Call, this will seem like a plausible explanation. The streets certainly are very narrow—even narrower than you will find in other parts of the town dating from the same period. So the case is closed, you might be tempted to think. "El Call" means the place of narrow and winding lanes.

However, go to Barcelona, where there is a small Jewish community, and ask someone from there about the word's meaning and more likely than not they will roll their eyes and laugh. "The word 'call' comes from the Hebrew word *kahal* (community or congregation)," they will reply. "Everyone knows that."

In fact, the *Gran Diccionari de la Llengua Catalana* gives both definitions for the word. However, as I was to find out later, this disagreement about what the word "call" means—narrow streets of stone versus a living Jewish community—is emblematic of a larger disagreement between some members of Barcelona's Jewish community and the non-Jewish public officials who are responsible for developing and maintaining Catalonia's Jewish Quarters.

At that moment, though, my mind wasn't concerned with present-day disagreements. This was my time to do what I had set out to do, to follow in the footsteps of the Ramban and try to discover what it is about Girona that caused the Ramban to say, "I left my soul and spirit here."

As I made my way down Carrer de la Forca, which was once one of the Call's main streets and marked its western boundary, my thoughts were already going back in time. Today, Forca Street is a pleasant pedestrian thoroughfare that is lined with upscale shops, but it's not the store windows that attracted my attention. Spontaneously, my eyes shifted to the doorposts, searching for some hint of an indentation on the right side of the shop's door.

An indentation, of course, is the telltale sign that a *mezuzah*—a small parchment scroll with verses from the Torah—once sat within the doorpost and that this was once a Jewish-owned store or home, or perhaps even the portal to the thirteenth-century synagogue that once stood on this street, but whose exact location has since been forgotten.

I was not alone in this endeavor, I discovered, when I met an Israeli couple. They too were searching the doorposts for some signs of Girona's once rich Jewish life. In fact, *mezuzah* hunting seems to be a favorite activity for just about all Jewish tourists who come to Catalonia, no matter where they are from or what their affiliation may be. However, neither I nor the Israeli couple had any luck. I will only "hit the jackpot" when I go to nearby Besalu and visit the home that once belonged to the Astruc family, one of medieval Catalonia's wealthiest and most influential families.

I gave up my search when I reached the street that is today called Carrer de Sant Llorence. This is the street I had seen in the photograph. As I stepped into the covered passageway, which was dark and tinted a gloomy gray at this hour, a shiver once again went down my spine. At this quiet hour, it was not impossible to imagine a robed and hooded figure rushing down the steep stairs, on his way to synagogue for the afternoon prayer service.

But even though I waited silently for a few minutes, no sounds of Jewish prayer greeted my ears. Only the creak of a shutter turning in the wind disturbed the early evening's silence. I therefore let my eyes follow the steps upward and I began the long climb up to the top. The street became narrower and narrower, but as I climbed a sliver of light began to peek through the roof tops. Then the light widened and intensified, and when I reached the top, which is close to the eastern boundary of the Call, I had left the darkness behind.

Perhaps it's trite, and probably I'm 100 percent wrong, but after climbing the 63 steps of Carrer Sant Llorence, I began to feel that it was obvious why Girona became a home for Jewish mysticism. Spiritual concepts such as "running and returning," "going from darkness to light," or "you're either going up the spiritual ladder or going down it," surely become more concrete and easier to internalize when you have to walk up or down 63 steps every time you go to synagogue or need to buy a little milk.

However, Catalonia, like other parts of Spain, is not all cold, grey stones and dark passageways. About halfway up the steps, there was a wrought-iron gate sitting within the right side of the wall. Through it I could catch a glimpse of the other side of Catalonia—a place of pleasant courtyards and beautifully landscaped gardens, where people could come to meet and share their joys. I had also come to the first place where there was a physical sign of a Jewish presence within the Jewish Call. I had reached the Museu Dels Jueus—Girona's Museum of the History of the Jewish People. There, embedded in the floor tiles of the museum's outdoor courtyard was a large *Magen David* (Star of David), proudly displaying its Jewish identity for all passersby to see.

A quick glance at my watch told me that the museum had closed a few minutes earlier. I would have to come back to continue my search for some tangible reminder of the past glory of Jewish Girona.

ii.

When I mentioned to my friends that I was going to Girona, I was met with a blank stare. Unlike Eastern European cities such as Prague or Warsaw, Girona doesn't have instant name recognition, not even among Torah-observant Jews.

"It's in Spain," I tried to explain.

"Ah, Spain," they replied.

But by the half-hearted sound of their voices I knew they still didn't understand. Although Girona has one of the best preserved Jewish Quarters in Europe, making it the jewel in the crown of Jewish Catalonia, the entire Jewish Quarter consists of just six narrow streets that form a rectangle in the heart of Girona's historic district. For the visitor on the run, the whole thing can be viewed in less than an hour.

I, however, was not in a rush. While doing research before the trip, I had come across several claims that had piqued my curiosity and I wanted to determine the veracity of these reports. More than one account had said that the place of the Ramban's yeshivah had been located and was now the site of a Jewish museum. Others talked about a treasure trove of medieval Hebrew documents that had been discovered within the bindings of old books dating from the fourteenth and fifteenth centuries.

What was true and what was false? To find out I made my way to the Centre Bonastruc ca Porta, the organization that operates the Museum of the History of the Jewish People, as well as the Nahmanides Institute for Jewish Studies. In an office overlooking the courtyard with the large *Magen David* I had seen the day before, I met with Mrs. Assumpcio Hosta Rebes, the Director of the Centre, who is also the Secretary General of the Red De Juderias De Espana (the Network of Spanish Jewish Quarters).

Mrs. Hosta has been with the project to reclaim Girona's Call since it began in the 1970s. In those days, Girona's historic district was a rundown area where only poor people lived. But as happened in many cities throughout the world, a few artists decided to leave Girona's newer and more expensive neighborhoods and set up their studios in the old part of town. Restaurateurs and shopkeepers followed, and one of them, a man named Jose Tarres, became convinced that the group of buildings he had purchased had formally been the site of Girona's Jewish Call.

At first, the Girona municipality was unconvinced, since no one had any solid proof about where the Call had been located. Some believe that when the Jews left Girona, they boarded up the windows and doors of their homes, hoping that one day they would be able to return and reclaim their property. It's also been suggested that the *anusim*, Jews who were forcibly converted to Christianity during the Middle Ages, moved to other neighborhoods, afraid that if they remained in the Call they would be accused of secretly practicing Judaism—a crime that came with a penalty of violent death during the days of the Inquisition.

For whatever reason, as the city changed and expanded, the memory of the Call grew dim. But once the idea of finding the lost Call was in the air, archeologists and historians began to search through the documents stored in Girona's archives. When solid evidence was found, the skepticism turned to belief and belief turned to commitment. Girona's mayor at that time, a history professor named Joaqim Nadal, asked a former student of his—Mrs. Hosta—to take charge of the project to rehabilitate the Jewish Quarter. The city couldn't afford to purchase all the property in the Call, which was, and still is, owned by private citizens, and so they concentrated their efforts on acquiring one central building.

"We started the project very slowly," Mrs. Hosta explained. "The houses in the Call go inside and out, meaning that our building has some little spaces that go underneath the houses belonging to our neighbors, and some of our neighbors live in parts of our building. That's the way the houses were in the Middle Ages. Also, some streets even went through the house itself. We know of a street here, within our building, which was a covered street within the house so that people could walk through it to the synagogue, for example, without having to go into a main street. That happens often in medieval Spain."

Tracking down the owners of all these "in and out" spaces took Mrs. Hosta almost four years. But finally the City of Girona and the County Council were able to purchase the property where the Centre now sits and start rehabilitating it. Today the building, with its beautifully landscaped courtyard, is an inviting place that houses the Jewish museum, whose exhibits and cultural activities attract approximately 100,000 people annually.

Many of these visitors are children, and Mrs. Hosta comments, "All of Girona's schools come once a year. We also have the schools from Barcelona and the surrounding areas."

The building is also the home of a research center which has a small library and offers classes in Hebrew and lectures on Jewish topics. However, according to Mrs. Hosta, 30 years ago a very different sight would have greeted a visitor to Girona.

"When we came to this building at the end of the 1970s, the lower part of the site had been abandoned," she said. "It was a ruin. People lived on the upper floors, in very modest apartments, but the area where the patio is today was filled with debris. The fact that the people living here didn't have any money to invest in renovating their homes was actually very fortunate. It meant that there was no money to destroy the medieval structures."

From information gleaned from historical documents, Mrs. Hosta could say with certainty that the building in which we were sitting was once a communal building which had a synagogue, and probably a Talmud Torah and *mikvah*, as well.

"But we don't know where the synagogue was located," she commented. "There are several areas in the building that have never been touched. When we will be able to excavate under the patio, we will probably find out much more.

"But we are talking about the last moments of the Call," she added, "the fifteenth century. A city is always changing."

My mouth drops open. Fifteenth century? So late? What about the many articles I had read that said that this building was located on the spot where the Ramban's thirteenth-century yeshivah had once stood?

"It's not true. We don't know where the Ramban's yeshivah was located," said Mrs. Hosta. "We hope that one day we will find it, but what's happening is that during the last three or four years several writers have written novels about Girona's medieval history and, as is happening all over the world, people are mixing facts with fiction. But we try to be very careful about our information. As soon as we know exactly where the Ramban's yeshivah was located, it will be something very special for Girona."

Disappointed, but not deterred, I next asked about what sort of artifacts were discovered during the renovations. I had written an article for *Mishpacha Magazine* where I mentioned a fifteenth-century ceramic Passover Seder plate found in Spain that had caused a sensation, since it was the oldest surviving Seder plate in the world, to date. If Girona had uncovered something similar, this would also be something "very special" for the city.

But even before I asked the question, I had a feeling it was unlikely. During a visit to the museum earlier that morning I couldn't help but notice that, except for some *mezuzos* and a collection of gravestones taken from the Jewish cemetery on nearby Montjuic (Mountain of the Jews), the vast majority of the items on display was either reproductions or came from places like Morocco or Tunisia.

Unfortunately, Mrs. Hosta confirmed my doubts. They haven't found a Seder plate or *Kiddush* cup, "but we do have some pieces that are currently being studied by the archeologists."

If a ceramic plate or cup was too fragile to survive, surely a book was made of sturdier stuff. So, batting zero, I made one last attempt to locate some tangible reminder of Girona's once glorious past. What about the hidden documents, I asked? The medieval documents in Hebrew that were found stashed inside the bindings of some old books? At last, I hit a home run.

The Hidden Documents

"We found more than 1,000 documents, both in Hebrew and Latin," explained Mrs. Hosta, "which are now stored in the Arxiu Historic de Girona (Historical Archives of Girona). We've already cleaned 368 documents, but it's a very time-consuming job because many of the documents were pressed together and had to be taken apart very carefully, one by one.

"We have translated only a few of them. They mainly pertain to daily life in the Jewish community—marriages, financial transactions, and things like that. Translating them isn't easy, because we need people who know medieval Hebrew and can translate them into Catalan."

Although there are a few people at the University of Girona who could do the job, their busy schedules haven't allowed them to translate more than 20 or 30 documents. It was only recently that the city found someone who was able to work on the project full time. While the translation of the first set of documents begins in earnest, the city hopes to start cleaning and photographing the next batch of 300 documents. The goal is to eventually place all the documents on a website devoted to the project, which is partially funded by the Hanadiv Charitable Foundation located in London, so that researchers and academics around the world can have easy access to them and start analyzing their contents.

Fifteen documents from the first batch have already been uploaded. About half pertain to the daily life of the Call, while the rest are fragments of pages from the Talmud, commentaries on the Talmud, and prayers.

"Our aim is to know what is inside these documents," Mrs. Hosta continued. "We do all our research through using documents. There is no other way. The history of the city is basically in the archives. From the documents stored in Girona and in Barcelona we have been able to learn a lot about the everyday life in medieval Girona that we didn't know before."

At this point it is worth mentioning that the archives in Barcelona and Girona are filled with documents in Latin and Catalan from the medieval period, including notarial documents that shed light on the day-to-day business affairs of the people. Historian Robert I. Burns, in his book *Jews in the Notarial Culture: Latinate Wills in Mediterranean Spain, 1250-1350* (Berkeley: University of California Press, 1996), compares the role of the medieval notary to that of the lawyer so ubiquitous in today's American society. The need for official documentation of transfers of property, deposits, loans, bills of lading, etc., as well as marriage contracts and wills, was a natural consequence of Catalonia's flourishing maritime trading empire. The proceeds of disputes which ended up in court, including the cases brought before the court of the Inquisition, were also painstakingly written down and entered into the communal records.

Historians have been flocking to these archives for more than a century. By sifting through the documents, a narrative begins to unfold. However, it is a story that is often tangled and incomplete, and is therefore open to interpretation. A case in point is the identity of the person who has lent his name to the name of the Centre Bonastruc ca Porta. According to nineteenth-century Jewish historians Heinrich Graetz and Joseph Jacobs, Bonastruc ca Porta is actually the Catalan name of Girona's most famous citizen—the Ramban, whose full Jewish name is Moshe ben Nachman.

The practice of having a Catalan name was very common for Catalan Jews during the Middle Ages, who had many interactions with the non-Jewish world. The Catalan name was used in business, etc., while the Hebrew name was used in the home and synagogue. The Catalan name would often have some connection to the person's Hebrew name, but not always. Therefore, even though the name "Bonastruc" can be translated as "good fortune" and doesn't seem to have a connection to the name "Moshe," that doesn't disqualify the evidence.

Thanks to the fact that Jacobs, who spent a month in Barcelona studying documents, stated his theory in an article for the influential *Jewish Encyclopedia*, published in 1906, the idea took hold and it became commonly assumed that Bonastruc ca Porta was the

Ramban's Catalan name. It should not come as a surprise, though, that there are historians who disagree with this interpretation of the documents. I therefore asked Mrs. Hosta for her opinion of the matter, wondering if the Centre had uncovered any conclusive evidence during their research.

"There are two theories about the name," she answered diplomatically. "One is that the Ramban and Bonastruc ca Porta is the same person. The second theory is that they are two separate people. But we don't know which theory is correct."

Even though there is an abundance of documents in Latin and Catalan, documents in Hebrew are considerably rarer. Therefore, there was considerable excitement when these documents were first discovered. Whether or not they will shed further light on the Ramban's life, and other matters pertaining to the Call, remains to be seen. But if the goal is to spread awareness, my next question is obvious. How can I see the documents?

Although a tourist can't visit the archives, Mrs. Hosta agreed to take me there. It took just one short phone call to make the arrangements, since the director of the archives, Mrs. Montserrat Hosta, just happened to be her sister. A few minutes later, I was holding in my hands a folder that had the year "1397" written across the top. Since her sister was on vacation, it was Mrs. Hosta who provided the background for how the documents were found.

"Three years ago, when they were moving the archive, the bindings of some of the books came open," she explained. "They discovered that documents in Hebrew and Latin had been used to pad the bindings. Because paper and parchment were very expensive during the Middle Ages, it was common for them to be recycled and used for other things, such as filler for bookbinders. It was like finding a treasure."

They sent a small batch of documents to Madrid for cleaning. When it took two years for them to get the documents back, they decided they would have to find another way to do the job. An institution in Israel offered to do the work for them, but when the Israeli institution insisted on retaining possession of the documents afterward, Girona turned down the offer.

"We didn't want to give them up," said Mrs. Hosta. "It's part of Girona's heritage."

Whose History Is It?

I stared at the fragment of a document that I was holding in my hands. On the page was written, in large letters, the Hebrew word *Selicha* — Forgive. What followed appeared to be a prayer. Was it a part of medieval Girona's version of the *Selichos* service — prayers of forgiveness — that are recited before *Rosh Hashanah* by Jews throughout the world? Or was it a personal entreaty written long ago by some unknown Jew who needed to receive forgiveness from a family member, business colleague, or his Creator?

Unfortunately, I didn't have time to decipher the unfamiliar cursive script. But at that moment we had stumbled upon a question that had been bubbling under the surface during my entire stay in Catalonia: Who does the Call — and its rich Jewish history — belong to? Who decides how its story, with all its nuances and room for interpretation, will be told?

It is not a purely academic question, I learned, when I traveled to Barcelona. There, in Barcelona's Call, I had an appointment to meet with a Jewish man who practically single-handedly restored a medieval synagogue in that city's Jewish Quarter. And it is in Barcelona that I would hear about the other Call. Not the Call of the silent narrow lanes and stone walls, but the Call of the *kehal* — Barcelona's modern-day Jewish community, which of course had something to say about the future of the Call's past.

iii.

It has been said that the Jews from Spain were different from other Jews. Unlike other Western European Jews who were continually uprooted from their homes and expelled from their host countries, Jews had been living on the Iberian Peninsula for more than a thousand years by the time they were expelled in 1492. And so, despite the terrible persecutions that occurred during the last few hundred years of that sojourn, the saying about the generation of Jews who left Egypt during the Exodus could be said about Spain's Jews, as well: You can take the Jews out of Spain, but you can't take Spain out of the Jews.

I was thinking these thoughts as I traveled from Girona to Barcelona. My journey was similar, in some ways, to the journey that the Ramban made more than 700 years ago, when he was ordered by King Jaume I to come to Barcelona and take part in a religious Disputation with a Jewish apostate by the name of Pablo Christiani.

Of course, I was traveling comfortably in an air-conditioned train and for me the trip from Girona took just 90 minutes. Still, I wondered if the view that was unfolding through my window was that much different. The Catalan countryside can be described in two words: postcard perfect. In the distance were the majestic Pyrenees Mountains, the mountain range that forms the border between Spain and France. Closer, and giving the landscape a softer contour, was a string of gently rolling hills. Some of the hills were covered in green, as this is an area blessed with abundant forests. Others had small, picturesque medieval towns carved into their side which, at least from a distance, looked impossibly unspoiled.

At the foot of the hills was a fertile valley that appeared, by turn, a golden brown or a lush green, depending upon what crop had been planted—wheat or grape vines, with a field of sunflowers thrown in here and there for good measure. To complete the scene were the solitary farmhouses that stood guard over the fields. Solidly built from the brown stone that is characteristic of the region, they lent an air of down-to-earth stability to an agricultural scene that is by nature always changing. It was all a serenely beautiful tribute to the Master Artist Who created it – and it was easy to understand why Spain's Jews loved this country so much and found it so difficult to leave.

However, I doubt that the Ramban paid too much attention to the wheat fields and the farmhouses on the summer day that he traveled to Barcelona. Unlike me, he surely had much weightier matters on his mind as he made his way to Catalonia's bustling capital city.

Hello, Columbus

After my train pulled into the station at Passeig de Gracia, I switched to Barcelona's efficient subway system and within minutes I was at a stop named Drassanes. This was the site of Barcelona's vast shipyards during medieval times, when Catalonia ruled the waters of the Mediterranean Sea. It wasn't the shipyards, though, I had come to see. My destination was the monument to Christopher Columbus, whose likeness soars 200 feet above Barcelona's Port Vell (Old Port).Columbus didn't set sail from this spot on his historic voyage in 1492. Most historians believe that the port city Palos, located in a southwestern Spanish province called Huelva, received that honor. But this is the spot where Columbus stepped ashore in 1493, after discovering the American continent, and so this is where Catalonia erected a monument in his honor in 1888, for the city's Universal Exhibition.

I usually try to avoid touristy sites like this one. However, this monument—a grandiose tribute in bronze to confused identity and ambiguous interpretation—is for me a symbol of everything that I find both fascinating and frustrating about Catalonia. Therefore, I handed over two Euros and took the cramped elevator up to the tiny observation deck.

At the time of the Universal Exhibition, Catalans claimed Columbus as one of their own. They were wrong—Columbus wasn't born in Catalonia—but even today Columbus's origins remain a mystery. There is even a theory that he was the child of Jews who were forcibly baptized by the Catholic Church. Even if he wasn't, he certainly must have felt comfortable in their company— and the company of Spanish Jews who had managed to remain true to their faith—because the records of his famous expedition are filled with their names.

For instance, Don Yitzchak Abrabanel, the famed Torah scholar and diplomat who had great influence at the court of Ferdinand and Isabella, championed Columbus's cause. Luis de Torres, who was baptized just a few days before the ships set sail, was the expedition's interpreter. And Avraham Zacuto, a Jewish scientist and mathematician who built the first metal astrolabe, served as one of Columbus's nautical advisors.

In addition to the mistake about Columbus's nationality, there is something else wrong with the monument. When Columbus disembarked from his ship, his destination was the Royal Palace in the Barri Gothic (Old Quarter), where he was given a triumphant reception by Ferdinand and Isabella. Yet the statute of Columbus stands so that the navigator has his back to Barcelona and the Royal

Palace. Neither is he facing the continent he discovered. Instead, as more than one person has noted, the navigator is facing southeast — and rather emphatically pointing toward Jerusalem.

No reason is given in the guidebooks for this anomaly, but a theory has been suggested for why so many prominent Jews and "New Christians" were so enthusiastic about Columbus's expedition: They were hoping he would find an escape route, and a safe refuge, for the hundreds of thousands of Jews who were facing an increasingly uncertain future in Spain.

The harbor was peaceful as I stood on the observation deck and tried to maneuver my digital camera through a small opening in the rain-spotted glass, so I could take a picture of the Old Port below. In the heyday of medieval Catalonia's maritime-based prosperity, the busy port would have been filled with merchant ships laden with silks and spices and other luxury items. Watching from the wharf would be Jewish and Christian merchants, who often jointly financed trading expeditions and became jointly enriched upon their successful return.

Those were the good times. The scene would dramatically change, however, on Tisha B'Av (July 31) of 1492, the date when the Jews were expelled from Spain. On that sad day, Port Vell would have been filled with rickety, rat-infested ships setting sail into the unknown.

I turned to the right and I saw Barcelona's Montjuic, an imposing mountain which is the site of Barcelona's medieval Jewish cemetery — and the last thing the expelled Jews would have seen as the Catalan coastline receded from view. Completing the panoramic tour was a view of La Rambla, the tree-lined avenue that is one of Barcelona's favorite places to see and be seen, and which reminded me that I had an appointment to keep in Barcelona's Jewish Quarter.

Be Careful What You Ask For

Although it was Girona that was called a "Mother City in Israel," because of its Torah scholarship and piety, it was Barcelona — the seat of Catalan government and commerce — that was considered to be the most important center of medieval Jewish Catalonia.

By the thirteenth century, Barcelona's original Jewish Quarter, today called the Major Call, couldn't house the growing population and so a Menor (Smaller) Call was built nearby. With only six or seven streets apiece, neither Call was very big. However, those streets were filled with a vibrant Jewish life.

The most outstanding leader of the Call was Rabbi Shlomo ben Aderet, the Rashba, who was considered to be the foremost rabbinic authority of his day. Other notables from Barcelona were Rabbi Nissim ben Reuven Gerondi (the Ran), Rabbi Isaac ben Sheshet Perfet (the Rivash), and Rabbi Hasdai ben Avraham Cresces, who wrote an account of the tragic events of 1391, when thousands of Jews were killed in bloody rampages against almost all of Spain's Jewish Quarters, and tens of thousands were dragged to churches and forcibly baptized.

The attacks that occurred in 1391 didn't come out of the blue. As in so many places, the success of Spain's Jews turned out to be their downfall. Having lived in Spain for more than a thousand years, the Jews spoke the same language, wore the same styles of dress, and felt perfectly at home with the Christians they did business with. To put an end to the ease with which the Jews intermingled with Christian society, during the thirteenth century the Church issued a series of edicts that served to separate, degrade, and marginalize the Jews, such as forcing them to live in separate neighborhoods and wear a distinctive badge on their clothing.

The Church also tried to take care of the "Jewish problem" by enticing the Jews to abandon their faith, and during this era a new "fad" took hold of Europe—the Disputation. In these religious debates a Christian (who was sometimes a Jewish apostate) was paired against a prominent rabbi. The point was to prove that the Jewish sacred texts themselves proved that the Messiah had already come. For the Jews, it was a lose-lose situation. If they lost the debate, the Jews would be forced to abandon their faith. If they won, the community would be at the mercy of the angry Christian mob.

The first Disputations were held in France, but it wasn't long before they swept over the Pyrenees and into Spain. In July of the year 1263, the Ramban was summoned to Barcelona's Royal Palace to engage in a four-day debate with the Dominican monk and Jewish apostate Pablo Christiani.

The Ramban won the debate, and King Jaume I—who according to most accounts was relatively good to the Jews who lived in his kingdom—went so far as to declare that he had never before heard an "unjust cause so nobly defended." But there are some historians who say that this Disputation signaled the beginning of the end for Spanish Jewry.

After the Disputation the Dominicans, who were becoming an increasingly powerful force in all parts of the Iberian Peninsula, claimed that they had won the debate. To refute this claim, the Ramban published an account of the debate in *Sefer HaVikuach* (*Book of the Dispute*). The Dominicans charged that there were certain sections in the Ramban's written account that were blasphemous and demanded that the Ramban be punished. To appease them, Jaume I ordered that the Ramban go into exile for two years and that the book be burned. However, the Dominicans weren't satisfied, and they forced the king to change the sentence to perpetual banishment. The Ramban fled Catalonia and eventually settled in the Land of Israel, where he lived until he passed away in the year 1270.

Jaume I died in 1276, and the next century was a period of economic decline for the Jews—and for all of Catalonia. In addition to years of famine, disease, and war, there were several bank failures, which ruined Barcelona's economy. All this led to sporadic attacks upon the Calls. The waters of the dam burst in 1391, when angry peasants stormed Calls throughout Spain and Catalonia, totally destroying many of them—including the Calls of Girona and Barcelona. Thousands of Jews were killed, and tens of thousands were forcibly baptized. According to Rabbi Cresces, the vast majority of Girona's Jews chose death over conversion. In Barcelona, there were some Jews who chose death—including Cresces's only son, who was about to be married—but the vast majority of Barcelona's Jews became "New Christians."

At first, the Church was overjoyed with its success. But there is an old saying that warns: Be careful what you ask for, because you just might get it. And, indeed, the mass conversions of 1391 created an identity crisis in Spain. The mass conversions created two types of New Christians, who were often referred to as *conversos*. Some were Christian in name only. They secretly continued to practice Judaism and kept up their ties with the Jewish community. They are the ones who are known in Hebrew as *anusim*, which means "forced ones." Many of them fled Spain as soon as they had an opportunity to do so and rejoined the Jewish faith. Others, however, completely severed their ties with Judaism, although it was more out of a desire to protect their lives and fortunes than out of enthusiasm for their new religion. They often intermarried with "Old Christians" and continued to amass wealth and hold positions of influence.

The Church began to worry that the apathy of these new converts, who could now move with complete freedom throughout Christian society, would have a negative influence on the Old Christians. This is why, according to several historians, the Spanish Inquisition was so much more terrible than Inquisitions in other countries; Spain was the only country that had witnessed mass conversions on such a grand scale, and so they had more "heretics" to haunt them.

The Barcelona Call Today

It's possible to visit the sites of both the Disputation and the court of the Inquisition. Both are located within the Royal Palace, which is now part of the City History Museum of Barcelona (MHCB). There's no sign to designate where the Disputation took place. But when I reached the outdoor courtyard of the palace, I heard the familiar sounds of Hebrew. A group of Israeli tourists had arrived a few minutes before me. As if on cue, as I approached the group their guide pointed out the spot.

Although the thirteenth-century structure no longer exists — it was replaced in the next century by the building still standing today — the exterior of the palace hasn't changed all that much. The courtyard where I was standing is the same courtyard that all visitors to the palace would have had to traverse, and Barcelona's Jewish community must have watched the Ramban climb up the stone steps with an anxious heart.

Next door is the Salo del Tainell, the great hall where Catalan kings were crowned and where Columbus received a triumphant welcome — and where the court of the Inquisition sat. Although a sign inside the museum tells about the coronations and fetes, there's no mention of the Inquisition and the misery that the walls of this hall have seen. The MHCB does include within its permanent exhibits a description of Jewish life in Barcelona during the Middle

Ages. It also has on display one of the Call's few remaining tangible reminders of its Jewish past, a plaque which commemorates the establishment of a poorhouse by a Rabbi Shmuel Hasardi, at No. 5 Carrer de Marlet.

This street was once the center of the Major Call, and that was my next destination. But if the Call was destroyed in 1391, what can the visitor see today? As the brochure published by the MHCB points out, very little. The streets are still there, and the buildings. However, in this relentlessly pretty city, where building after building glows with a fashionably faded Mediterranean charm, the Call's buildings stand out like a gaggle of ugly ducklings: dark, dirty, and undistinguished.

One building, which happens to be located at No. 5 Carrer de Marlet, sticks out, literally, more than the others. Jutting out into the street at an odd angle, it almost seems to be straining to see something that is going on at some point southeast. And, indeed, despite its grimy façade, this is no ordinary building. According to Miguel Iaffa, who personally restored parts of its interior, this building is none other than the Major (Great) Synagogue of the medieval Call. The reason, of course, why it is built at such a funny angle is so that it will face Jerusalem.

Despite its name, the Major Synagogue is just two small rooms, so the visitor shouldn't expect anything grand. It's also no longer a functioning synagogue, although there is an *aron kodesh* (Ark) and a Torah scroll, as well as other ritual items and pieces of artwork that give the space a Jewish feel.

Before Miguel explained how he got involved in this project, he insisted on making something clear. "I was born in Catalonia," he said empathically. "You'll understand why that's important a little later."

Miguel's father was a Lithuanian Jew who came to Catalonia in the late 1930s to fight in the Spanish Civil War against the fascists. After the war, Miguel's father married a young woman who came from an *anusim* family. Not long afterward, Miguel was born and the young family left Spain and moved to Argentina. Miguel grew up in Argentina, but he returned to Catalonia and settled in Barcelona in the 1970s.

Jews were first allowed back into Spain in the late 1880s, as part of a pledge by the government to practice religious tolerance, and synagogues were opened in Barcelona and Madrid. However, when General Francisco Franco came to power in 1939, the small Jewish communities kept a low profile. In 1968, Franco's government allowed Madrid's Jews to open a new synagogue, and at the opening ceremony the government officially repealed the Expulsion edict. To commemorate the 500th anniversary of the Expulsion in 1992, King Juan Carlos repeated the repeal in a symbolic ceremony.

Today, there are about 4,000 Jews living in Barcelona, which has the second-largest Jewish community in Spain, after Madrid. There is an Orthodox community, as well as a Reform community. Miguel is a member of the Reform community, as is the young man who served as our interpreter, Andres Fajngold, who is also from Argentina.

When the Jews returned to Barcelona, they set up residence in newer areas of Barcelona, which were far away from the Call. In fact, the memory of the Jewish Call, which had become a commercial area filled with shops and restaurants, had disappeared from public consciousness. It was only in the year 1987 that a respected Catalan historian named Jaume Riera did some government-sponsored research and published his findings.

One person who read the pamphlet with interest was Miguel, who described what happened next. "I came to this building with my compass. From the street, I could see that it had a wall facing southeast, toward Jerusalem. I thought to myself, 'Okay, I've seen what is here. Someone will now come and rehabilitate this place.' But it didn't happen. No one was interested. I never expected that I would be the one to do it."

Major Synagogue, Major Disagreement

There are a few theories as to why the Barcelona municipality didn't take action to restore the Call after Riera published his findings. For one thing, the city had been selected to host the 1992 Olympics and so it was busy preparing for the games. Another theory is that Barcelona is a big city with many attractions — including its distinctive Art Nouveau buildings — and so restoring the little Call just wasn't a priority.

Miguel had his own theory, however, about his adopted city. "Many people don't want to uncover the Jewish past that is here in

Barcelona, because they don't want to discover their own Jewish past. This isn't about anti-Semitism. It's about identity."

Whatever the real reason was, eight years after Riera's study, the Call was still waiting for someone to take an interest in it. By this time Miguel's children were grown up, and so he had time to assume that role—a role which bears something of a likeness to a modern-day Don Quixote tilting against the windmills of indifference and denial.

"The first time I saw the inside of this building was in December of 1995, and the place was in very bad shape," he continued. "A month later, I saw that there was a 'For Sale' sign. When I heard that some people wanted to buy the building and convert it into a pub, I thought to myself, 'This place cannot become a bar.'"

Miguel contacted a member of Majorca's *anusim* community, whose family had been persecuted during the Inquisition. This man loaned Miguel the money he needed to take out a mortgage and begin the renovations. However, repairing the ceiling to make the structure safe and cleaning up the site quickly used up all the money for renovations.

"One night I was thinking, 'I need another break.' And I remember feeling sure that it would happen—that God would help me."

The next morning he entered a subway car and he noticed an empty seat, which was the only one left in the car. When he sat down, he realized that he was sitting opposite the man who was then the mayor of Barcelona, Pasqual Maragall. Miguel didn't know the mayor personally, but he's not shy and so he invited the mayor to see the synagogue. The mayor agreed to go with Miguel, and by the end of the morning Barcelona's journalists were broadcasting the story of the rediscovered synagogue all over town.

However, Miguel's triumph was bittersweet. When the mayor discovered that none of the city's historians and bureaucrats had made any effort to discover the synagogue, he became very angry with them. This created bad feelings between them and Miguel, which continues to have ramifications even today. Although Miguel eventually received 77,000 Euros from the city, which allowed him to pay back the mortgage and paint the interior, there are still some influential people who don't believe that the building at 5 Carrer de Marlet is the site of the Major Synagogue. The City History Museum of Barcelona, for example, doesn't mention the synagogue in its brochure about the Call.

"I opened the site to the public in 2002 and a lot of official people visited it," said Miguel. "They came with their compasses to look around, to see if the wall is really facing southeast. But the people from the City History Museum of Barcelona continue to deny that this is the site of the synagogue. They say that because I'm from South America, I've let my imagination run wild. That's why I said in the beginning that it's important that people know that I was born in Catalonia – I am from here, just like them."

Both Miguel and Andres said that they haven't ever experienced any anti-Semitism, although Andres pointed out that since they dress like everyone else no one would know that they are Jews. According to Miguel, the synagogue has been the object of only two minor attacks during its five-year existence: a Pakistani drew a swastika on the door and once a few neo-Nazis came by and shouted some things. On the other hand, thousands of non-Jewish Catalans have visited the synagogue.

They also made a distinction between the media — which is very anti-Israel — and the people. "In 2006, the year of the war with Lebanon, you could walk in the streets as normal. No one was going to kill you," said Miguel. "And during the Intifada there was an opinion poll in Barcelona to see how the public felt. I thought that 90 percent of the people would be against Israel, but the results were half and half.

"In other parts of Spain, the results of the opinion polls were different, but this is why I say that the problem here in Barcelona is because of identity, and not because of anti-Semitism. The reason why they didn't discover that this is the location of the Major Synagogue is because they weren't interested in discovering it — and now they are too embarrassed to admit their mistake."

The disagreement about the synagogue isn't the only thing causing friction in the Call. Barcelona's municipality plans to open up a center that will provide information about the Call's history and host activities. According to a JTA news article, there are several members of Barcelona's Jewish community who are disappointed that the municipality hasn't asked for their participation in this new project or been receptive to their efforts to become involved.

Pilar Rahola, a non-Jewish former legislator from the Catalan Left Party who wrote a book in support of Israel, in which she discusses the issue of Judeophobia in Spain (she is also the person on the Barcelona city council who was responsible for getting Miguel the 77,000 Euros), is quoted in the JTA article as saying, "With respect to City Hall, the government of Barcelona, like the government of Spain, prefers 'Jewish stones' to living Jewish people."

When I asked Mrs. Hosta, who as will be recalled is the Secretary General of the Spanish Network of Jewish Quarters, the nonprofit organization responsible for restoring and promoting Spain's Jewish Quarters, about these issues, she commented, "Barcelona is only right now starting to develop their Jewish Quarter and find the pieces of the puzzle. In this puzzle, Miguel and the synagogue he opened have to be fit in. They will have to find an agreement between a private person and the municipality. I'm really convinced that this will take place soon. We have to minimize the differences in order to maximize the Jewish Quarter."

One can only hope that the argument over the identity of the little building at No. 5 Carrer de Marlet will be peacefully resolved very soon. One can also hope that the other puzzle that Miguel Iaffa mentioned, the puzzle of people's identities, will also be resolved at last. According to some estimates, there are tens of thousands of *bnei anusim* (descendants of the original crypto-Jews) living in Spain and Portugal — and there are some who believe that their 500-year exile from the Jewish people is about to come to an end.

iv.

"How can I get to Breslov?" I asked the young woman at the tourist office in Girona.

"Where?" she asked politely, but with a puzzled look on her face.

"Breslov."

"Maybe you should show me on a map."

She unfolded a map of Catalonia and I pointed to the place where I wanted to go.

"Ah, Besalu!" she said with relief.

I laughed at my mistake. Although some day I would like to see this city where the chassidic leader Rabbi Nachman of Breslov lived, it will have to wait until I make a trip to Ukraine. Yet my slip of the tongue had more to it than just a confusion of letters. Much to my surprise, I felt very much at home during my brief stay in Catalonia. The people were very friendly, and despite their lack of English everyone I asked for assistance made a heroic effort to help me get where I wanted to go.

Of course, there are some who believe that at least 50 percent of the Catalan population has some Jewish blood in them, so perhaps my feeling of being not a total stranger wasn't so farfetched. But I knew better than to openly voice those sorts of observations. The people of Girona are pretty emphatic about making the point that there aren't any Jews living in their city today. And according to Jewish law, this is absolutely true.

The young woman handed me the bus schedule for Besalu and wished me a pleasant journey. Her good wishes were fulfilled. It took just 45 minutes by air-conditioned bus to be transported back in time to this tiny medieval city that is home to one of the oldest *mikvahs* in Europe.

A *Mikvah* and a *Mezuzah*

Even for someone like me, who can get lost in an American supermarket, it's impossible to miss the stop for Besalu. Not long after the bus turns off the main highway, a large and impressive stone bridge, complete with a stone tower and a serious-looking iron gate, signals the approach to the town. In medieval times, the only way to enter Besalu was by this bridge, and visitors had to pay a fee for the privilege of doing so. Today, Besalu is much more open to strangers. A chance finding in 1964 not only turned this sleepy town into a national historic site, but also into a popular day-trip destination for tourists.

As the story goes, a factory located on the edge of town, near the Fluvia River, wanted to dig a well in its floor. To the surprise of the workers, they discovered that someone had dug out a hallow cavity in the ground long before them. Even more surprising, this hallow cavity had dozens of steps which led down to a smaller cavity. Archeologists were called in to examine the strange structure. The archeologists consulted with a few rabbis and it was agreed that they had discovered a Jewish ritual bath dating from the twelfth century, making it one of the oldest *mikvaos* in Europe and the only one of its kind that has been discovered in Spain.

Since the guided tour of the *mikvah* wasn't scheduled to begin until 1:30 pm (the door to the *mikvah* is kept locked), I decided to take a quick tour of the town's historic quarter beforehand. Signs pointed the way to Call, which is easy to find since the street leading to it is thoughtfully lined with tourist shops displaying their wares. Once inside the area of the Call, I made my way down a narrow street and came upon the site where Besalu's medieval synagogue once stood — or at least that's what the sign said, since there was nothing left of it to see.

The synagogue is located next to the *mikvah*, but of course I couldn't see that until I returned with the tour. As I made my way back to the square, I passed by the second most interesting Jewish site in Besalu — an impressive Romanesque house, whose presence explains the heavily fortified bridge that guards the entrance to this small town. In the fourteenth century, Besalu was the capital city of the province and this house is where the governor lived. But a sign explains that the history of this house goes back even further. In the beginning of the fourteenth century, the house was owned by a wealthy Jewish family named Astruc, and one can still see the indented space in the doorpost where the family's *mezuzah* once sat.

Although the sign pointing out the space for the *mezuzah* doesn't explain how the Astruc's mansion passed into the hands of the governor, it's possible to fill in the blanks from other explanatory signs scattered around Besalu's Call. In 1415, walls were built around the Jewish Quarter to separate the Jews from their non-Jewish neighbors. Other discriminatory and oppressive acts followed, and by 1436 Besalu's Jewish citizens, who had comprised approximately one-fourth of the town's 1,000 residents, left Besalu and took up residence in other Jewish communities.

At 1:30 pm the guide for the tour of the *mikvah* appeared and greeted the group, which consisted of just me and four women who spoke Catalan. I was impressed both by his punctuality and by the effort he made to translate what he was saying into English.

Since I didn't need to be told what a *mikvah* is, I silently took in the impressive site while our guide talked with the others. On that hot day in late June, the cool air of the underground *mikvah* was a welcome respite. However, I supposed that it must feel very different in winter, when cold gusts of wind blow in through the tiny sliver of an opening cut through the upper wall—the only source of natural light. The water would be freezing, but of course today there are no Jews left in Besalu and so the *mikvah* is empty and there's no need to worry about the Jews catching cold.

After about 20 minutes, our guide signaled that it was time to go. We climbed up the steps and he locked the door behind us. I stood for a few minutes on the newly-paved floor of what used to be the synagogue. I had an excellent view of the bridge and its tower. Only now the view was leading me back through the gate and to the road leaving Besalu. I couldn't help but think back to that day in 1436 when the door to the *mikvah* was locked for the last time by Besalu's Jewish community and the small group trudged across the bridge in search of safer quarters.

The Call Vanishes

After the year 139_, safe quarters became increasingly difficult to find. That was the year when anti-Jewish rampages swept throughout the Iberian Peninsula. The destroying force, which had turned into a popular uprising against the governing authorities, arrived in Catalonia in August. After the rampages, King John I of Aragon (1350-1395) rounded up 25 of the mobs' ringleaders and had them executed, but it was too little too late. The Barcelona Call had been completely destroyed, and most of its Jewish population was forcibly baptized. In Girona, the majority of the Jews chose death.

Some of Girona's Jews did succeed in fleeing from the mob, and they were given refuge in a fort located on the outskirts of the city, called the Gironella Tower. They remained there for 17 weeks, under the protection of the city's officials. When it was finally safe for them to return to the Call, there was very little left to return to, since their homes and synagogues and study halls had all been destroyed.

During the next century, the dwindling and impoverished community would suffer a series of repressive measures, such as being forced to wear distinctive clothing and listen to priests' sermons. By 1492, the year of the Expulsion, there were only 20 Jewish families left in the Girona Call, which had once been home to more than 800 Jews. Half of the families chose physical exile and left Spain; the other half chose spiritual exile and converted.

The Gironella Tower isn't mentioned on the tourist map put out by the municipality, so it's good to know that the way to reach it is through a green and shady oasis called the Jardins d'Alemanys. Once there, it's possible to climb to the top of the Tower and enjoy a breathtaking view of the countryside. There's also a breathtaking view of Montjuic, where Girona's medieval Jewish cemetery is located.

This should be the end of the story. Those who died sanctifying the Divine Name are now at rest. As for what happened to the more than 100,000 Jews who left Spain in 1492, that tragic chapter in Jewish history is, as the saying goes, another story.

But even though the descendants of those Jews who "chose" baptism over death drop out of Jewish history books after the 1600s, when it became practically impossible to determine who was of Jewish lineage according to Jewish law, it's impossible to forget them in Catalonia. It's not anything overt. It's more a presence, a restless energy, a reading between the lines.

I think of the thousands of "Hidden Documents" that are now stored in Girona's public archives. For hundreds of years these Hebrew fragments were hidden within the bindings of non-Jewish books. Then one day, which was not so long ago, the bindings burst open and the fragments tumbled out. Could this happen with the thousands of *bnei anusim*, as well? Could it happen that one day they will break through their outer disguise and publicly reveal the tiny spark that still connects them to the Jewish people?

I knew better than to pose this question in Girona. But if I were to follow the Ramban's path to the end — to Jerusalem — I knew that I would likely find an answer to this question there.

A Time to Wake Up?

When the Ramban was exiled from Catalonia, after the 1263 Disputation, he turned adversity into opportunity and set out for Jerusalem. Although he must have felt joy about traveling to the Holy Land, it was a joy tinged with sorrow, for he wrote: "I am the man who felt the stab of pain. I left behind the table that was spread for me. I went far from friends and companions; the journey is long and full of trials. I, who was a prince among my brothers, live now in an inn for travelers. I left my family. I forsook my house. There, with my sons and daughters, the sweet, dear children whom I brought up on my knees, I left also my soul. My heart and my eyes will dwell with them forever."

The Jerusalem he found upon his arrival was a city that had been devastated by the Crusades. There weren't even ten adult Jewish males left in the city, the number needed to form a *minyan* (quorum) for communal prayer. In a letter to his son Nachman, the Ramban wrote about the Holy Land: "Many are its forsaken places, and great is the desecration. The truth is that the more sacred the place, the greater the devastation it has suffered. Jerusalem is the most desolate place of all."

The Ramban set to work rebuilding the Jewish community. First he constructed a synagogue. Next he established a yeshivah. As word spread, Jews began to trickle back into the city and the rebuilding of Jerusalem was underway.

There is a synagogue in the Jewish Quarter of the Old City that is named after the Ramban, but that wasn't my destination. Once I was back in Jerusalem, I didn't need to search out stones, or indentations in the doorposts; synagogues and *mezuzahs* can be found everywhere. Instead, it was to hear about a new "trickle of Jews" that brought me to the building located next to Jerusalem's Great Synagogue, where the offices of an organization called Shavei Israel are located.

Shavei Israel works with *bnei anusim*, as well as other populations, to help them strengthen their connection to Judaism. It also helps smooth the path for those who decide to return. Before my trip I had spoken with Michael Freund, who founded Shavei Israel in 2004 and currently serves as its director, and who gave me some background on the topic.

According to Mr. Freund, no one knows how many *bnei anusim* there are today. "It's an issue of definition," he explained. "During the first few hundred years after the Expulsion, it was still possible to trace a person's lineage and see if the person was Jewish according to Jewish law. Today, it's much more complicated.

"In Palma de Mallorca, there are about 15,000-20,000 Xuetas — *anusim* who until recently could only marry among themselves because of discrimination against them. The Xuetas are perhaps the exception, though, because their identity has been preserved.

"From a strictly biological point of view, if 20 percent of Portugal's population was Jewish at the time they were all forced to convert in 1497, there are some who will say that everyone in Portugal has Jewish blood. That doesn't mean that they're all *anusim*, but there could be hundreds of thousands of *anusim* in Spain and Portugal. In Brazil, they say there are millions. But some may not be aware of their Jewish lineage. Of those that are aware, many may not be interested. Of those that are interested, many don't do anything about it. So even though there may be millions of *anusim* out there, that doesn't mean that they are all seeking a way to come back to Judaism."

Shavei Israel has emissaries in places where there are large concentrations of *anusim*, such as Lisbon, Palma de Mallorca, and Recife, Brazil. In addition to serving as local rabbis, they offer seminars about Judaism several times a year. In Palma, for example, each seminar attracts about 80 *anusim* from Spain and Portugal.

It doesn't sound like a lot, but Mr. Freund is optimistic that this is just the beginning of a larger awakening that will take place in the future. Citing the Abrabanel, who wrote in his commentaries on *Devarim* (*Deuteronomy*) and *Yeshiyahu* (*Isaiah*) that one day the *anusim* will come back to the Jewish people, Mr. Freund listed several factors as to why he feels that return will finally happen during our own times.

"It was only in the 1970s that Spain and Portugal became democracies and the power of the Catholic Church began to diminish. As the general society grows freer, individuals within the society feel freer to explore their roots and be different from others. Second, people like to say that we are living in a post-modern world, and so people are searching for connection and for an identity.

"Finally, there is the Internet. In Spain and Portugal, people are still afraid to come out and admit they are Jews. They are afraid of how it will affect their career and their social standing. Before the Internet, if someone wanted to explore his Jewish roots, he had to do it in public. He had to go to a library or a synagogue. Now people can explore their roots from the privacy of their own homes. The Internet gives them a window to the wider world, where they can see that they're not alone, and this gives them confidence."

The Shavei Israel seminars are just the first step in a very long process that can entail a great deal of soul-searching. For those who are ready to make the step to return to Judaism, the organization has an institute in Jerusalem called Machon Miriam. Those who complete the intensive one-year program go before a Jerusalem *Beis Din* (Jewish court of law).

To date, about 90 former *anusim* have returned to Judaism through Machon Miriam. One of them is a man called ... well, let's call him Joao, because as he told me in the Shavei Israel office, he doesn't want to be publicly identified. His family back in Portugal is still very afraid.

Fire and Light

Joao's earliest memory of knowing he was different from some of the other people in his village revolves around food. Namely, his mother told him that if she ever caught him eating a certain kind of food she would make him fast for a week.

Not long afterward, the five-year-old child heard a rumor that his family was Jewish, "which was not a very positive word," he explained. He began to notice that his family did many strange things, and he decided to ask his great-grandmother for an explanation.

"She was very closed, and afraid. All she said was that we were different. So I went to my brother and I asked him if we were Jews, and he insisted, 'We're not Jews!' Next I went to my mother and she said, 'Yes, we are Jews, but this is not the sort of thing that you speak about outside of the family, because you can put a person in danger. Many years ago, people were burned alive for being Jewish and it can happen again today.'"

However, the young Joao was both curious and persistent, and so his great-grandmother began to teach him some of their family's traditions, but in a very subtle way and never saying outright that these were Jewish traditions. Joao explained that although there are some doubts about his father's lineage, his mother is unquestionably Jewish. The families she comes from will marry only with each other, something that has been going on for generations. Furthermore, in the area where his family lives, which is near the border with Spain, many Jewish traditions have been preserved.

Although the traditions will vary from village to village—and everything is passed down from memory from one generation to the next—many of the *anusim* from these villages in northern Portugal do perform *bris milah* (circumcision), for example, bless the children by saying the *bircas Kohanim* (Priestly blessing), take *challah*, and say a prayer over the New Moon. Although they don't celebrate *Purim*, they do observe the fast of Queen Esther. For Passover, they bake *matzos*, using special water, read some parts of the Bible, and drink wine, although they haven't preserved the tradition of the four cups of wine.

When they kill chickens, they cover the blood with soil and inspect the organs to make sure they are healthy. Upon arising in the morning, they wash their hands. They have many prayers, which are in Portuguese. In one of them there is an illusion to the Inquisition, which speaks of the fact "that we couldn't raise our heads." When they must enter a church, for appearance's sake, they silently say, "I don't worship stone or wood, but the Great God Who rules the world."

According to Joao, they also have a kind of *Havdalah* ceremony after the end of Shabbos, where they pray that the new week should be the week of their redemption. This mention of the end of Shabbos naturally brings up the question of what they do to signal its beginning. There are so many stories about the *anusim* hiding their Shabbos candles behind closed cupboards. Were these stories true?

"We light Shabbat lights using olive oil and wicks made from linen," Joao replied noncommittally.

"Yes, but where do you light?" I persisted. "Are the lights on the table?"

"We light just one candle," Joao corrected me. "We put the wick in olive oil—the best quality olive oil we can find on the market. The best! The mother lights it without looking, when the sun touches the horizon. Then we put the light inside a pot and we hang the pot inside the inner part of the chimney, which is in the kitchen. This chimney is cleaned and painted with white chalk every Friday before Shabbat, after we've finished cooking. When the pot is hanging inside the chimney, we ask the children to look at the light. It is just a little light. Someone who came into the kitchen wouldn't see it unless they looked inside the chimney, because it's not visible from the outside."

I tried to imagine this scene—the entire family gathered around the hearth, and the mother and father instructing the small children to look up inside the dark chimney to catch a glimpse of this little light. I couldn't help but ask the question that was on my mind: If these people are so stubborn about clinging to their Jewish traditions, why don't they take the next step and return to being Jews?

"People are still afraid," he explained.

Joao then told about the time when he was still a young boy and he decided that he wanted to learn Hebrew. His mother bought him a book, but when his great-grandmother saw it, she asked him, "What are those strange letters?" Joao replied, "This is Hebrew, the language of our ancestors."

"She began to tremble and weep," Joao continued. "She said, 'Where did you find that book?' I told her that my mother gave it to me. 'Oh. I should have known that your crazy mother would make this kind of mistake. But do you want to end your life in the fires?'

"I said that all that happened many years ago and she said to me, 'Shut your big mouth. During the last world war, thousands of people were burned, and their books, and it will happen again.'

"She asked me to put the book away and I did it, because I was afraid she would have a heart attack. My family still believes that there is always someone who wants to kill Jews. When I began to study for my conversion, they said to me, 'Why do you study to become a Jew and go to the synagogue? Look, there is a new crazy guy, Osama bin Laden. Open your eyes.'

"I promised my family that I would make my conversion here in Israel, and not in Portugal, because they are still afraid of the danger—of a second Inquisition. On the one hand they are happy, because they see that with me there is hope for the future. On the other hand, they are afraid that one day all of my descendants could be exterminated overnight. It's a kind of trauma."

The People of the Nation

Joao did have an Orthodox conversion in Israel, with the help of Shavei Israel, and today he is learning in a yeshivah in Jerusalem. However, nothing about the process was easy, at least in the early stages.

"The first time I heard that I had to convert, I was in shock. I thought it must be a joke—a joke in very bad taste. But when I realized that people were serious—that I would have to convert if I wanted to be recognized in the synagogue as a Jew—I did it."

He recalls another incident that occurred on the often bumpy road that led him to his return to the Jewish people. It was Shabbos and a group of American tourists entered the synagogue in Lisbon where he would often go to pray. After the prayer service, they plied Joao with questions about his community and their customs.

"The *anusim* seem so romantic," one of the members of the group said.

"Romantic?!" Joao said to me, with a tone of voice that managed to convey irony, exasperation, and real pain all rolled up together in that one word. "It's really hard. There's nothing romantic about it. It's traumatic. Imagine you are eating fish every day, and every day people are asking why you are eating fish. Every day people are suspicious of you, because you have funny habits."

This suspicion, in turn, makes the *anusim* suspicious of anyone who is a stranger. "We never say the word 'Jew,'" Joao explained. "We call ourselves 'The People of the Nation.' This is a kind of code. If you go to a village where there are *bnei anusim*, you should never make the mistake of asking people if they are Jewish, because they will immediately close up. That will be the end of the conversation. But if the conversation is indirect, people will be very curious and ask a lot of questions. And they will send messages, such as tell you that the Israeli government needs to be tougher with the Arabs, and that they need to rebuild the Temple. Through these messages, you will know that in this place there are Jews."

How do people know where these villages are located? According to Joao, an infallible way to find out is to ask the people who go from village to village, selling things from their truck. "You ask them, 'By the way, do you see that there are some places where your pork products don't sell so well?'

"They say, 'Now that you mention it, there are a few places like that.' So when you go to that part of the village, you look at the people and it's visible on their faces that they are Jews. You find out that they will only marry amongst their families. If you ask the non-Jews of the village, they'll tell you, 'Yes, they are dirty Jews.' But if you ask these people, they'll say, 'No, no. There are no Jews in this village.'

"Perhaps it sounds funny, but that is the situation today."

A Community on the Verge of Extinction — or Rebirth?

And what about tomorrow? According to Joao, the traditions of the *bnei anusim* are on the verge of extinction. He explains that after the Industrial Revolution, communities began to break up and the people moved to where there were more economic opportunities, whether that was a big city or a different country. Traditions that had been preserved for hundreds of years started to become lost, and that process has already taken its toll in the large cities of Portugal and Spain.

So that those traditions won't be entirely lost, Joao is currently writing a book — a little book, which can be hidden easily in the pocket — about the Portuguese *anusim* and their traditions. The book, which will be published by Shavei Israel, will also talk about the ideas of Exile and Redemption. And who is the book for, if the younger generation is clueless about their past?

"I believe that the return will happen first with those who are the most assimilated — and not with the ones who have some knowledge and traditions," he said. "It's the ones who are the most disconnected who are the ones who are most prone to considering conversion."

I left Joao to continue with writing his book. I thought back to my conversation with Michael Freund, where he said, "I believe that we are at the beginning of a massive wave of return, where we will see the return of tens of thousands, if not hundreds of thousands of *anusim*."

Maybe this sounds a little crazy, but it's not impossible. In Catalonia, at least, the people are known for coming down, every now and then, with a *cop de rauxa* — a burst of crazy inspiration that shatters everyday complacency and hurtles the person into the unknown. So why shouldn't thousands of *anusim* suddenly get it into their heads to start learning about Judaism and return?

After all, we have a King in Heaven and in the weekly Torah portion called *Netzavim*, which is always read the week before *Rosh Hashanah* and the beginning of the Ten Days of Repentance, it says: "Hashem your God will turn your captivity and have compassion upon you, and will return and gather you from the nations, where the Lord your God has scattered you."

According to the Abrabanel, the first return from captivity refers to Jews who remained Jews throughout the long Exile. The second "return," though, refers to the *anusim*. Someday they will also be gathered up, and follow in the footsteps of the Ramban, here to Jerusalem — may it be speedily and within our days.

— September 2007

Sighs, Sugar, and Slaves: What Happened to the Children of Sao Tome?

They were some of the littlest victims of the Expulsion from Spain, those 2,000 Jewish children who were torn from the arms of their parents and exiled to a malaria-infested island located off the coast of West Africa. But they haven't been forgotten. Until today, historians are trying to unravel the mystery of what happened to the children of Sao Tome.

They call it "Paradise on Earth," in the tourism brochure. And for the world-weary traveler who really wants to get away from it all, the tiny island of Sao Tome, located in the Atlantic Ocean about 150 miles west of mainland Africa and a smidgen north of the equator, is a tropical playground filled with miles and miles of unspoiled beaches and rainforests.

But for a group of Portuguese settlers who were banished there in the year 1493—a group that included some 2,000 Jewish children, as well as adult convicts and other social outcasts—the island was anything but paradise. Separated from their families, and with little hope of ever returning to their homes, their dreary mission was to turn the forest-covered island into a profitable colony for the Portuguese king.

Amazingly, they succeeded. Within one generation large swaths of land had been cleared and Sao Tome had become the world's largest exporter of sugar. But what happened to the Jewish children? Did any of them manage to escape from their island prison? Or, if they remained in Sao Tome, were they able to retain at least some connection to the Jewish religion—and leave a trace of their Jewish heritage behind? The truth is that only scattered fragments have been discovered about the children and their fate. But from these fragments we can try to piece together their story.

Do You Know the Way to Sao Tome?

I was seriously thinking about asking *Mishpacha Magazine* to send me to Sao Tome, until I learned two things about the island: malaria is still a danger, and the one European airline that flies there, TAP Portugal, has only one flight to Sao Tome a week. That plane makes its way from Lisbon to the Gulf of Guinea early on a Friday morning, lands and refuels at Sao Tome's tiny airport before breakfast, and then hurries back to Lisbon so quickly that there is still plenty of time to prepare for Shabbos. Did I really want to stay for a full week in such an isolated place?

The truth is that I probably needn't have worried, provided I took anti-malaria medicine beforehand. Crime is practically non-existent, perhaps because the local population is so poor that there is little to steal (although they hope to soon become very rich since oil deposits were recently discovered off the coast). And even though the country has experienced economic hardships and several coups in the three decades since it gained independence from Portugal, an event that occurred in 1975, the approximately 150,000 people who live in Sao Tome and the neighboring island that makes up the other half of the country, Principe, have a reputation for being polite and friendly.

That politeness and friendliness is perhaps something of a miracle, given the country's often harsh colonial past. A breakdown of Sao Tome's main population groups reveals that history in brief: *Mestiços*, or mixed-blood persons, are descendants of the Portuguese colonists and African slaves who were brought to the islands from nearby Benin, Gabon, and Congo during the early years of settlement; *Angolares*, who are thought to be descendants of Angolan slaves; *Forros*, descendants of slaves who were freed when slavery was abolished in 1875; and *Serviçais*, contract laborers from Angola, Mozambique, and Cape Verde, who live temporarily on the islands.

One group that is noticeably missing is the Portuguese, who left the country en masse when Sao Tome e Principe gained its independence. However, Portuguese continues to be the official language—even though many of the people speak Farro, a form of Luso-African Creole—and reminders of the island's colonial past can be seen at the plantations that once provided Sao Tome with its main sources of income.

Some of those plantations are still producing crops of cocoa and coffee today, while a few of them have been converted into upscale hotels. Many of them, though, were deserted after 1909, when the international community boycotted the island's products due to the plantation owners' harsh treatment of their workers, and the rainforests have since reclaimed the once-cultivated land.

There is, of course, another group that is missing from the island's population roll call: Jews. But before we can discover what happened to the Jewish children who were among the island's first settlers, we must recall how they got there in the first place.

The First Exile: 1492

To the very end, the Jews of Spain prayed for a miracle; perhaps the cruel Edict of Expulsion would be annulled. But when the miracle didn't materialize, about half of Spain's Jews boarded rickety, rat-infested ships and set sail for Italy, the Ottoman Empire, and various ports in Northern Africa. The other half fled to nearby Portugal.

King Joao II of Portugal didn't open his country's border because he had a kind heart. He was preparing for a war against the Moors and he needed money. He therefore granted permanent residence to some 600 Jewish families who were able to pay a fee of 100 *cruzados*. Some 30 craftsmen whose skills could be used in the upcoming campaign were also allowed to stay. The rest, about 100,000 souls, were allowed into the country on the condition that they pay a "transit fee" and leave Portugal within eight months. If they didn't leave, they would become the king's slaves.

When the eight months elapsed most of the impoverished Spanish Jews were still stuck in Portugal. They were given a brief reprieve in 1494, when Manuel I became the new king and granted the enslaved Spanish Jews their freedom. However, when Manuel decided to marry the daughter of Ferdinand and Isabella of Spain, the Catholic monarchs insisted that he first expel all the Jews from his kingdom. Manuel was in a dilemma, since the Jews were a source of wealth and skilled labor that he didn't want to lose. He therefore embarked upon a project that was as cruel as it was ambitious: he forcibly converted all of the Jews living in Portugal, both the Spanish exiles and the native Jewish-Portuguese population. By October of 1497 he was able to announce to his future in-laws, "There are no more Jews in Portugal."

The Exile to Sao Tome

Amidst all the heartbreak of those years, one incident was especially poignant. In 1493 King Joao, anxious to populate and cultivate a recently discovered island off the coast of West Africa, decided to seize some 2,000 Jewish children, whose parents were among the poor Jewish exiles from Spain. After the children were forcibly baptized, they were shipped off to Sao Tome.

Samuel Usque, whose family was among the Spanish exiles and who wrote a history called *Consolation for the Tribulations of Israel*, described the scene, some 50 years after the event took place (translation by David Raphael, *The Expulsion 1492 Chronicles*):

When the luckless hour arrived for this barbarity to be inflicted, mothers scratched their faces in grief as their babies, less than three years old, were taken from their arms. Honored elders tore their beards when the fruit of their bodies was snatched before their eyes. The fated children raised their piercing cries to heaven as they were mercilessly torn from their beloved parents at such a tender age.

Several women threw themselves at the king's feet, begging for permission to accompany their children; but not even this moved the king's pity. One mother, distraught by this horrible unexampled cruelty, lifted her baby in her arms, and paying no heed to its cries, threw herself from the ship into the heaving sea, and drowned embracing her only child.

Later historians have charged Usque with being overly dramatic. But the basic facts of the story are confirmed by Rui de Pina, an official chronicler of the Portuguese kings. In his *Chronica D'El Rei Dom Joao II*, which was completed sometime before 1504, de Pina writes (translation by David Raphael):

In this year of 1493, ... the king gave to Alvaro de Caminha the Captaincy of the Island of Sao Tome of right and inheritance; and as for the Castilian Jews who had not left his kingdom within the assigned date, he ordered that, according to the condition upon their entry, all the boys, and young men and girls of the Jews be taken into captivity.

After having them all turned into Christians, he sent them to the said island with Alvaro de Caminha, so that by being secluded, they would have reasons for being better Christians, and [the king] would have in this reason for the island to be better populated, which, as a result, culminated in great growth.

What happened to the children when they reached Sao Tome? According to Samuel Usque, they were abandoned on the shore, where most of them were either eaten by crocodiles or died of starvation. However, according to Rabbi Yitzchak Abrabanel, who left Spain in 1492 with the exiled Jews and settled in Naples, the children met a very different fate. In his commentary to the Torah, *Shemos* (*Exodus*) 7:28, he writes:

The king of Portugal forced many children of the Spanish exiles to adopt his faith. He sent them to [Crocodile Island] fourteen years ago; all of them children without any blemish, boys and girls, more than two thousand souls. They have already multiplied there, and most of the island is inhabited by them. The island is not far from the equator.

Which is the true account, the one written by the Abrabanel that says the children lived, or the one written by Samuel Usque that says that most of them perished? Could both be right? Or is neither accurate? And how did they know what happened to the children?

To begin our search, we first turn to a Jew from our own times, Professor Moshe Liba, who arrived in Sao Tome in the year 1994 not as an exile or a slave, but as Israel's first non-resident ambassador to the modern-day country that is known as Sao Tome e Principe.

What Do We Know?

In addition to being an Israeli diplomat, Prof. Liba is the author or editor of dozens of books and articles. One of them, *Jewish Child Slaves in Sao Tome*, is a collection of scholarly articles that were presented at a 1995 international conference on the fate of the Jewish children, which was organized by Prof. Liba.

One of the purposes of the conference was to see if scholars could agree about some of the basic facts concerning the children. The problem, of course, is that many of the historical sources present conflicting evidence. As an example, Prof. Liba mentions that although there is a general agreement that the children were seized and baptized in the year 1493, there is a question as to how many children were abducted, their ages, and if only boys were seized or also girls. The consensus seems to be that both boys and girls were abducted. Although Rabbi Shlomo ibn Verga mentions just boys, three other sources mention both boys and girls: the Abrabanel's commentary on *Shemos* 7:28; the last will and testament of Captain Alvaro de Caminha, dated April 24, 1499; and the 1634 diary of a Catholic priest who lived on the island, Padre Rosario Pinto.

How many children were sent into exile? Most sources claim that about 2,000 children were forcibly baptized and put on the boats, along with a motley collection of *degradados* (convicts), priests, soldiers, and sailors. But some sources mention just 600 children. How can this discrepancy be resolved? One possible explanation is provided by Padre Pinto, who wrote that 1,400 children died during the voyage because of "the difficulties of the trip." Thus, out of the original group of 2,000, only 600 children made it to the island alive.

Why did so many of the children perish during the voyage? This raises an additional question about the logistics of transporting so many people at that time. The will and testament of Alvaro de Caminha states that there was food on board for only 1,000 people. Did this mean that the real number of Jewish children sent into exile was less than 1,000? Or does it mean that the children were cruelly and intentionally left to die of hunger and illness on board the ship? On this issue, Alvaro de Caminha is silent.

The question of the children's ages is important, because it would have had an impact on the ability of the children to retain some vestige of their Judaism in a totally alien environment — and pass on some knowledge of their Jewish heritage to future generations. Again, the historical records vary, but the general consensus is that the children were between the ages of two and eight.

Even though we would like to believe that these little children stubbornly clung to their Jewish faith, is there any evidence? When I posed this question to Prof. Liba during a phone interview, he fairly bristled with indignation.

"The children who were sent to Sao Tome were small children who were abducted from their parents, put on a ship, and sent to a place that had no access with the outside world. They were put in a Christian school and educated by priests with the goal of turning them into Catholics. They remained slaves, who were not allowed to marry amongst themselves. Instead, they were forced to intermarry with the African slaves who were also brought to the island, as part of the King of Portugal's plan to create a new race on the island, which was intended to be a prosperous colony to fill the king's coffers.

"These children were not *anusim*, at least not in the sense that we usually use the term, which is to refer to Jews from either Spain or Portugal who were forced to become Christians. The *anusim* had their families and their communal structure. They had women who passed down their traditions from mother to daughter. They also had some written documents, although not many, which they passed down from one generation to the next. But this was not the case with the children who were sent to Sao Tome. Therefore it is nonsense to speak about the children hanging on to their Judaism, or about there being any remnants of synagogues or traces of Jewish customs on the island. It makes me want to cry when I hear people speak such nonsense."

It's a harsh answer, and when I hang up the phone I refuse to accept it. But my refusal doesn't stem from the fact that when I'm not writing articles for *Mishpacha* I'm writing historical novels. It's because I happen to know, from my research, that Sao Tome wasn't as isolated as Prof. Liba has suggested.

History Sweet and Sour

If the story of the children exiled to Sao Tome is only a footnote in historical accounts, the story of Europe's attempted colonization of the African continent is the subject of numerous books and scholarly articles. One of them, Richard Hull's *Jews and Judaism in African History*, even tells the story from the Jewish perspective. In a chapter titled "The Atlantic Slave Trade," Hull, a professor of African history at New York University, discusses Sao Tome in great detail.

When the first Portuguese settlers arrived on the uninhabited island in 1485, they almost immediately began sailing to the lands located around the Gulf of Guinea. There they did a brisk business with the African natives, trading Portuguese wares for African gold, ivory, and pepper. They also engaged in a more sinister business — selling African slaves.

Slavery was a part of life for several African tribal nations, so the Portuguese can't be blamed for introducing it to the continent. They did, however, quickly take advantage of the situation. For instance, when the settlers discovered that the soil of Sao Tome was good for growing sugarcane, but that the island lacked sufficient manpower for performing all the backbreaking tasks involved with planting and harvesting the crop, the Portuguese solved the problem by importing African slaves from the mainland.

By the 1520s Sao Tome had become a busy transit point for slaves bought in the Kingdom of Kongo, who were then sold in the Gold Coast (present-day Ghana) to Islamic slave traders and to plantation owners on other Portuguese islands. In the 1530s a new market opened up, the Spanish Caribbean, and the trans-Atlantic slave route was set in motion. Sao Tome continued to be the hub of this ugly business until the 1570s, when internal turmoil in the Kingdom of the Kongo forced the Portuguese to move their operations further south.

What does this have to do with the children of Sao Tome? For one thing, it shows that the island was hardly an isolated speck on the map. Between the years 1510 and 1540, for example, it is estimated that there were between four to six slave ships running continuously between the island and the African mainland.

On the African mainland, those ships would be greeted by *lancados* — middlemen who were at home in both the Portuguese and African languages and culture. *Lancado* is actually a Portuguese word that means "thrown out," and so it should come as no surprise that some of those outcasts/middlemen were New Christians who had either been exiled to West Africa as punishment for some petty crime or who had willingly left Portugal in the hope of finding greater freedom on the African continent.

During this same time period, Sao Tome was building up its sugar industry. In addition to slave labor, the island needed knowledgeable people to act as plantation managers and technicians. According to Prof. Hull, those jobs were filled by New Christians, or *conversos*, from Portugal, who had learned the sugar industry in nearby Madeira and Cape Verde.

Did the children of Sao Tome have any contact with these *conversos*? Were the *conversos* able to teach the children about Shabbos, or keeping kosher, or the holidays?

I can already hear Prof. Liba warning me to not write nonsense. It seems that many *conversos* — at least the ones who willingly came to West Africa — were more interested in making their fortune than in preserving their Jewish traditions. Otherwise, they would have fled to North Africa or the Ottoman Empire, where there were established Jewish communities. In addition, Prof. Liba has told me that Alvaro de Caminha, in letters he sent to Portugal, spoke of the children in the best possible light. The priests also left records that praised the children. This written evidence, which can be found in Lisbon in Portugal's National Archives, seems to prove that the children submitted to their fate, despite the presence of other Portuguese *conversos* in the area. So, to put it in Prof. Liba's words, "As for observing Shabbos and kashrus, you can forget about it."

On the other hand, after 1497 all Iberian Jews, now dubbed New Christians, became masters of deception. With so many *conversos* wandering up and down the West African coast, was it possible that not one of them still had a "Jewish heart" and concerned himself with these children?

To see if there is another way to view the historical record, I turned to Norman Simms, an associate professor at New Zealand's University of Waikato, editor of the scholarly journal *Mentalities/Mentalite*, and the author of an article whose title immediately caught my eye: "Did Any of the Captive Jewish Orphans of Sao Tome Ever Leave the Island?"

Caution: Speculation Ahead

"It is a *mitzvah* for me to help perpetuate the memories of these children," Professor Simms begins, "but first let me say that the history of these Jewish children cannot be proved in a strictly historical way. There is a lot of guess work, but intelligent guess work, I hope. We know they were manumitted, or partly so, in about 1512, on condition that they marry with black slaves and remain on the island. After that, the evidence is patchy, and almost everything I will say is more or less speculation."

He then paints a possible psychological portrait of the children, based upon what we do know from the records, saying, "These children, the ones who survived the rough treatment and diseases, would be a hardy group. They came from poor and therefore non-professional Castilian-Jewish families. Their parents were the Jews who refused to convert. They would have had some Jewish education, and this minimal training would be what they passed on over the next century or so.

So the children were able to hang on to some semblance of their Jewish faith and practices?

"This is very hard to know, because the only way to survive as a secret Jew was to maintain the secrecy. Nevertheless, we know that periodically the Church and the Crown sent to the island Inquisitorial agents to root out the Judaizers.

"There also may have been merchants and sailors who passed through who were secret Jews and carried the news back about these children of Sao Tome, since there were accounts recorded about their ordeal. These visitors may have brought back some of the 'children' with them. We may also suppose they passed on a little Jewish knowledge and kept the secret community somewhat aware of conditions in Europe and elsewhere in the Portuguese Empire."

Did any of the children ever manage to leave the island?

"It is likely that some of the children—20, 30 years later, of course—did leave the island, for we find them arrested by the Inquisition in Italy and charged with Judaizing."

Is there any record of what happened to the children after they grew up?

"The most surprising thing is that by the turn of the sixteenth into the seventeenth century the descendants of the original Jewish slaves almost completely disappear—and re-appear in Brazil. The documents state that Jews from Sao Tome came to South America to help develop the sugar industry, and Brazil quickly out-produced Sao Tome in this regard; their sugar was also of a higher quality thanks to the climate and soil."

In the mid-1600s, the Dutch wrested Brazil from Portugal and set up a short-lived colony where Jews were able to live openly as Jews. While some of the *conversos* might have returned to Judaism, it seems that many did not. Their fears were perhaps justified when Portugal regained control in 1654.

According to Prof. Simms, the *conversos* from Sao Tome then most likely did one of three things: retreated further into the Brazilian wilderness, where they continued to live as *conversos*; fled to nearby Surinam and joined a short-lived autonomous Jewish republic in the jungle known as Jodensavanne; or returned to Europe with the Dutch Jews.

Although the historical record agrees with Prof. Simms that sometime in the mid-1500s New Christians from Sao Tome went to Brazil to help build that country's nascent sugar industry, a new question arises: Who went to Brazil? Were they really the descendants of the children of Sao Tome? Or were there other New Christians on the island?

Robert Garfield, author of *A History of Sao Tome Island*, believes that the descendants of the children became some of Sao Tome's wealthy and powerful plantation owners. So would they have left behind their families and plantations to go off to the wilds of Brazil?

Another wrinkle is provided by historian Malyn Newitt, who believes that Portugal continued to use Sao Tome as a place of exile for *conversos* until the year 1535. Indeed, Prof. Hull, in his book, claims that by the 1540s, when *conversos* left Sao Tome for Brazil, the *conversos* were the dominant group on the island. So was it a different group of *conversos* who went to Brazil—and eventually returned to Europe—while the children's descendants remained in Sao Tome? We will probably never know.

What Remains Today?

When Prof. Liba was in Sao Tome back in the 1990s, the country's then-prime minister, Miguel Trovoada, said to him, "Ambassador, we have common roots. The Jewish children brought here as slaves from Portugal were the first settlers of this island."

Roots, yes. But what about branches? Does a trace remain of either the Jewish children or their descendants on the island, which is today a mostly poor and very isolated place?

Neither Prof. Liba nor other scholars are encouraging. It's true that some of the country's approximately 150,000 citizens are light-skinned, but it's just as likely that they are descendants of the Portuguese *degradados* as the *conversos*.

What about physical or cultural traces? Prof. Liba recalls an encounter he had with Bishop Abilio Ribas, who was then the head of the Catholic Church on the island. Prof. Liba asked if the Bishop knew where the children were buried—those that had died from malaria or from the crocodiles or snakes. Bishop Ribas replied, "Near the Cathedral."

Bishop Ribas then explained that some 20 years earlier, when the Presidential Palace, which is located next to the Cathedral, was being built, the excavators discovered two things: the sword of Alvaro de Caminha and the burial place of the Jewish children. Naturally, Prof. Liba rushed to the site.

"The story sounded plausible," he recalls. "It's a Christian tradition to have the graveyard near the church. But behind the church there was a small garden—and nothing else. No signs, no graves, no cross, no gravestone." Prof. Liba adds that he never saw a trace of the sword, either.

During his exploration of the island, Prof. Liba did see two Jewish graves located off to one side of Sao Tome's main cemetery. However, they date to the late 1800s (the Inquisition was abolished in 1821) and belong to two Moroccans of Portuguese descent, Arao

Gabai and Avraham Cohen, who were most likely merchants visiting the island on business.

He also saw a *Magen David* (Star of David) embedded in the floor of a chapel located near a cocoa plantation called Agua Ize. But, as Prof. Liba points out, it proves nothing since a six-pointed star wasn't a uniquely Jewish symbol until fairly recently. A later report of a second *Magen David*, this one engraved into a pillar, turned out to be a false alarm: it had only five, and not six, points.

Some islanders have said that the influence of the Jewish children can be seen in certain local customs and rituals, particularly in the island's burial customs. However, most scholars agree that if such influences do exist, it's more likely due to later Jewish and *converso* settlers. In the opinion of Prof. Liba, who has discussed the topic with an expert on the island, "Such claims aren't serious enough to write about in a newspaper."

So what can we say about the children of Sao Tome? Although we still know little about their lives, and nothing about their deaths, we can say with some certainty that they never forgot that they were Jews — and that they passed on a stubborn resistance to the Catholic Church to their children. How can such a claim be made?

The historical records tell us that the prejudices that haunted the New Christians in Portugal and elsewhere in Europe eventually found their way to Sao Tome. In other words, some of the *conversos* were accused of being "Judaizers." While some scholars believe that these charges had more to do with financial competition and petty jealousies than any real effort on the part of the *conversos* to practice the Jewish religion, nonetheless at least one document from the year 1632 states: "… the island (Sao Tome) is so infested with New Christians, that they practice the Jewish rites almost openly" (*L'ancien Congo d'apres les archives romaines, 1518-1640*, J., Cuvelier and L. Jardin).

Another document, this one dated April 24, 1691, and written by a local priest named Giuseppe Maria da Busseto, laments, "In this city, which has no bishop, if there are two priests, including the Reverend Father Prefect, they are almost too many, since not many people come to our church."

Prof. Simms therefore sums up the children's legacy by saying. "While it is a terrible tragedy — a narrative of slavery, child abuse and religious persecution—it is also an amazing story of Jewish survival in a variety of forms."

* * *

What Happened to the Crocodiles of "Crocodile Island"?

Were you to visit Sao Tome today, you might have to share your island getaway with lizards, mosquitoes, and sharks, but one thing you wouldn't have to worry about is crocodiles. So why did the Abrabanel write: "... and today we know of an island whose inhabitants are natives of Sefarad (Spain) and the kingdom of Portugal, and its name is the Island of the Crocodiles ..."? And what about Samuel Usque, who wrote about "great lizards that swallowed the children"? Were they both deceived by false information?

"I asked in Sao Tome about the crocodiles and the lizards," says Prof. Moshe Liba. The answer he received was: "Here there are only snakes."

Not content with that answer, which contradicted the Jewish sources, Prof. Liba searched for more information. He found it in an article that appeared in a 1975 bulletin published by UNICEF, which said: "A sailor that arrived at the island in the fifteenth or sixteenth centuries wrote of crocodiles in great number, as well as poisonous serpents. The crocodiles are gone, but the serpents continue to be a danger for the plantation workers."

So for once the UN agrees that the Jewish version of a story is correct.

—October 2010

Cowboy Colony: The Crypto-Jewish Province of Nuevo Leon

The northern Mexican countryside was so wild that none of the "Old Christians" wanted to try to tame it. But for the anusim, *the crypto-Jews of Spain and Portugal, subduing the warlike Indians of the New World seemed like a much easier task than dodging the fanatical priests of the Spanish Inquisition.*

As I walked out on the streets of Laredo,
As I walked out in Laredo one day,
I spied a young cowboy all wrapped in white linen,
Wrapped in white linen as cold as the clay.

"Oh, beat the drum slowly and play the fife lowly,
Play the dead march as you carry me along;
Take me to the green valley, there lay the sod o'er me,
For I'm a young cowboy and I know I've done wrong.

—"Streets of Laredo," traditional American song
also known as "The Cowboy's Lament"

A cowboy who wants to do *teshuvah* (repent)? And in Laredo, Texas, of all places? What on earth is going on? If one had to think of a place that was the antithesis of traditional Jewish values and culture, Laredo—a former western frontier outpost—would seem to fit the bill nicely. Yet odd as it might seem, Laredo was founded by the descendants of *anusim* — Spanish and Portuguese Jews who had been forced to convert to Christianity.

During the sixteenth century, the Kingdom of Spain claimed the territory around the Rio Grande as its own. However, because of the fierceness of the native Indians, Spanish forces had been unable to establish a foothold. Spain's king was therefore forced to make an extraordinary concession: "New Christians" were granted the right to colonize the territory, and they jumped at the chance.

The colony that these crypto-Jews founded, Nuevo Leon, was practically an autonomous state, due to its remoteness from even New World civilization. And even today, traces of Sephardic culture are still present along the banks of the Rio Grande.

The Great Escape

On March 15, 1391, an angry mob burst into the Jewish Quarter of Seville, Spain. Although the original source of the peasants' unrest was economic, they vented their rage upon the defenseless Jews. The rebellion quickly spread throughout the Iberian Peninsula. By the time the rampage ended, practically every Jewish community had been destroyed. Thousands of Jews were killed, and tens of thousands were forcibly baptized.

Many of these "New Christians," known to Jews as the *anusim* (the forced ones), only pretended to be good Christians. Behind closed doors, they continued to secretly practice their Jewish religion. However, this ruse became increasingly dangerous after the Castilian monarch Isabella I re-instituted the Inquisition in 1478. The community's despair increased even further after the Jews who had managed to escape conversion were expelled from Spain in 1492.

The news that Christopher Columbus had discovered a "new world" gave them renewed hope. During the 1500s, Spanish colonization of Nueva Espagna (present day Mexico) began in earnest. The government needed someone to settle the colony, and crypto-Jews, who jumped at the chance to escape from the Inquisition, left Spain en masse. In fact, according to many estimates, by the middle of the sixteenth century there were more crypto-Jews living in Mexico City than Spanish Catholics.

The Catholics were not amused by this turn of events. Officials wrote letters to the Spanish government complaining that Mexico would become Jewish if the flood of crypto-Jewish immigrants wasn't stopped. A new law was instituted: the Blood Purity Law. From then on, only people who could prove that their families had been New Christians for at least the last three generations could immigrate to Mexico. This law was followed by an even more serious edict in 1571 — the establishment of the Mexican Inquisition.

Crypto-Jewish immigration to Mexico came to halt. Undergoing a rigorous examination of the family tree was a risky business, since nearly everyone had more than a few "backsliding skeletons" in their closet. And once the Inquisition set up shop in Mexico, there was little reason to take on the additional dangers that went with settling in the New World.

However, there is a Father in Heaven Who is compassionate, and He sent the crypto-Jews help from an unlikely source: the Apache Indians.

A Colony of Their Own

Spanish conquistadors were usually able to subdue the indigenous Indian population without too much trouble. After they paved the way, the settlers followed. Despite the hardships, there were reasons why even Catholics left their comfortable homes in Spain. Mexico was blessed with mineral wealth, including silver, and the conquered Indians provided the Spanish settlers with a cheap source of labor. Another source of wealth for the settlers was raising livestock. Many of them established sprawling *ranchos* (ranches), and once again the Indians were used to perform the menial tasks.

There was one area, however, that the Spanish had not been able to conquer. The native tribes — and especially the Apaches — put up such a fierce fight that the Spanish, led by Captain Alberto del Canto, who some historians believe was a crypto-Jew, had no choice except to retreat. However, this area — an expanse of land that stretched across much of northern Mexico, as well as much of what is today south-central Texas and New Mexico — was too large to ignore. Therefore, when a Portuguese royal accountant by the name of Luis Carvajal de le Cueva offered to try again to settle the territory, the King of Spain was willing to listen to his proposition.

Carvajal, who came from a family of crypto-Jews, although he himself was a sincere Catholic, was familiar with the region and so he knew what he was getting into. He also knew that there were few others who would be willing to risk their lives to settle the lawless territory. He therefore felt confident that the King of Spain would grant his audacious request without asking any questions: let any New Christian settle this region, without having to prove his lineage.

The gamble paid off. On May 31, 1579, El Nuevo Reyno de Leon (the New Kingdom of Leon) was established. Cavajal was given the title of First Governor-Captain General and granted full colonization rights. Under the terms of the agreement, Cavajal was able to bring over 100 soldiers and 60 married laborers, as well as their wives and children. Everyone who sailed with him on the *Santa Catalina* was a member of his own extended family, and they were mostly all crypto-Jews. After the colony was established, many crypto-Jews from settlements in southern Mexico who wanted to escape the clutches of the Inquisition joined the original settlers. Therefore, a case can be made that Nuevo Leon was a crypto-Jewish Kingdom in the New World.

Carvajal succeeded in his task, and he established several permanent settlements in the territory he had been given. But his hopes for establishing a safe refuge for his family and other crypto-Jews were dashed after only a decade. A property dispute with a neighboring colony led to intrigues at the viceroy's court in Mexico City. Questions were raised about Carvajal's family background and the Inquisition was called in to investigate the goings-on in the colony.

Carvajal, his sister Francisca and four of Francisca's grown children were arrested in 1590. Carvajal died in prison. The others, who were tortured during their interrogations, were "rehabilitated" after agreeing to give up their Jewish practices. A few years later Francisca and her children were once again arrested for Judaizing. One of them, Carvajal's nephew, who was also named Luis, recorded his family's experiences in a memoir, making him the first Jewish author in the Americas. Francisca, Luis and the others were sentenced to death at an *auto da fe* in Mexico City in December 1596 and burned at the stake.

The Inquisition decided to make an example of the Carvajal family. For the next 50 years they hunted down the family members, one by one, until the family was almost entirely destroyed. Although the Inquisition left the other crypto-Jews alone, for the most part, many decided that the time had come to move on. Some followed the trade routes further west. Others headed north.

Go North, Young Man

In the mid-eighteenth century, Jose de Escandon was appointed governor of the province Nuevo Santander, located along Mexico's northern coast, and given the task of settling the lands along the lower banks of the Rio Grande River. One of his ablest assistants was a colorful crypto-Jew who went by the name of Captain Tomas Sanchez.

Sanchez's ancestors had helped found Nuevo Leon a century earlier. After establishing a series of successful settlements along the lower Rio Grande, he decided to ask for his reward. Escandon approved Sanchez's request to privately develop land on the northern bank of the Rio Grande on May 15, 1755. The new settlement was called Laredo.

Laredo, which is considered to be the oldest independent settlement in Texas, started small. It had just three families, all of whom were related to Sanchez. Even when it grew to a population of 85, about half the people were Sanchez's relatives. It was operated as a family *rancho*, where cattle, sheep, horses, mules, and oxen were raised. Pigs were conspicuously absent. Another absence was noted by a Spanish government inspector who visited the ranch in the 1700s. In his report, he wrote that the community didn't have a priest.

Certainly Sanchez and the other crypto-Jews who lived on the ranch didn't mind the lack. However, when the Archbishop of Guadalajara passed through Laredo in 1759, he was shocked to discover that most of the children weren't baptized. Although he called Sanchez in for questioning, suspecting that he had uncovered a heretic, by this time the Inquisition, which would be abolished in 1821, was already losing its power.

Yet even though he couldn't arrest Sanchez, there was something the Archbishop could do: he announced that he was going to send a priest to Laredo. However, even in this, the clergyman was thwarted. Escandon protested, stating that the missionary living in nearby Revilla could take care of Laredo's spiritual needs and that there was no need to disrupt the stability of the settlements because of religious disagreements.

Laredo continued to grow and prosper. In 1767 it received the official status of *villa* (a city). A central public square, or *plaza mayor*, was constructed. Plots of land facing the plaza were designated for public use, while plots facing the river were parceled out to the heads of households. It also became an important frontier outpost during the late eighteenth century. Located on the Camino Real (King's Highway), a 700-mile route that stretched from Monterey, Mexico to Robline, Louisana, Laredo played a part in the cross-country cattle drives that made the region wealthy — and gave birth to the local phenomenon that would later become known as the "Texas Cowboy."

Are We There Yet?

For some crypto-Jews, the lower banks of the Rio Grande weren't far enough away from the suspicious eye of the Inquisition.

When Luis Carvajal was arrested, the Lieutenant Governor of the colony, Gaspar Castano de Sosa, who may have been a crypto-Jew, gathered together about 170 crypto-Jews and followed the Rio Grande north, to uncharted territory which is today part of New Mexico. They were forced to return to Nuevo Leon by the Spaniards. Some of the group became the founders of the city Monterey, but Castano was convicted of treason for the illegal expedition and died in exile.

A few years later, though, the Spanish King decided that he did want to establish settlements in that unknown area. He assigned the task to Don Juan de Onate, who is also considered to be a crypto-Jew by some historians. Some of the members of the earlier expedition joined Onate and they eventually settled in northern New Mexico, where they became the founding members of Santa Fe, the oldest capital city in the United States.

The Franciscans who were responsible for running the Inquisition in New Mexico were more interested in fighting with the civic authorities than uncovering heretics, and so the little group was able to find what had eluded so many of their brethren — the ability to live in peace and quiet.

A Few Lingering Customs

Mexico gained its independence from Spain in 1821. In 1845, the United States annexed Texas, which led to the US-Mexican War. The United States won, and the Rio Grande became the boundary between the two countries. People who wished to retain their Mexican nationality moved south of the border. Descendants of Sanchez remained in Laredo, where they continued to play an important role in the town's development, but as the years passed their crypto-Jewish roots were forgotten.

Yet according to author Richard Santos, the original crypto-Jewish founders had a profound influence on the development of the culture and customs of the Rio Grande territory, and this deserves to be remembered. As he writes in *Silent Heritage: The Sephardim and the Colonization of the Spanish North American Frontier, 1492 – 1600*, "...they were Sephardic by culture. They were the ruling class and landed aristocracy. As such, their culture, worldview, cuisine and lifestyle were imitated not only by their Christian counterparts, but by the converted and assimilated Native American Indian cultures."

* * *

Cowboys and Indians: The Truth Behind the Myth

Lounging there at ease against the wall was a slim young giant, more beautiful than pictures. His broad, soft hat was pushed back; a loose-knotted, dull-scarlet handkerchief sagged from his throat, and one casual thumb was hooked in the cartridge-belt that slanted across his hips....No dinginess of travel or shabbiness of attire could tarnish the splendor that radiated from his youth and strength.

– "The Virginian"

It all began in the late 1800s, when the twin forces of increased literacy and cheaper printing processes created a publishing phenomenon known as the "dime novel." The stories usually took place in the American frontier, and as the genre developed a new American hero emerged on the horizon: the cowboy.

Owen Wister, who penned the best-selling novel *The Virginian* in 1912, was the one who created many of the most enduring details of the myth. His cowboy hero was a young man who was daring, but who had integrity and fortitude. He was a loner, since being a champion of justice and a defender of the powerless tends to be an unpopular job. And needless to say, he was white and a Protestant.

Of course, the myth created by Wister — which was copied by dozens of authors after him, and immortalized in hundreds of movies and TV programs — was just that, a myth. But as it sometimes happens, the truth is even stranger than fiction.

Smile When You Say That

The Virginian's pistol came out, and his hand lay on the table, holding it unaimed. And with a voice as gentle as ever, the voice that sounded almost like a caress, but drawling a very little more than usual, so that there was almost a space between each word, he issued his orders to the man Trampas: "When you call me that, SMILE."

– "The Virginian"

When the Spanish crown granted settlement rights in Mexico, the *hacienda* system of medieval Spain was transplanted in the New World. Each *hacienda* was like a little feudal kingdom, which was ruled by a wealthy *patron* and his family. Below them were the *peones* (serfs) and *campesinos* (peasants), Native Indians who had been rendered powerless by the often brutal Spanish conquest of their lands. *Peones* worked the lands that belonged to the *patron*, while the *campesinos* were tenant farmers.

When cattle ranching was introduced to the area in the 1500s, the *patron* needed someone to keep an eye on the cattle as they grazed and drive the herds of cattle to market. That person was the horseback-riding *vaquero*.

The Spanish word *vaquero* means "cow-man," and its origins come from the Latin word *vacca*, which means "cow." In any language, the work was hard and the pay was low. Therefore, most *vaqueros* were either Native Indians or *meztizos*, people of mixed European and Indian blood.

When Texas was annexed by the United States, the word *vaquero* was gradually replaced by the word "cowboy." In California, the term that was commonly used was "buckaroo" — which has its roots in the Hebrew word *bakar*, which means "cow," and the similar word in Arabic, *bakara*. Despite the English-language name given to the job, the pay was still pitifully low. Therefore, even during the heyday of the cowboy period during the mid-1800s, it is estimated that perhaps 50 percent of the cowboy population was comprised of people of Hispanic descent, newly freed black slaves, and American Indians of the southwest. There is also a Jewish connection.

Don Juan de Onate, who may have been a crypto-Jew, is credited with being the first one to transport some 7,000 animals, including sheep and long-horned livestock, across the Rio Grande into what is now the American southwest, thus founding the lucrative cattle business on US soil. Crypto-Jewish ranchers such as Tomas Sanchez and his descendants, who made a fortune from their dealings in livestock, would have been typical employers of the *vaquero*/cowboy.

Thus, crypto-Jews played an instrumental role in laying the foundations for what would later become the cowboy of myth and popular culture. But should you decide to enlighten some modern-day cowboy walking down the streets of a Texas town like Laredo about the Jewish origins of his profession, here's a piece of advice: When you say it, smile!

—September 2007

A Bright Light in the Jodenbuurt:
Amsterdam's Portuguese Synagogue

Amsterdam's Portuguese Synagogue, the 335-year-old Esnoga, is one of the few still-standing reminders of that city's pre-Holocaust Jewish community. It's also a moving tribute in wood, stone, and candlelight to the "stiff necks" of its founders – descendants of anusim *who refused to give up their Jewish faith.*

"Where is it?"

"Over there."

"Where?"

"There!!"

For a moment, I think the nice but exasperated young man would like to throw me into one of Amsterdam's ubiquitous canals. Or maybe push me into the path of the dozens of bicycles whizzing by us – the bicycle being the preferred means of transportation for many Amsterdam residents, both young and old.

But I'm really not trying to tax his patience. It's just that I'm totally jet-lagged after a sleepless plane ride from Detroit to Amsterdam, and I don't see anything that looks like a synagogue in the direction where he is pointing.

"You mean that long row of short buildings? That's the Portuguese Synagogue?" I ask, trying to mask my disappointment and dismay. After all, the main reason why I decided to do a 13-hour layover in Amsterdam was to see this synagogue, which is supposed to be one of the most beautiful in Europe.

"Yes," the helpful citizen replies. "It's being renovated. See?"

I look again. And then I see it: a massive square structure that is "gift-wrapped" in some sort of green construction material. The Portuguese Synagogue has been hiding from me all the time, which somehow seems appropriate for a synagogue that was founded by descendants of *anusim*, crypto-Jews from Portugal and Spain who were forced to hide their loyalty to the Torah.

I gingerly cross the street, careful to avoid both the bicycles and cars, and enter another world. Despite the sounds of construction going on outside, the interior of the Portuguese Synagogue immediately casts its spell; it is an oasis of sublime calm. Yet the inside calm is as misleading as the green wrapping material on the outside, because during its heyday, the synagogue was an active, noisy gathering place for a "Nation" of Jews who were at the center of Holland's Golden Age.

A "Dutch Jerusalem"

The Portuguese Synagogue had its inauguration in 1675, but its story actually begins much earlier — in the year 1391, when pogroms broke out on the Iberian Peninsula. Many of Spain's Jewish communities, some of which had existed for hundreds of years, were decimated and the quarters where the Jews had lived were destroyed. Thousands of Jews were forcibly dragged to baptismal founts. The survivors of 1391 who remained Jewish were increasingly targeted for taxation and degradation during the century that followed. This led to even more Jews converting, out of duress, and the rise of a new class within Spanish society: the *anusim*, or crypto-Jews, who appeared to be Christians on the outside, but still secretly clung to the Jewish faith.

The Expulsion of the Jews from Spain in 1492 forced many of Spain's remaining Jews to flee to nearby Portugal, which seemed to offer a safe haven. But that illusion of security was short-lived; in 1497 all Jews living in Portugal were forcibly converted. In the years that followed, those who could, fled to other countries.

Crypto-Jews, whose first concern was to rejoin a Jewish community, often tried to escape to lands ruled by the Ottoman Empire, both because the Turkish sultan welcomed them and because there were already well-established communities. However, many of the Portuguese Jews, who were wealthy merchants, preferred to remain in Europe. Some fled to Antwerp, where commerce was flourishing. Because Antwerp was ruled by Spain, they reestablished their businesses there under the guise of being "New Christians."

In the late sixteenth century, the Dutch staged a revolt against Spain. While Antwerp's economy wilted under a Spanish blockade that crippled its international trade, the Protestant Northern Provinces successfully declared their independence under the Union of Utrecht. In addition to being a proclamation of independence, the Union of Utrecht guaranteed freedom of religion for every resident—the first time such a declaration had been made on European soil. And so when in 1595 a few of Antwerp's crypto-Jews closed up shop and moved to the city of Amsterdam, they were able to live openly as Jews.

By the early 1600s Amsterdam was a thriving metropolis, a great center of international trade and business. The German poet Phillip von Zesen described the polyglot character of the Amsterdam Exchange by writing that one could find there, "Poles, Hungarians, Walloons, Frenchmen, Spaniards, Muscovites, Persians, Turks, and even, occasionally, Hindus." He might have added Portuguese Jews, since the community was growing by leaps and bounds.

But even though the Portuguese Jews were able to start engaging in trade at once, reestablishing a Jewish *kehillah* (community) wasn't as easy. After all, as the grandchildren of *anusim*, they had never had the opportunity to live in a Torah community and most of them knew little about what was required. The little *kehillah* therefore asked Rabbi Moshe Uri HaLevi of Emden to move to Amsterdam and be their spiritual leader. Rabbi HaLevi accepted the offer and in 1602 he came to Amsterdam with a *Sefer Torah* (Torah scroll), which it is said still sits in the synagogue to this very day.

By 1609 there were about 200 Jews living in Amsterdam and the community had two synagogues, Beth Jacob and Neve Shalom. These synagogues weren't officially recognized by the authorities— the freedom of religion granted by the Union of Utrecht extended only as far as private worship. But the overall air of tolerance in the city extended to the Jews, who were allowed to hold their prayer services "in private" at their synagogues without molestation.

That tolerance was almost sunk when the conservative Dutch Reformed Church tried to get the Catholics and the Jews expelled from the Netherlands. But unlike in Catholic Spain, it was decided in 1619 that the Portuguese Jews — many of whom were extremely wealthy merchants — added too much to the economic wellbeing of the country, and so they were allowed to remain. However, they did not yet enjoy full rights as citizens. For instance, the Portuguese Jews were barred from entering many professions and trades and from holding public office. To make sure a degree of social separation remained, Jews were prohibited from hiring a non-Jewish domestic servant, sending their children to a non-Jewish school, intermarrying, and — interestingly enough — they were commanded by the city authorities to strictly observe the "Laws of Moses."

In the year 1618, the growing community established a third synagogue, Beit Israel. But by 1639, when the community numbered approximately 1,000 souls, they decided that it was better to pool their resources and the three synagogues became one, under the name Talmud Torah. In addition to the synagogue, the community supported an extensive *chesed* (charity) network that aided both poor *anusim* from Portugal and Spain who were newly arrived in Amsterdam and needy communities in other countries.

By mid-century the Portuguese community could boast not only of having great wealth, but also of having created a "Dutch Jerusalem," a thriving center for Torah learning and Hebrew book printing. (Amsterdam had also become home to a large group of Ashkenazic Jews, who had fled from the 1648 Chmielnicki massacres in Poland and the Thirty Years War that raged in what is today Germany. But since the two groups remained separate on the whole, their history is another story.) Rabbi Yitzchak Uziel, author of a book of Hebrew grammar called *Maaneh Lashon*, gave a weekly lecture on Shabbos, which attempted to instruct the former crypto-Jews in the ways of the Torah. Rabbi Menasseh ben Israel, one of Rabbi Uziel's students and another leading figure, went to London to plead for the re-admittance of Jews to England. Rabbi Isaac Aboab da Fonseca, another student, sat on the city's *beis din* (Jewish court of law) and was one of the scholars responsible for excommunicating the renegade philosopher Baruch Spinoza.

The order of excommunication placed on Spinoza in 1656 exposed the dark side of the generally rosy picture that was Jewish Amsterdam during the "Dutch Golden Age." While many of the New Christians made a wholehearted return to Judaism soon after they arrived in Amsterdam, there were those who continued to live as Christians and eventually assimilated into that society. There was also a group that vacillated between the two groups, too filled with spiritual doubts and confusion to find their place in either community.

Even the wealthy members of the Portuguese Synagogue who had made a wholehearted return to Judaism had their fears and insecurities, due to the Inquisition, which was still raging in the Catholic countries where they often did business. In tolerant Amsterdam they could revel in their Portuguese heritage and create a mini-Lisbon in the Jodenbuurt (Jewish Quarter) where they lived, worked, and prayed. And they could proudly refer to themselves as "Hebrews of the Portuguese Nation," to distinguish themselves from their brethren from Poland and the Germanic countries, who were, in their eyes, much poorer, both financially and culturally. However, when it came time to do business, those same Portuguese Jewish merchants who gloried in their supposedly superior culture often felt compelled to hide their true identity by assuming a Dutch secular name. This was to protect both themselves and their relatives and business associates who were still living in Portugal or Spain from the dark side of Iberian culture—the Spanish Inquisition.

A Longing for Redemption

The year 1666 was supposed to be the year when *Mashiach* (the Messiah) revealed himself and the Jewish People would be redeemed, according to certain Jewish mystics and Christian millenarians. Instead, of course, it was the year when Shabbtai Tzvi, the false messiah who had dazzled much of the Jewish world, converted to Islam.

Amsterdam, like so many other places, had been swept up in the messianic fever. Rabbis such as Isaac Aboab da Fonseca had been enthusiastic supporters, and the city's Jewish printing presses had been active in disseminating Shabbetean pamphlets and prayer books. Yet once it became certain that Shabbtei Tzvi was a fraud, the Sephardic *maamad*, or governing board, acted quickly to go back to "business as usual." In 1670, under the direction of Rabbi Aboab, they purchased a piece of land with the intention of building a new synagogue for the community—an act that showed in stone and wood that their dream of being carried to the Holy Land on the wings of the false messiah was over.

The community spared no expense. The architect for the project, which is today commonly known as the Portuguese Synagogue, was Elias Bouwman, who also helped design the Great Synagogue of the Ashkenazim. Bouwman took as his inspiration a model of the *Beis HaMikdash* (Holy Temple) built by Rabbi Yaakov Yehuda Leon, who taught at the Talmud Torah school. And like the *Beis HaMikdash* in Jerusalem, this replica in Amsterdam towered high above everything around it. To build such a massive structure in water-logged Amsterdam required a feat of engineering: the building is supported by 3,000 wooden piles, which carry the six foundation vaults, five of which can only be reached by boat. The construction of the inside was just as impressive. Although the interior is not ornate — Amsterdam tastes leaned more to a classical style defined by simple geometric forms, sparse decoration, and strict symmetry — its sheer size inspires a sense of awe.

The *heichal* (Ark) for example, which was donated by the wealthy merchant Moshe Curiel, is 25 feet tall and constructed from *Jacaranda* wood (Brazilian rosewood) that was imported from Brazil. The impressive *teivah* (bimah platform), which stands at the opposite end of the long room, was constructed from *Jacaranda* wood, as well. Massive chandeliers made from brass, each one supporting dozens of candles — electricity was never installed in the main sanctuary — loom overhead, adding gleaming flights of illumination to the mostly somber interior.

The main sanctuary can seat about 1,200 men, while the *ezras nashim* (women's section) has room for about 450 women. Sand was spread over the wood floor of the sanctuary — although this wasn't done to muffle the noise of the congregation from the Inquisition's agents, like in hidden synagogues used by *anusim* still living in Catholic countries. The building was obviously much too grand to hide. Instead, covering the wood floor with sand was a Dutch tradition, whose purpose was to both absorb noise and dust and moisture from shoes.

The seating is arranged so that the rows of wooden benches on either side of the center aisle face each other. Each place has its own *gaveta*, or storage place for the owner's prayer book and *tallis* (prayer shawl). Each place also has its own candleholder — and a candle still sits in each holder. Rising above the rows of benches belonging to the regular members of the *kehillah* is the bank of benches for the *parnassim* — the wealthy merchants who were members of the synagogue's executive board. Made of sturdy solid oak, the "Parnassim Bench" was a strong visual reminder of who was in charge of the *kehillah's* communal affairs.

When the building was completed, at a total cost of 186,000 florins, it was the largest synagogue in the world. It also became the model for other Sephardic synagogues, such as the Bevis Marks Synagogue in London, the Touro Synagogue in Newport, Rhode Island, and the Sheerith Israel Synagogue in New York City.

The inauguration ceremony took place on the tenth day of the Jewish month *Menacham Av* 5435/1675 — the day after the fast commemorating the destruction of the Holy Temple in Jerusalem — which was the eve of Shabbos *Nachamu*, the Shabbos *of Comforting*, reflecting the solace that the new synagogue brought to a community that had suffered both the terrors of the Inquisition and the disappointment of the Shabbtai Tzvi debacle. The festivities, which were attended by both Jewish and non-Jewish dignitaries and included sermons by the city's leading rabbis, lasted for an entire week.

The Dutch printmaker Romeyn de Hoogh created a commemorative copperplate engraving of the inaugural event, and when looking at the print one can almost feel the excitement. On one side of the sanctuary are members of the *kehillah* who are circling the sanctuary and carrying Torah scrolls in their arms. On the other side is the choir. In the middle is the *chazzan* (cantor), who is leading the prayers. The names of the all-powerful *maamad* members, as well as the names of the building committee members, are inscribed on either side of the picture, preserving for posterity the names of the community's wealthy merchants who were at the height of their prosperity.

A Showplace of Their Own

The Portuguese Synagogue was depicted several times in Dutch paintings and copperplate engravings. Amsterdam's most famous artist, Rembrandt van Rijn, who lived in the Jewish Quarter and often painted the Jewish residents, had passed away a few years before the synagogue was built and so there is no picture painted by his hand. But other artists of the era did paint it and the building was considered to be important enough to be included in the 1680 book *All the Most Important Buildings of the Famous Merchant City of Amsterdam*. Forty years later, the synagogue played a starring role in Bernard Picart's *Ceremonies of the Jews*, the first of an eleven-volume series that looked at the customs and ceremonies of various peoples around the world. Thanks to Picart, we have a glimpse of what *Rosh Hashanah* and *Sukkos* looked like at Amsterdam's most majestic Jewish house of worship.

But even while artists like Picart were busy drawing the Jewish community and the Portuguese Synagogue was a "must see" for foreign visitors to the city, Amsterdam's fortunes were on the wane. During the 1700s, the Netherlands was plunged into a series of disastrous wars. That, combined with the collapse of the Dutch East India Company, a major source of wealth for Jews and non-Jews alike, led to the end of Dutch supremacy in international trade and a steep economic decline. By the end of the century, more than half of the Jewish population, including both Sephardim and Ashkenazim, depended upon charity.

Although the 1800s saw some improvements on the economic front, the Jewish community was hit by another blow: assimilation. King William I successfully dismantled the traditional communal organization and took away the power of the wealthy merchants. He also instituted compulsory secular education for Jewish children and fought the use of Yiddish, which was spoken by the Ashkenazic Jews, who had been in the majority since the late 1600s.

And so by the time the Germans occupied the Netherlands on May 10, 1940, the glory days of Amsterdam's Sephardic community had long been a thing of the past. Only about 4,300 Sephardic Jews lived in the country (the Ashkenazic community numbered about 135,000 souls). Of that number, only about 800 survived the war.

A Lonely Survivor

In 1943 the last members of the Portuguese Synagogue's choir, called Santo Servico, were deported and killed. The synagogue, however, was spared, making it one of the few synagogues in Amsterdam—and all Europe—that survived the Nazi inferno totally unharmed. What was the cause of its good fortune? According to Margriet Kotek, a member of the Jewish Historical Museum's communications staff, the real reason is unknown. But, of course, there are theories. One story goes that it was because of the building's tall windows. During wartime all windows were supposed to be blacked-out to prevent enemy bombers from seeing their targets. Since the synagogue's windows were too tall to be blacked-out, and too numerous, the Nazis couldn't use it for their own purposes and so they left it alone. Another, perhaps more fanciful, story says that the synagogue was spared thanks to the quick thinking of a young Jewish boy.

When the synagogue was built back in the seventeenth century it was lit by candles. Even when electricity became available, a decision was made in the 1920s not to install electricity in the main sanctuary. That meant, of course, that on a gloomy winter's day the sanctuary was both cold and dark. But the *maamad* wasn't unduly concerned. The low row of buildings that surrounded the main building on three sides housed not only the world-famous Etz Haim library but also a smaller synagogue that did have heat and lights. The people could gather there for prayers, thereby preserving the unique atmosphere of the candlelit main sanctuary—a visual reminder of how the sanctuary would have looked during the *kehillah*'s most prosperous period. And so when the Nazis decided to turn the Portuguese Synagogue into a barracks for their soldiers, this Jewish boy told the officer in charge that the building wouldn't do. The German soldiers wouldn't be at all comfortable in a building that lacked running water, heat, and electric lights. The officer was convinced by this argument and the building wasn't touched.

Is this story true? Maybe, maybe not. Yet the fact that it was candles that might have saved the Portuguese Synagogue from destruction somehow typifies the community that built it and prayed there. Living proof that the *pintele* Yid (Jewish spark) is never extinguished, those hardy, quick-thinking Portuguese descendants of the *anusim* showed the world that darkness is no match for the bright light of a Jewish soul.

* * *

If You Go ...

If you have a layover in Amsterdam of at least six or seven hours, you will have ample time to visit the Portuguese Synagogue and other sites in the Jewish Quarter. A commuter train connects Amsterdam's Schiphol Airport to the Central Station in the city center. If you feel up to tackling the automated ticket kiosks at the airport, have fun. I was too tired, so I paid a few extra Euros to buy a round-trip ticket at the tourist information center. (But don't buy the city map there. You can get a free one at the ticket office of the Jewish Museum.)

Outside the Central Station is another information center for tourists, where you can buy tickets for the trams. The stop for the No. 9 tram to Waterlooplein, the closest stop for the Jewish Quarter, is just a few steps away—so do be sure to watch out for the oncoming trams that will be coming at you from all directions. If the tram conductor announced the stops along his route, I didn't hear him. So ask a fellow passenger when to get off, because it's a fairly short ride.

The tram will let you off on the sidewalk of a busy street. If you're not too blurry-eyed from the flight, watch out for the signposts that will direct you to the Jewish Museum and the Portuguese Synagogue. If you don't see them, ask for the Joods Historisch Museum (Jewish Historical Museum), "Joods" being easier to pronounce correctly than "Portugees"—especially if you look like an Ashkenazic Jood.

If you decided not to ask and you find yourself walking in a charming neighborhood with cobblestone streets, you're probably lost. Not much remains of the old Jewish Quarter, which was heavily damaged during the Second World War. Most of what was left was torn down for redevelopment in the decades that followed. The area is definitely not charming, especially when the skies are overcast, a light drizzle is falling, and you step by mistake into the bicyclists' lane.

But once you get yourself pointed in the right direction, the Jewish Museum is easily recognizable. It's the building that has a big painted sign above the entrance that says Joods Historisch Museum. The Portuguese Synagogue is just across the busy street. It's the building wrapped in green, at least while renovations are being made to the buildings that house the Etz Haim library, etc.

Since most of the 600 present-day members of the synagogue live outside of the city center, there aren't regular prayer services, but the synagogue can be contacted through its website for more information. On the day I visited it, there were only four other tourists and three groups of schoolchildren, so don't count on putting together an impromptu *minyan* (prayer quorum) during the week, at least not during the winter.

If you visit Amsterdam after the present restoration work is completed, you will have an opportunity to see the synagogue's dazzling collection of more than 800 ritual objects, which includes objects made from gold and silver, textiles, and rare books and manuscripts. But even if you visit while the collection is still under wraps, you can still enjoy the informative free audio tour of the main building. And do try to imagine the synagogue as it was on that inaugural day back in 1675, when the synagogue was packed with people. Because even though the synagogue may be mostly silent today, if you listen closely you might just hear an echo of the joyous songs of thanksgiving and praise that were sung by the jubilant members of the "Portuguese Nation" who no longer had to hide the fact that they were Jews.

—December 2010

"Holy Queen Esther" and the *Anusim*

Purim *might be a minor holiday for the Jewish people, but for the* anusim *it became one of the most important days of the year. And so no matter where they fled, the* anusim *took with them the memory of "holy Queen Esther," whose story so closely paralleled their own.*

It started off as a honeymoon trip. Samuel Schwarz, a Jewish-Polish mining engineer employed at a tin mine in Spain, and his new wife, Agatha, the daughter of a Jewish banker from Odessa, decided to vacation in Portugal after their wedding. While they were sightseeing, World War I broke out.

Practically overnight the borders between Europe's countries closed, leaving tens of thousands of people stranded, including Samuel and Agatha. Since they couldn't return to Eastern Europe, they decided to stay in Portugal and make the best of things — and continue to explore the country. In 1917, they struck gold. No, they didn't find a mine filled with those shiny yellow-colored nuggets that people like to turn into necklaces and rings. Instead, this mining engineer found something much more precious: A "lost" community of *anusim*, descendants of Jews who had been forced to convert to Christianity during the era of the Spanish Inquisition.

It was a meeting fraught with suspicions on both sides. In the early years of the twentieth century, few people in the Jewish world knew that there were still *anusim* around. The common thinking was that either the *anusim* had returned to Judaism centuries earlier, or they had fully assimilated into Christian society and disappeared.

For its part, the little community of *anusim*—which had made its home in an isolated part of northern Portugal, near the tiny town of Belmonte—were sure that they were the last Jews in the world. So naturally they were suspicious when Schwarz turned up and told them that he was also a Jew.

It was only when Schwarz began to recite the *Shema* and said the word *Ad-onoy*—one of the names of God and one of the few Hebrew words that the Portuguese-speaking *anusim* recognized—that they believed him. The elderly women of the community opened their doors to Schwarz and spoke to him about their customs and prayers. His findings were published in 1925 in the book *The New Christians in Portugal in the Twentieth Century.*

Along with hearing stories about the "holy little Moses," who was forced to hide his Jewish identity while growing up in Pharaoh's palace, Schwarz learned about another hidden Jew who loomed large in the secret religious world that the *anusim* had been forced to construct: The "holy Queen Esther," whose fast and feast became some of the most important days of the *anusim* calendar.

When February Comes In ...

When *anusim* first went undercover, so to speak, they couldn't take anything Jewish with them: no volumes of the Talmud, no prayer books, and no Jewish calendar. For a time, some were able to maintain a secret connection with their Jewish relatives. But when the Jews were expelled from Spain and Portugal, their last living link with the Jewish community was severed. As the years passed and their memories faded, the struggle to maintain a connection with Jewish practice became harder and harder. But perhaps nowhere do we see more clearly the *anusim*'s determination to cling to some semblance of Jewish observance than the holiday of *Purim*.

Since the Jewish month of *Adar*, like the other Jewish months, no longer existed for them, the Fast of Esther was observed on the full moon of the month of February instead. When the *anusim* feared discovery by the Inquisition's agents, the Fast of Esther and *Purim* were moved to March. When that ruse didn't work, some communities—such as the ones in Toledo and Granada—sometimes moved the Fast of Esther to July. But fast they did, and not just for one day. Like Queen Esther, who fasted for three days in the month of *Nisan*, many of the *anusim* also fasted for three days.

Professor Moshe Orfali, dean of Bar-Ilan University's Department of Jewish Studies, has pointed out that, in general, the *anusim* observed more fast days than even the *Chassidim* of Eastern Europe, who tended to fast quite often. He surmises that the *anusim* felt that since they were forced to violate the laws of the Torah every day, they needed to fast often to achieve atonement and be cleansed of their sins. Prof. Orfali further notes, like many other scholars, that the Fast of Esther was so central to the *anusim*'s observance of *Purim* that it was perhaps more important than the festive meal held on *Purim* day. It was through fasting, and not feasting, that they hoped to achieve a personal *geulah* (redemption) for themselves, as well as the Final Redemption for all the Jewish people.

Eliezer Segal, a professor of religious studies at the University of Calgary, suggests another reason why the Fast of Esther took precedence over *Purim*'s other *mitzvos*: It was safer. Gathering together to read *Megillas Esther* or sending *Shlach Manos* (gifts of food, one of the *Purim* customs) to neighbors was dangerous. Fasting, on the other hand, didn't require any special activity and so no one—and especially not the agents of the Inquisition—had to know that they were doing anything unusual. Therefore, the fast became a substitute for many of *Purim*'s other rituals.

But did the *anusim* really fast for three consecutive days, or was that merely a legend?

What becomes clear from the records of the Inquisition and from the testimony of modern-day descendants of the *anusim* is that the Fast of Esther was primarily a women's fast and there were many ways to observe it. Gabriel de Granada, for instance, a 13-year-old boy who was interrogated by Mexico's Inquisition in 1643, revealed the custom of his mother, Dona Maria, and his other female relatives concerning the Fast of Esther, "which they keep by eating, the previous evening at supper, fish and vegetables and going the following three days without eating anything, until the night of the last day." However, he also mentioned that the women of his family didn't always fast for all three days. Instead, they would sometimes split the three days between them, and have some members of the family fast on the first day, others fast on the second day, and the rest on the third day.

Leonor de Pina, a Portuguese woman who was arrested in 1619 for being a "Judaizer," offers another explanation for how the three-day fast was observed. She told her interrogators that she and her daughters fasted for three days "without eating if it was not dark, or else eating things other than meat." In other words, they fasted during the day, but ate at night, or their fast consisted of refraining from eating meat for three days.

One reason why women might not have fasted for the entire three days was because it could be dangerous; there are recorded instances of women who died while attempting to complete the fast. Yet whether the women fasted the entire three days, observed a partial fast for three days, or split the days of the fast between them, what is clear from the historical record is that the Fast of Esther was second in importance to only that other great fast day of the Jewish calendar — *Yom Kippur*. And like *Yom Kippur*, it was a solemn fast that was taken very seriously.

"Holy Queen Esther"

Although the three-day Fast of Esther was at the center of the *anusim*'s *Purim* observance, *Purim* wasn't entirely a solemn holiday. The family did gather together for a festive meal on *Purim*, and a memory of what that meal was like in more modern times was recorded by Professor Janet Liebman Jacobs, who made an ethnographic study of descendants of the *anusim* who live in the American Southwest.

According to one of the people that Prof. Jacobs interviewed, a woman who lives in New Mexico, "The festival of Saint Esther is mainly a women's holiday in our way of doing things. Usually this holiday is dedicated to mothers teaching daughters the ways of the home and such. Pastries, rolled *empananitas* made with fired bread and pumpkin, were prepared along with elaborate meals."

Although it's very possible to see how *empananitas* were substituted for *hamentashen*, a traditional *Purim* cookie that is often filled with poppy seeds, a person could be forgiven for wondering how Queen Esther became "Saint" Esther! Prof. Jacobs posits that this is an example of how an oppressed people survive spiritually. They disguise their own religiously important figures within the garb of the dominant religious culture. Since the Spanish brought both Catholicism and the Inquisition with them to the New World, Queen Esther had to go into hiding along with the *anusim*.

Perhaps a more interesting question, though, is why did the "Holy Queen Esther" play such a lofty role in the *anusim*'s spiritual world?

One answer, of course, is that Queen Esther, like them, "did not reveal her people or her kindred" (*Megillas Esther* 2:10), when she was forced to live in a non-Jewish environment. For the *anusim*, secrecy was as necessary as breathing and eating. It was therefore perhaps only natural that the *anusim* would identify so intensely with Esther, who was forced to conceal her identity and observe kashrus and Shabbos and the other Torah commandments in secret.

However, Prof. Orfali goes even further and suggests that there was an even deeper reason for the *anusim*'s admiration for Esther: She was willing to die *al kiddush Hashem*, for the sanctification of the Divine Name. "If I am to perish, I shall perish," Esther says in chapter 4, verse 16. Those words became a sort of rallying cry for the *anusim*, who were fully aware of what was in store for them if they were caught committing the "crime" of "Judaizing."

Keeping an "*Anusim* Home"

The Spanish Inquisition, which began in the year 1478, lasted for more than 300 years. Tribunals were set up not just in Spain and Portugal, but also in the New World. Although modern scholars estimate that "only" a few thousand people were burned at the stake, no one disputes the fact that tens of thousands of people were arrested and interrogated. The terror of being caught permeated the entire community. The question must therefore be asked, from where did the *anusim* get the strength to cling to Jewish customs and traditions throughout all those terrifying years?

The answer, it seems, is from the women.

Even when it was no longer possible for the men to pray together in their synagogues, learn Torah in their study halls, or concern themselves with Jewish communal matters, the women could still perform their rituals, which were centered in the home. Although these rituals had to be done in secret or given a disguise — the Shabbos lights were hidden in a cupboard or in the chimney, the words "kosher" and "*treif*" became "clean" and "unclean" — both daily and holiday rituals could be passed down from mother to daughter. And they were. As the woman from New Mexico mentioned, *Purim* became an important day for transmitting vital information from mother to daughter about keeping an "*anusim* home."

However, as time went on and memories grew dim, the women took on additional roles. They became the ones who both composed and transmitted the community's prayers. They were also the ones who ensured that the community's sons didn't marry non-Jewish women.

Their role in preserving Jewish tradition was noted by Rabbi Yom Tov ben Moshe Zahalon, also known as the Maharitatz, who wrote, "The pious Portuguese women, in whose heart the Law of Israel is planted, are the ones who teach the men and bring them close to the Law of Israel, as we have heard and seen."

"These Days of *Purim* ..."

Although Rabbi Yom Tov wrote those words in the seventeenth century, women were still the primary transmitters of their traditions when Samuel Schwarz stumbled upon a community of Portuguese *anusim* in 1917. As he noted in his book, he gleaned most of his information from the women. They were the ones who knew the prayers by heart. They were the ones who knew the details concerning how to prepare for and observe Shabbos and the holidays.

And just as Queen Esther didn't forget her connection to the Jewish people, the *anusim* didn't forget their connection to Queen Esther. From Spain to New Mexico, and from Portugal to Peru, they fulfilled the words of the *Megillah*: "These days of *Purim* will never leave the Jews, nor will their remembrance ever be lost from their descendants."

* * *

A Twist of "Fate"

When Samuel and Agatha Schwarz found themselves stranded in Portugal during World War I, they most likely bemoaned their fate. However, when the war ended, they decided to remain. Samuel continued to take a great interest in both the *anusim* and Portugal's small Jewish community, and he even excavated and renovated a fifteenth-century synagogue located in the city of Tomar at his own expense.

Samuel Schwarz donated the synagogue to the State of Portugal in 1939. In return, Portugal granted Samuel and Agatha Portuguese citizenship. And so their unplanned extended stay in Portugal turned out to be the very thing that protected them during the Holocaust.

—February 2009

Shalom, Ladino!

Mama loshen. *Those two simple words encapsulate so much about the subject of language. More than a means of communication — more than being the most effective way of expressing thoughts such as "Pass me the ketchup," or "Please come to our* Seder,*" or "How much does it cost?" — language is part of our identity. It "speaks" to who we are, and expresses who we wish to be.*

It also suggests the idea of an inheritance, on a communal level. Language doesn't develop in a vacuum. It is both a response to the events that a people experiences and a way to give meaning to those experiences.

As a people who experienced Sinai, it is the Hebrew language that best describes what is most important to us when we endeavor to live a full Jewish life. But during the long years of exile other languages replaced Hebrew as the means by which we express our everyday needs and dreams. Yiddish is one of those languages. Today, English is another.

Yet several centuries ago there was another language that was the most widely-spoken language in the Jewish world, a language that carried with it the memory of the scent of lemon trees in blossom and turns of phrases that sang with a Castilian lilt. That language was Ladino, and after the Jews were expelled from Spain it went into exile with them.

"Buenos dyas. Avlates Ladino?"

Not so very long ago, a person could have walked into a synagogue in Salonika or Sarajevo or even Seattle, Washington, and gotten a positive response to their question, "Do you speak Ladino?"

Today, however, Ladino is on the "severely endangered" list of UNESCO, the cultural agency of the United Nations that tracks such things. What exactly does this mean?

Although "severely endangered" isn't the worst category for a language—"extinct" languages hold that honor—it does mean that practically no children speak it as their first language. And if today's children aren't using it, the language has no future. It will be on the "extinct" list before the century is out.

Why should we care? Sephardic communities are thriving. Does it matter that the first language of these children is Modern Hebrew or English or Turkish or French?

If we regard language as just a convenient way to give and obtain information, or express an emotion, it really doesn't matter what language we use. But if we see language as a repository of a people's history, culture, and spiritual aspirations, then perhaps we shouldn't be so quick to bid Ladino a hasty goodbye.

Adio, Sefarad

When the Jews of Spain were expelled in 1492, they took with them two languages: Hebrew and Castilian Spanish. Hebrew, of course, was the language of the synagogue and the house of study. Castilian Spanish was the language that they used at home or in the marketplace.

During the next two centuries, these exiles from Spain and their descendants settled in an astounding number of places, such as Jerusalem, London, Amsterdam, Venice, Sarajevo, Salonika, Istanbul, Tunis, Algiers, Fez, Recife (Brazil), Jamaica, New York, and Quebec. But wherever they went, they took with them *el espanol maestro*—"our Spanish"—which reminded them of the country where their ancestors had lived for nearly a thousand years, and the cultural milieu that had given the Jewish world such outstanding scholars as the Rambam, the Ramban, Rabbeinu Yonah, and the Abrabanel.

Although the exiles who settled in places like Amsterdam, England, and Italy maintained contact with Spain and, therefore, new developments in the Spanish language, the Sephardic Jews who settled in lands ruled by the Ottoman Empire were more isolated. The result was that their everyday language retained many of the older forms of Spanish and at the same time began to borrow words from their surrounding culture—Turkish, Arabic, French, Greek, and the like. It is this hybrid language that developed in the Ottoman Empire that is today referred to as Ladino.

Ladino, like Yiddish, also had many words that came from Hebrew. Another similarity with Yiddish is that Ladino was written in Hebrew letters, often using Rashi script—a semi-cursive script that first appeared on the Iberian Peninsula—until the beginning of the twentieth century, when Latin letters began to be used instead.

Over the centuries, Ladino developed a rich legacy of folk tales, proverbs, and songs. For instance, just as Yiddish stories have their "wise men of Chelm," so too can Ladino-speakers "boast" of a fool of their own: Jocha, or Ejoha, who is sometimes a wise fool and sometimes a foolish fool, but always entertaining. But Ladino literature wasn't just for passing the time on a long summer's evening. Works of Torah were also written in the language, including the classic commentary on the Torah, the eighteenth-century *Me'am Lo'ez*.

The reason why a commentary on the Torah was needed in Ladino, as well as translations of the prayer book, the *Shulchan Aruch,* and other basic texts, was simple. Many of the members of the community were former *anusim*—Jews who had been forced to convert to Christianity back in Portugal and Spain—or their descendants. And so, in the words of Rav Yaakov Culi, who initiated the *Me'am Lo'ez* project in the year 1730, many people "do not understand the holy tongue, and even those who do know the words do not know what they are saying; and from day to day, there are fewer and fewer readers, and the Law and the customs of Judaism are being forgotten."

At its height, it is thought that Ladino was spoken by some 80 percent of Jews living outside of the Land of Israel. During the 1600s and 1700s, it was the common language of commerce in ports that dotted the landscape of both sides of the Mediterranean Sea. Later, it became the lingua franca for conveying the news to Sephardic communities in Europe, and during the early years of the twentieth century more than 300 periodicals written in Ladino were published in Turkey and the Balkans alone.

The Holocaust dealt a lethal blow to Ladino, and unlike Yiddish the language never recovered. Important centers of Sephardic life, such as Salonika and communities in the Balkans, were completely annihilated. Even though the Jews of Turkey were spared the horrors of the Holocaust, during the war years there were forces at work that made some of them hide their beloved Ladino in a secret corner of their lives. A fear of an anti-Semitic reaction was one reason. Another reason came from the Turkish government, which had been promoting for many years the use of Turkish among all its citizens. In order to appear like loyal citizens, the Jews began to use Turkish as their first language.

After the war, Ladino-speaking survivors once again scattered to practically the four corners of the earth. Some went to South America, where they quickly became fluent in modern Spanish. Others settled in Israel and bowed to governmental pressure to adopt Modern Hebrew as their new mother tongue.

There were also many who immigrated to the United States and became English-speaking citizens. Like the Sephardim who came to the United States in the early 1900s, the new generation found it difficult to preserve their unique heritage. The Ashkenazic culture was the dominant one in Jewish-American life, and so many Sephardim chose to try to fit in.

Estimates vary as to how many Ladino-speakers there are today. Some say there are as few as 110,000 people. Others give a more optimistic estimate of 300,000 souls. Israel has the largest population of Ladino-speakers, with Turkey coming in second. All agree, though, that the majority of these people, wherever they live, have only a limited, basic knowledge of Ladino, since it's not their first language. A second point of agreement is that the vast majority of these people are over 50 years of age. Finally, it is generally agreed that there is not even a single person left in the world who claims Ladino as their primary, everyday language.

For any other people, that would surely spell the death knell of their language. But did we mention that Ladino is a language of the Jewish people? Since "stiff-necked" is our middle name, it should come as no surprise that there are still some Ladino speakers who are not going to give up without a fight.

Kuando mas eskurese es para amaneser. (**When the sky darkens, it heralds dawn's arrival.**) - Ladino saying

Rachel Amado Bortnick still recalls the time when she came to the United States as a young foreign student from Izmir, Turkey, even though it occurred some 50 years ago. The college she was to attend, Lindenwood University, was located in St. Charles, Missouri, which wasn't too far from St. Louis, but was hardly a thriving center of Jewish life.

"No one knew Sephardim like me existed," she says, as she recalls the Jewish community of St. Louis as it was back in the late 1950s. "When people asked me the first time if I spoke 'Jewish,' I replied, 'Do you mean Ladino or Hebrew?' They thought I was crazy. But I didn't know there was such a thing as Yiddish."

Her lack of knowledge about Yiddish didn't prevent her from finding her future husband, Bernard Bortnick, in St. Louis. After they were married in Izmir, the young couple lived in Holland, Israel, and several cities in the United States, before settling down in Dallas, Texas, where they still live. A teacher by profession—she teaches English as a Second Language—Mrs. Bortnick naturally fell into the role of teaching the world about Ladino, the language she spoke in her home back in Turkey. And so for the past several decades she has lectured at various venues, introducing her audiences to both Sephardic culture and the language that Sephardim once used.

Ladino got a boost in 1999 when an international conference sponsored by the National Authority for Ladino and its Culture (NALC) was held in Jerusalem to decide upon a common way to write the language in Latin letters. The conference attracted both native Ladino-speakers such as Mrs. Bortnick and non-Jewish academics from Spain who have a scholarly interest in the language. It was while listening to a talk given by Moshe Shaul—one of today's foremost proponents of Ladino, as well as a vice-president of NALC and the editor of the organization's Ladino journal, *Aki Yerushalayim*—that she got the idea for a way to give new life to what many people saw as a dying language: Ladinokomunita, the world's first Ladino correspondence group on the Internet.

"Ladinokomunita is the only place in the world where Ladino is being used every day," she explains. "We now have more than 1,200 members, who live in about 40 different countries."

Most of the group's members, some 60-65 percent, are Sephardic Jews, who grew up hearing Ladino in their homes. The rest are either Spanish-speaking people, Jews and non-Jews, alike, including Ashkenazic Jews, who are interested in the language; descendants of *anusim*, who find that Ladino provides them with a way to reconnect with their Sephardic roots; and academics, who follow the discussion to study how a native speaker uses the language.

Most of the group members are older, and so it's not surprising that many of the topics of this moderated discussion group revolve around memories of Sephardic life back in the "Old Country." The latest news coming from Israel is another topic that generates a lively discussion. And then, of course, there is Ladino itself. Members will discuss the origins of certain sayings and songs, as well as give their opinion about how words should be spelled.

"Ladino brings a sense of community to the Sephardic world, in general," Mrs. Bortnick comments, "and Ladinokomunita provides this sense of community for our members. It's the language that binds us together. For many of the members of the group, the language is our sense of Jewishness."

Since many of the group's members have relatives that perished in the Holocaust, or they lost contact with relatives after the war, Ladinokomunita has also become a way for Sephardic Jews to find out about family members who remained in Europe. In one dramatic reunion, a member of the group enlisted the help of other members to determine if an elderly aunt of his was still alive. She was, and so he went to Turkey to meet her and her children—cousins that he didn't even know he had.

When I ask Mrs. Bortnick if this means that Ladino is still developing and adding new vocabulary—if it is still alive—she replies, "Yes, it's definitely growing and changing. When we need a modern word, we will usually take it from Spanish. But sometimes we make up our own words.

"Some of us older people don't like to see it change too much," she adds, "so we have some very interesting discussions."

Although Ladinokomunita enables Ladino-speakers around the world to use the language on a daily basis, even an optimist like

Mrs. Bortnick admits that, "Ladino was the communal language when I grew up, but it can't continue to live as the daily language of friends and family because the communities don't exist anymore. The only place where a community does still exist is in Turkey. However, the younger generation has adopted Turkish as their everyday language. Ladino is therefore lost as a language spoken in the home."

However, if Ladino will never again be heard around the Shabbos table or in the corner grocery store, Mrs. Bortnick refuses to believe that it will ever completely die out.

"I see it living on in two ways. The first is through music. Through music, I believe that Ladino will live on forever. To date, it's mainly been the old songs that have been recorded, but these songs comprise only about ten percent of the 3,000-4,000 old songs that are registered at the National Authority of Ladino. There are still a large number of songs from different parts of the Ladino-speaking world still waiting to be performed and recorded. In addition, new songs are being composed in Ladino all the time. There is a real enthusiasm for composing songs and writing poetry in Ladino, which I hope will continue. These people don't necessarily speak the language, but they contribute to its preservation."

The second group involved with preserving Ladino is academics, who learn the language so that they will be able to study classic Ladino texts. University courses exist in Israel, the United States, Spain, and elsewhere. Even though this group won't use Ladino as their everyday language, their interest in it will help to ensure that the language isn't totally forgotten.

"Our language is so exciting," she tells me in conclusion. "It holds within it our history. The words and the expressions that came from Spain, Turkey, Greece, and other countries where there were once flourishing Sephardic communities, are the words that tell our story — the story of the Jews who were expelled from Spain and their descendants."

Cada uno sabe su salmo, ma el Hazan sabe dos. (Everyone knows his own one psalm, but the cantor knows two.) – Ladino saying

Although Ladino will most likely live on in music and scholarly journals, there are some Sephardim who believe Ladino is already a "dead letter" in terms of being the primary means to preserve a healthy identity for today's generation of Sephardic children.

Back in 1973, Rabbi Marc Angel, rabbi emeritus of Congregation Shearith Israel, the historic Spanish and Portuguese Synagogue in New York City, had this to say about attempts to revive bygone aspects of Sephardic life: "When a culture is about to die out, it first experiences a resurgence in nostalgia among its members. There is one last burst of creative energy before it gives way to new and different patterns of life."

Even though Ladino popular culture remains popular more than 30 years later—with Ladino-inspired festivals of music and food being held around the world—the current Hazzan (Cantor) at Congregation Shearith Israel, Rabbi Ira Rohde, agrees with that earlier assessment.

He tells me that although the synagogue held language classes in Ladino for many years during the 1990s, a time when that "resurgence in nostalgia" was operating at full steam, they stopped giving them several years ago, due to a lack of interest. And that this isn't necessarily the end of the world for Sephardic Jewry, in his opinion.

"Today, when many, many Jews have some knowledge of Spanish, an international language—and when Ladino is so close to Spanish—does it really make sense to keep alive the 'old forms' of Ladino, along with its loan words from Turkish, Greek, Hebrew, even French, etcetera, as a separate language? Most who want to study the language don't really want to learn it with any degree of thoroughness. They just want to keep alive vestiges of the language, and its culture, as a component of a healthy Jewish/Spanish-speaking identity."

As one component of that identity, Rabbi Rohde does believe that some vestiges of Ladino, such as its music, will have a future. But he believes that the question of how to use language to help preserve cultural identity goes deeper than the study of Ladino.

"I like to say that Sephardic culture has always been very classically-oriented and multi-lingual, and this is the aspect of our culture that we should encourage in our youth today. As long as we teach our children to speak the best Hebrew, Aramaic, Spanish,

Arabic, English, and other world languages—like our *hahkamim* (Torah sages) did throughout the generations—a good Sephardic identity will survive. It's more important to generally cultivate an ear for languages and knowledge of the languages' *dikduk* (grammar), which has always been a hallmark of Sephardic culture, than to concentrate on teaching Ladino."

Aboltar cazal, aboltar mazal. (A change of scene, a change of fortune.) – Jewish saying

Although Rabbi Rohde doesn't make the teaching of Ladino the centerpiece of his educational efforts, he does employ the Ladino language, with its songs and sayings, as a way to introduce the synagogue's very Americanized children to their Sephardic heritage and build their Sephardic identity.

And what about the Ashkenazim? Are there any lessons for Yiddish-speaking communities in Israel, the United States, England, and elsewhere to learn from the long journey of Ladino?

This author, at least, believes that there are two. The first is recognizing the importance of teaching Yiddish to our children. The second is that it takes an entire community to keep a language alive.

* * *

Avlates Ladino?

Do you speak Ladino? If you think the answer is no, think again. If you know a little Hebrew, you already know more Ladino than you think, and here are three easy lessons to teach you even more.

Ladino – Your first ten words:

alefbet — alphabet
asur — prohibited by religious law
beraxa — blessing
El Dio — God (The Spanish word "dios" was modified, because the final "s" looked like a plural suffix to the Jews.)
maase — story, event; as in *kontar un maasè*—tell a story
mabul — deluge, downpour, torrent; as in, *No kyerro tanto, me dátes   mabul.* — I don't want so much, you gave me plenty.

mazal — star, destiny
mazalozo — happy
sedaka — charity
tefila — prayer

Your first conversation:

Shalom. Me yamo _____. Avlates ladino?
  (Hello. My name is ____. Do you speak Ladino?)

No entiendo. No avlo byen ladino. Adio.
(I don't understand. I can't speak Ladino very well. Goodbye.)

Buen dya.
(Have a good day.)

Speak like a native at your Passover Seder table, with these sayings:

De una pulga lo hacen gamello. — Don't make a camel out of a flea.

Ya llevo' los males de Paro'. — He's had as many woes as Pharaoh.

Si neviim no somos, de neviim venimos. — We may not be prophets, but we descend from them.

Quien mucno pensa, no se le fada YeruSalai'm. — He who hesitates will never reach Jerusalem.

—April 2010

The Khazars: The Jewish Empire of the East

For the final essay in this section, we go back in time to the Golden Age of Spain — a time when Jewish intellectual, artistic, and spiritual life flourished on the Iberian Peninsula. Yet despite the richness of the life in Spain, there were Jews who knew in their hearts — and were reminded by others — that the Jewish people were still in Exile.

One of them was the high-ranking Spanish diplomat Hasdai Ibn Shaprut, who couldn't believe his eyes when he received a letter from someone calling himself the king of a Jewish kingdom. A Jewish kingdom? A land where Jews could observe their religion in total freedom, and protect themselves from danger? Was someone trying to make a fool of Ibn Shaprut, or was this rumor about the Kingdom of the Khazars really true?

"You're the smartest diplomat I've ever met, Hasdai. But you're a Jew, and your people have been rejected by the Al-Mighty. That's why you don't have a kingdom of your own to serve."

Hasdai Ibn Shaprut should have been used to such words, but each time he heard them they pierced his heart like a dagger. And it didn't matter if the taunt came from the lips of a Christian diplomat such as John of Gorze, the ambassador of the German emperor Otto I, or a Muslim courtier from Arabia. It also didn't matter that things were relatively good for the Jews living on the Iberian Peninsula.

For the times were good in tenth-century Spain. The Muslim Ummayad rulers had established a magnificent seat of culture in Cordoba, located in what is today the south of Spain. Hasdai held one of the highest positions at the caliph's court. Not only was he the personal physician of the caliph—first serving Abdarrahman II and then Hakam II—but he was also the inspector-general of customs at Cordoba's prosperous riverside port. Yet even that description doesn't paint the complete picture, for Hasdai was actually the caliph's closest confident and acted as his foreign minister.

Hasdai used his wealth and influence to help his fellow Jews. In a letter sent to the Byzantine empress Helena, he pleaded with her to grant religious liberty to the Jews living in her empire, pointing out that Christians were treated well in Muslim Spain. While he sent generous gifts to the yeshivos located in the Babylonian cities of Sura and Pumbedita, he was also instrumental in opening up centers of Jewish learning in Cordoba, so that Iberian Jews wouldn't have to be dependent upon the Babylonian scholars. He also personally supported several scholars and imported books from the East to raise the level of Jewish-Iberian scholarship.

Yet despite his achievements and the comfort he lived in, Hasdai was very aware that something crucial was lacking. The Jewish people were in exile. They were homeless. They were at the mercy of whoever ruled over them. After almost 1,000 years of wandering, there were even some Jews who were starting to believe the taunts of the non-Jews that God had abandoned His people.

Therefore, when messengers arrived from Constantinople with news that a Jewish king ruled over the land of the Khazars, Hasdai listened avidly to their words. If such a king truly existed, that surely meant that the Jewish people had not been entirely forsaken!

This was not the first time such a rumor had floated over Europe and landed in Spain. An earlier messenger had mentioned rumors about the kingdom, but Hasdai thought he was just trying to flatter him. These messengers, on the other hand, said they had personal knowledge—that their country traded goods with the Jewish kingdom and that there were diplomatic relations between the two countries. But were they telling the truth?

There was only way to find out. Hasdai called for one of the scholars he supported, Menachem ben Saruk—who was known for his literary gifts—and asked him to compose a letter to the King of the Khazars. The text of that letter has come down to us, and it displays Menachem's skill in conveying what was in Hasdai's heart.

For this is not just a correspondence between a diplomat and a foreign ruler. It is a letter written from one Jew in exile to another, and so it begins:

"I, Hasdai, son of Isaac, son of Ezra, belonging to the exiled Jews of Jerusalem in Spain, a servant of my lord the King, bow to the earth before him and prostrate myself towards the abode of your Majesty from a distant land. I rejoice in your tranquility and magnificence and stretch forth my hands to God in heaven that He may prolong your reign in Israel. ...."

The letter goes on to describe the condition of Spain's Jews and Hasdai's position at court. It then asks for details about the Jewish ruler's kingdom. Towards the end of the letter, Hasdai openly reveals what is gnawing at his heart:

"We live in the Diaspora and there is no power in our hands. They say to us every day, 'Every nation has a kingdom, but you have no memory of such in all the land.' But when we heard about our master the King, the might of his monarchy, and his mighty army, we were amazed. We lifted our heads, our spirits returned, our hands were strengthened, and my master's kingdom was our response in defense. ..."

The letter was dispatched, but it didn't reach its destination. Hasdai's emissary, Yitzchak ben Nosan, was stopped in Constantinople by suspicious Byzantine officials and he was forced to return to Spain.

Two Jews who worked for the ambassador from Germany suggested that Hasdai try a northern route instead: send the letter across Germany to Hungary, and then on to Bulgaria and Russia, where it could be delivered to Khazeria. The second attempt was successful and a German Jew named Yitzchak ben Eliezer had the honor of delivering the letter to Yosef, the King of the Khazars.

The irony, as historians point out, is that Hasdai established contact with the Jewish kingdom just a few years before it was crushed by invaders. Yet long after the Kingdom of the Khazars ceased to exist politically, it continued to flourish in the hearts and minds of the exiled Jewish people.

A Refuge in the East

"Every schoolchild in the West has been told that if not for Charles Martel and the battle of Poitiers there might have been a mosque where Notre Dame now stands. What few schoolchildren are aware of is that if not for the Khazars … Eastern Europe might well have become a province of Islam."

With these words from his book *Khazar Studies*, Professor Peter Golden of Rutgers University sums up the importance of the Khazars — an importance not only for the Jews, but for all of Europe.

The Khazars, a people of Turkic origin, first appear on the world stage in the seventh century CE, after the collapse of the Gokturk Empire, which stretched from the Crimea in the west to the northwestern border of China to the east. In the struggle that ensued over the next century amongst the various tribes of the former empire, the Khazars became the dominant power.

Their first task was to stop the northward expansion of the Arab Umayyad regime, which was trying to gain control of Central Asia and the Caucasus. The Khazars won a major victory in 650, when they defeated an Arab force outside the Khazar town of Balanjar. The Arabs tried again in the 710s, and this time their forces were successful. However, instability within their own empire forced the Arabs to retreat and the Khazars regained their independence around the year 740. A relatively peaceful period followed, which has been dubbed the "*pax khazarica.*" During this time various tribes, including the Slavs, expanded their settlements in the Eastern European steppes, forming the basis of what would later become well known Ukrainian cities and towns, including Kiev.

The Khazars were remarkably tolerant and they opened the doors of their empire to Jewish refugees fleeing from persecution in Byzantine, Persia, and elsewhere. They also happened to be remarkably fortunate in terms of their location, because their lands were situated on an important trade route between Europe and China, later known as the Silk Road. Naturally, the Jews played an important role in helping the Khazars make the most of their excellent geographic location.

A Fair Trade

During the early Middle Ages, Christian Europe and Muslim countries often refused to do business directly with one another. Therefore, an intermediary was needed—a people who didn't belong to either religion. That role, of course, was fulfilled by the Jews.

A group of Jewish merchants known as the Radhanites traveled back and forth between Europe and China using four main trade routes, all of which began in France's Rhone Valley and ended in China, and which passed through Christian, Muslim, and pagan countries along the way. According to a contemporary account written by Ibn Khordadbeh, an Arab Director of Posts and Police during the late 800s, the Radhanites transported steel weapons, furs, and slaves from Europe to China. On their return trip home they brought back luxury items such as spices, silks, perfumes, and jewelry.

Some historians believe that the Radhanites helped to establish Jewish communities along their trade routes, including in Eastern Europe, Central Asia, India, and China. It is also very possible that they played a role in an extraordinary event that occurred in the ninth century: the conversion of the Khazar royal family, and large parts of the general population, to Judaism.

Why Be Jewish?

The jury is still out as to why the Khazars decided to convert to Judaism en masse. Modern historians of a practical bent note that since the empire was sandwiched between Christian Europe to the west and Muslim countries to the east, the best way not to be swallowed up by either one was to remain neutral. Since both Christianity and Islam recognized Judaism to be the "mother" religion, the theory goes that the Khazars thought their neighbors wouldn't mind if there was a neutral Jewish kingdom lodged between their borders.

Khazar tradition gives an entirely different reason. In King Yosef's response to Hasdai Ibn Shaprut's letter, he describes how an early Khazar king, King Bulan, rejected paganism and began to search for the true faith. He invited representatives from

Christianity, Islam, and Judaism to present the case for their respective religions, and:

"On the third day he called all the sages together and said to them. 'Speak and argue with one another and make clear to me which is the best religion.' They began to dispute with one another without arriving at any results until the King said to the Christian priest 'What do you think? Of the religion of the Jews and the Muslims, which is to be preferred?' The priest answered: 'The religion of the Israelites is better than that of the Muslims.'

"The King then asked the kadi [a Muslim judge and scholar]: 'What do you say? Is the religion of the Israelites or that of the Christians preferable?' The kadi answered: 'The religion of the Israelites is preferable.'

"Upon this the King said: 'If this is so, you both have admitted with your own mouths that the religion of the Israelites is better. Wherefore, trusting in the mercies of God and the power of the Almighty, I choose the religion of Israel, that is, the religion of Abraham.'"

The tradition related by King Yosef forms the basis for the best known work about the Khazars, *The Kuzari*, which was written by the twelfth- century religious Iberian poet and philosopher Rabbi Yehuda Halevi. Although *The Kuzari* is not a history book—its purpose is to prove that Judaism is the one true faith—it describes a series of fictionalized meetings between the pagan king of the Khazars and a Jewish sage, whom the king has asked to teach him about the Jewish religion.

The annals of history do suggest that such a Jewish sage may have existed. Medieval Jewish sages, including the Ramban and the author of *Sefer HaEmunos*, mention a Rabbi Yitzchak HaSangari, whom they believe was a companion of the Khazar king and played an instrumental role in converting the Khazari people to Judaism. *Sefer HaEmunos* also mentions that Rabbi Yehuda Halevi had access to Rabbi Yitzchak's writings and used them as the basis for the discussion in *The Kuzari*.

However, there is yet a third possible explanation for the Khazars' conversion to Judaism. In the late 1800s, the scholar Solomon Schechter was sorting through the findings of the Cairo Geniza and he ran across a badly damaged letter that has come to be known as the "Schechter Letter." In this correspondence, which is between an unnamed Khazar author and an unknown Jewish dignitary, the author explains how the Khazars converted to Judaism.

According to this account, after Jews from Persia and Armenia fled to the Khazars' lands, the Jews intermarried with the Khazars and totally assimilated. Many years later a strong warrior leader called Sabriel became the ruler of the Khazars. It so happened that this Sabriel was descended from those early Jewish settlers. His wife Serach convinced him to convert to Judaism, and afterward his people followed him.

Some historians believe that the Schechter Letter was written by a Khazar based in Constantinople, who had learned of Hasdai Ibn Shaprut's first unsuccessful attempt to contact King Yosef and decided to communicate with the Spanish diplomat. However, there is no way to prove the veracity of this theory.

At any rate, what is known today, as opposed to what was believed a generation ago, is that Judaism was not just adopted by the royal family, but also spread throughout the entire empire. Recent archeological digs at Khazar burial sites have discovered that the Khazars' burial practices began to change in the mid-800s, reflecting a turn away from the pagan practice of placing material goods in the grave. By the year 950, the pagan practice had totally disappeared among all classes of Khazar society, suggesting Judaism's pervasive influence.

Contemporary sources also speak about the widespread nature of the Khazars' conversion to Judaism. Ibn al-Faqih, a tenth-century Persian historian, put it simply when he said, "All the Khazars are Jews." An even earlier source, the ninth-century monk Christian of Stavelot, writing in *Expositio in Matthaeum Evangelistam*, says: "At the present time we know of no nation under the heavens where Christians do not live. For [Christians are even found] in the lands of Gog and Magog—who are a Hunnic race and are called Gazari (Khazars) [they are] circumcised and observing all [the laws of] Judaism."

Despite Ibn al-Faqih's comment that all the Khazars were Jews, it is known that the Jewish kingdom actually allowed people of other faiths to freely worship their own religions. Therefore, although the dominant religion was Judaism for nearly three centuries,

Christianity, Zoroastrianism, and various pagan cults were also practiced.

A World Power To Be Proud Of

The Khazars were a wealthy nation. A ten percent tax was levied on all goods passing through its borders. The central government earned so much from tax revenues from the Silk Road trade, as well as from tribute money paid by vassal states, that the citizens didn't have to pay any taxes.

In addition to their wealth, the Khazars were known for the fairness of their court system. Their supreme court had seven judges, who represented the kingdom's major religions: Judaism, Christianity, Islam, and Slavic paganism. In addition, a citizen had the right to be tried according to the laws of his religion.

The height of the kingdom's influence occurred in the ninth century, when the *pax khazarica* reigned and a steady stream of goods traveled peacefully over the lucrative trade routes. By the tenth century, however, the empire was coming under attack. Strong rulers, such as Aharon II and Yosef (the king that Hasdai wrote to) were able to squelch local revolts and fend off tribal invaders for a while. However, the Khazars had seriously offended Christian Byzantine when the kingdom converted to Judaism, and the Byzantines were waiting for their chance to get back. The Byzantines formed alliances with various smaller states and had these states attack the Khazars from all sides. The final blow came from the north when the Rus, a former pagan ally located in northwest Russia that was beginning to become Christian, attacked the Khazars.

"I have to wage war with them [the Rus]," King Yosef wrote to Hasdai Ibn Shaprut, "for if I would give them any chance at all they would lay waste the whole land of the Muslims as far as Baghdad."

After a series of battles, the Khazars' capital city, Atil, was captured by the Rus in 967 (or possibly 969) and destroyed, signaling the end of the Jewish kingdom. No one knows for sure what happened to King Yosef, although it is assumed that he fell in battle.

After the Fall

No one really knows for sure what happened to the Khazar people either. Some of them probably assimilated into the various Christian and Muslim communities. Those who remained Jewish might have become the ancestors of the Mountain Jews who lived in the Caucasus. There is a tradition that some moved to Hungary. Former Israeli foreign minister and author Abba Ebban suggested in his book *My People* that many of them moved to Slavic lands, where they helped to establish Jewish communities in Eastern Europe. The British historian Martin Gilbert suggests that they moved to Lithuania, where they established a community in Vilna.

What is certain is that the Jewish people have never lost interest in the Khazers. For the kingdom of the Khazars was the real thing. Its army was powerful, its wealth was substantial, and its civic spirit of justice and respect was practically unparalleled in the medieval world. It's no wonder, then, that news of this kingdom caused such a sensation in Hasdai's Spain—and still arouses our admiration even today.

—September 2007

WOMEN'S WORK

Dehiya, Al-Kahina, Queen of the Berbers

She fought off an Arab invasion in the seventh century and inspired a cultural revolt in the 1990s. Who was the mysterious "Al-Kahina" — and why does her legend still hold such power today?

The invading Arab forces seemed to be unstoppable. Just one decade after the death of the founder of Islam, in the year 632, Muslims from Arabia took on the Byzantine Empire and conquered Syria, Egypt, and the Land of Israel. They also targeted the Persian Empire for conquest, first capturing Iraq and then, in 642, forcing the once mighty Persia to surrender.

Although an internal civil war halted their continued expansion for about a decade, once that conflict was resolved the Arabs looked westward. Under the leadership of Uqba ibn Nafi, the Muslims swept across North Africa and reached the shores of the Atlantic, where legend has it that Uqba thrust his sword into the water, frustrated that there were no more lands to conquer.

That wasn't entirely true. The Christian Byzantines had managed to retain hold of some of their North African coastal cities, including one of the most important Byzantine cities at that time — Carthage. In addition, a stubborn group of insurgents was causing trouble in lands that Uqba had already conquered. During his return march across North Africa in 683, Uqba was killed in battle by these rebellious Berber tribes, who were just as determined to drive out the Arabs as the Arabs were determined to conquer them.

It would take the Arabs another two decades to subdue the unruly Berbers, the rugged people who made their homes in the equally rugged Atlas Mountains. One of the Arabs' fiercest opponents in that struggle, unbelievable as it might seem, was a Jewish woman called "Al-Kahina," who was Queen of the Berbers until her army was defeated by the Arab forces.

Who was Al-Kahina, and how did Jews come to live in an area which is still isolated even today? Although much of the history is shrouded in mystery, there are enough facts to piece together the story of the woman whom one historian called "the Deborah of the Berbers."

A Little Jewish Geography

No one knows for sure when the Jews first came to the Maghreb, the Arabic word which means "place of the sunset" or "western." In Old Arabic, the Maghreb was used to describe the area in North Africa that lies between the coast of the Mediterranean Sea and the Atlas Mountains, which stretch across Tunisia, Algeria, and Morocco. What is certain is that there were Jews in the area long before the Arabs gave it a name.

According to an oral tradition in Morocco, the first Jewish presence in lands west of Egypt was established around 1300 BCE by Joseph's son Ephraim. Some Moroccan Jews believe that they are descended from Ephraim, and that this kingdom continued to exist, in one form or another, until around 1147 CE.

However, historians believe that Phoenician traders were the first to colonize the North African coast, and that this occurred during the ninth century BCE. Although there is some speculation that Israelite traders followed in their wake, there is no material evidence to support this claim. Other historians believe that the Jews first settled in the area after the destruction of the first *Beis HaMikdash* (Holy Temple) in the year 586 BCE, as part of the Babylonians' resettlement plan. Yet another theory places the date even later—after the conquest of Judea by Alexander the Great in the fourth century BCE.

What does seem to be certain is that there were flourishing—and relatively autonomous—Jewish communities in North Africa well before the year 146 BCE, when the Romans conquered Carthage, the Phoenician's capital city. Substantiating these claims are Phoenician reports about trading with the local Jews, who engaged in commerce and agriculture, as well as linguistic evidence that these Jews spoke

Hebrew until the fifth century CE—and not Aramaic, which gradually began to replace Hebrew as the lingua franca of Judean Jews after their exile to Babylonia.

The Jewish population of the North African coastal area was further increased after the destruction of the second *Beis HaMikdash* (approximately 70 CE). According to the historian Josephus, the Roman emperor Titus exiled about 30,000 Judeans to Carthage. Subsequent uprisings in Judea, including the Bar Kochba revolt, led to more Jews being exiled to North Africa, where they were sold as slaves.

During those times, when the Romans forbid many Jewish practices—such as studying Torah, *bris milah* (circumcision), and Shabbos observance—the Talmud relates that Rabbi Akiva traveled to the communities of North Africa to strengthen them.

Rabbi Akiva probably traveled to Cyrenaica, the coastal area of modern-day Libya, which Josephus tells us had a Jewish population of about 500,000 during the first century CE. After the Roman suppression of a Jewish rebellion in Cyrenaica, circa 117 CE, many of these Jews fled west to the Maghreb, further swelling its Jewish population. The westward migration continued during the following centuries, when rule was transferred from the Roman Empire to the Vandals, who were subsequently vanquished by the Christian Byzantines.

Life under the Christians rulers, who obviously saw Judaism as a threat, became increasingly worse for the Jews. In 414 CE, the Jews were expelled from Alexandria, which had once been the largest and most important Jewish community in North Africa. Like others before them, they fled west, but there was little security in their new homes. In 535 CE the Byzantine ruler Justinian issued an edict where Jews were officially turned into second-class residents of the Christian Roman Empire. In addition to being barred from holding public office, the Jews were prohibited from practicing their religion. Synagogues were turned into churches and torture was commonly used to force the Jews to convert.

To escape the clutches of the Byzantines, many Jews fled inland, to the Atlas Mountains. In particular, they settled in the area of the Aures Mountains, located in eastern Algeria and considered to be one of the most isolated spots in that isolated region. There the Jews encountered the native Berber population, a loose confederation of tribes who were still pagans, due to the fact that Byzantine rule was mainly centered in the coastal areas.

The mountain Berbers welcomed the Jews with open arms, recognizing the Jews' vast technological knowledge, as well as their scholarly erudition. In fact, about eight of these tribes were so impressed by the newcomers that they decided to put their pagan practices aside and convert to Judaism. United by religion as well as by an intense desire to remain a free people, these tribes banded together to form a small but mighty Jewish kingdom.

The Mystery of the Berbers

If the origin of the Jewish presence in North Africa is shrouded in mystery, it is in good company. Even the origin of the region's indigenous population, the Berbers, is unknown. In fact, no one is even quite sure how the Berbers got their name.

It's assumed that the word "berber" comes from the Latin word for barbarians. However, the Greeks called them Libyans and the Romans referred to them as being Numidians and Moors. It was the Arabs who gave them the name "Al-Babar," which may sound like it comes from the Latin word barbarian but it is almost certain that the Arabs didn't give their conquered people Latin names!

According to the fourteenth-century Muslim historian Ibn Khaldun, the Arabs believed—or at least created a myth, according to their tradition—that "the Berbers were the descendants of Ham, the son of Noah, the son of Barbar, the son of Tamalla, the son of Mazigh, the son of Canon."

Interestingly enough, the Sages of the Talmud also believe that the Berbers were the descendants of Ham, whose son Canaan founded a dynasty that included the Girgashite nation. In Tractate *Shevi'is* of the Jerusalem Talmud (6:1) it discusses Joshua's war against the Canaanite nations, saying: "Rabbi Shmuel bar Nachman said: three decrees were sent out into the land of Israel before they went into the land. Whoever wishes to leave should leave. To make peace, should make peace. To make war, should do so. The Girgashi left, and believed in the Holy One, Blessed be He, and went to Afriki …"

The Berbers actually call themselves the Imazighen, which means the "free people," and they refer to their territory as the

Tamazgha (land of the free people). A semi-nomadic people, they grew vegetables and raised livestock and also built small villages where they developed local industries such as working with iron, copper, and lead, making pottery, and weaving. Ever true to their name, each village was autonomous. However, they could band together during times of need.

Yet even though they could be fierce warriors, they were not predominately a warlike people. They allowed the Phoenicians, Greeks, Romans, and Byzantines to set up their colonies on Berber land, but all the while they held on to their own culture and sense of identity. It was only in the Middle Ages that they briefly became a conquering force of their own.

Most Berbers were originally pagans. Some converted to Christianity when the Byzantines conquered the coastal area. However, according to the third-century church leader and author Tertullian, the Jews had been alarmingly successful with converting Berbers to the Jewish faith. He noted that many Berbers observed Shabbos, the Jewish holidays and fast days, and kashrus.

In an era where the powerful Christians were trying to convert as many non-Christians as possible, the success of the Jews was seen as a slap in the face. Tertullian therefore wrote a polemic against the Jews called *Adversus Judaeos*, which became the basis for the vilification of the Jews and Judaism throughout Christian lands.

According to Ibn Khaldun, the Jews attracted the most converts in the mountainous areas located in the central Maghreb (today's Algeria,) which were inhabited by the nomadic Berber tribes. One of these tribes was called the Jerawa, which became famous throughout North Africa as being the tribe of Dehiya, Al-Kahina.

The Legend of Dehiya, Al-Kahina

It should be noted from the start that there are some modern historians who disagree with the widely accepted theory that Dehiya, Al-Kahina, was Jewish. Indeed, she is not mentioned in any Jewish sources. However, even today the Berbers, who have regulated her to the status of national hero, claim that she was a Jew. The well-respected medieval Arab historian Ibn Khaldun—who was admired by Edward Gibbon, author of *The Decline and Fall of the Roman Empire*—also writes that she was Jewish.

The modern Jewish historian Salo Baron agrees with most of Ibn Khaldun's account, even though it was written some 700 hundred years after the events occurred and relies heavily on folk legends. Baron writes, "Nevertheless this account is essentially confirmed and amplified in many significant details in the more recently published chronicle of an older Arab writer, 'Ubaud ibn Salih ibn 'Abd al-Halim."

Therefore, those who claim she was a Jew are in good company. However, the controversy is not yet over as further disagreement revolves around her origins. One account states that she was descended from the Jews who had fled from Cyrenaica after the Jewish revolt to the mountains, to escape from the Romans. Another account states that her family was new to the area, suggesting that they were Jews fleeing from Christian persecutors. It is also possible that she and her tribe were recent converts to the Jewish faith. The Israeli historian Nachum ben David Shlomo Slutz, whose literary biography of Dehiya closely follows the Ibn Khaldun version, says that she was the daughter of a priestly family who ruled in Jerawa. We will probably never know for sure, as solid historical fact is silent on this point, just as it is silent about much of her life.

Monroe Rosenthal and Isaac Mozeson, who in their book *Wars of the Jews* say that she was born to a poor Jewish family who lived in a cave in the mountains, provide us with another biographical detail. A chieftain of another Judeo-Berber tribe began to terrorize the Jerawa tribe and demanded that Dehiya marry him. When she refused, he retaliated by slaughtering several members of her tribe. To save her people from further slaughter, she agreed to marry him. However, on their wedding night she emulated the Biblical heroine Yael and drove a nail through his skull.

Whether this story is true or not, there is general agreement that she did marry and she had two natural sons and one adopted son, of whom we will hear more about later. According to Ibn Khaldun's chronicles, she lived for 127 years and governed the tribe of Jerawa, with the aid of her sons, for 65 years. How did she rise to this position of prominence? Perhaps a hint can be found in the title that the Arabs bestowed upon her: Al-Kahina (the Kahina).

Although a few believe that the word "kahina" comes from the Hebrew word *kohein* (priest), most historians believe that the term comes from the Arabic word *"kahin,"* which means "soothsayer" or "prophetess." Slutz mentions how she was an only child, and so her priest/soothsayer father taught her all his wisdom, including how to predict the future. And according to Slutz and Ibn Khaldun, Dehiya was able to predict the future with uncanny accuracy. This ability, along with her charismatic personality, made her an inspiring leader during uncertain times. It also sparked fear in the hearts of the Arabs, and she was sometimes described as being a fearsome sorceress in their legends.

When the Arabs began their invasion of North Africa, the Jewish Berbers formed an alliance with the pagan Berbers who lived in the mountains and the Christian Byzantines who lived along the coast. The Jewish tribes crowned Al-Kahina as their queen and appointed her their military leader. After the leader of the non-Jewish Berbers was killed in battle, she became the queen and military commander of all the Berbers, where she gained a reputation as being a fierce warrior.

The Arabs, under the leadership of Uqba, were unprepared for this strong resistance. As mentioned earlier, Uqba was killed in a Berber ambush. However, the Arabs were not deterred. They made a second invasion, this time under the leadership of Hassan ibn Numan, whose army of 40,000 horsemen captured Carthage.

The tide turned against the Arabs when they encountered Queen Kahina's forces for the first time. Slutz recounts the story of that fateful battle that took place outside the town of Bagia. After escaping from the besieged city through a series of secret passageways, Queen Kahina led her forces to a high place where they had an advantage over their enemy. She ordered her cavalrymen to remain in their saddles all night, which forced the Arab invaders to do the same. The difference, of course, was that the Berber troops were well rested and on familiar territory, while the Arabs were exhausted from their battles and strangers in a foreign land.

At dawn, the Berbers attacked from the front, while the townspeople attacked from the rear. The result was that Queen Kahina defeated Hassan's troops so thoroughly that he was forced to retreat first to Libya and then to Egypt, where he remained for five years. After this triumph, Queen Kahina liberated Carthage and other cities and villages, some of which had been conquered by the Arabs and some of which were still under Byzantine rule. Christians hailed her as the one who had liberated them from Arab rule, while the Jews were grateful that she had put an end to Byzantine domination of the region.

For the next five years the Berbers were the rulers of their own lands, making it a rare period in the history of North Africa when the indigenous people enjoyed freedom from foreign domination. However, the alliance did not last.

According to Slutz, disagreements broke out between the semi-nomadic Berbers and the city-dwellers, something that often happens when two very different ways of life encounter one another and clash. The disagreements were further exacerbated by the fact that the nomads were either Jewish or pagan, while many of the city-dwellers were Christians. When news of the internal grumblings reached the ears of the Arab general Hassan, he made preparations for yet another attack.

What happened next is unclear. According to Ibn Khaldun and other Muslim historians, when Queen Kahina learned about the planned invasion, she decided to deter the Arabs by pursuing a scorched earth policy. Declaring that the Arabs wished to conquer North Africa only because of the wealth of its coastal cities, she ordered the nomadic Berber warriors to completely destroy the cities and orchards of the sedentary Berbers.

Slutz suggests that she may have pursued this policy because she was bitter about being betrayed by her former Christian allies, who had rebelled against her and had gone over to the Arab side. Other historians find it hard to believe that a person as obviously intelligent as Queen Kahina would engage in such a destructive policy, which alienated even many of her pagan allies. Instead, they think that Hassan, angered by the fierce Berber resistance, destroyed the cities and orchards himself and then placed the blame on Queen Kahina. Yet another theory says that the destruction of the coastal area was a result of hundreds of years of warfare in the area, and not due to one general's strategic decision.

Whichever version is correct, North Africa was turned into a desert and the coastal city-dwellers and pagan Berbers turned against their Queen. Another blow, according to some accounts, came from a member of her household, a young Muslim captive that she had adopted, named Khalid ibn Yessid El Kaisi. In one version of the story, Khalid secretly passed along to Hassan the Berbers' battle plans, as well as the locations of their encampments and hideouts. He left the Berber camp before his treachery was exposed and became a deputy commander in Hassan's army.

According to the Arab historian Ibn Nuvairi, when the final showdown between Queen Kahina and Hassan occurred, perhaps in the year 703, the fighting was fierce. He writes that it was only because of the "will of Allah" that the Muslim forces triumphed. As in life, the historical accounts differ as to how Queen Kahina met her death.

Some say that she died on the battlefield, sword in hand. Others say that she was taken captive. When Hassan commanded her to either convert or become his vassal, she refused both and was beheaded. Yet another version has it that she swallowed poison and committed suicide. Slutz, following the Ibn Khaldun version, says that she threw herself into a well, rather than be taken captive. Legend has it that the well is located in the Aures Mountains at a place called Bir-al-Kahen (Al-Kahina's well), which still bears the same name today.

However she died, after her death the Berber tribes surrendered. The majority of the Jewish troops were slaughtered. According to Slutz, Queen Kahina had foreseen this end, as well. In his version, she tells her adopted son Khalid to take her two sons to Hassan and beg for mercy, even though this will mean that the two young men will have to convert to Islam. The Arab general accepts the young men and they join Hassan's army.

The Conquest of Spain

In his book on the history of North Africa, Charles-Andre Julien posits that Queen Kahina told her sons to convert to Islam because the survival of her family was more important to her than her religion or Berber independence. However, Slutz presents another possible theory.

During this time, the Christian Visigoths ruled over the Iberian Peninsula, causing untold misery to the Jews living there. These brutal overlords would often drag entire Jewish communities to the baptismal fount and forced them to become Christians. Although the Arabs could act brutally toward the leaders and armies of their enemies, they had a different policy for the general population.

People were given a choice: they could either convert to Islam and become first-class citizens or retain their religion and become *dhimmis*, second-class citizens.

Slutz posits that Queen Kahina told her sons to go over to Hassan's forces for two reasons. One, she retained a hope that one day they would be able to free their people from the Arab invaders and return to power—and their Jewish faith. She also wanted to help free the Iberian Jews from Visigoth domination. Indeed, her sons, as well as the remnants of the Jerawa tribe, subsequently joined the forces of the Arab general Tarik, who gave his name to Gibraltar (Tarik's Rock) and who led the successful conquest of Spain.

Whether or not Slutz's theory is true, what is true is that the Iberian Jews welcomed the invading force and worked to ensure their success. And they had good reason to do so. Although the Jews were considered to be *dhimmis*, at least they were no longer forced to convert to another religion. Furthermore, the Ummayad rulers of Muslim Spain were more tolerant than the Christian leaders of the rest of Europe. For almost three centuries, the Iberian Peninsula enjoyed a golden age where science and the arts flourished, and where Sephardic culture reached its zenith.

The Legend Today

A Jewish-Berber presence in the Maghreb came to an end after the establishment of the State of Israel, when the vast majority of the region's Jews immigrated to the Jewish state. Although at one point there may have been more than 100,000 speakers of the Judeo-Berber language, which was used both in the home and as the language of instruction and culture, today there are only a few elderly people who remember the language.

However, according to Dr. Bruce Maddy-Wesitzman, a Senior Research Fellow at the Moshe Dayan Center for Middle Eastern and African Studies, Jewish-Berber culture is being kept alive in a very surprising place: the Maghreb. Some Berber nationalists in Morocco, Algeria, and Tunisia are ardently against the Arab-Islamic nationalism that has gripped their lands—and forced their own culture underground. They also openly express admiration for the

State of Israel, which successfully revived Hebrew as a spoken language and granted autonomy to the Jewish people.

Since poems and songs in Arabic about Al-Kahina have existed for centuries and are part of Berber folklore, it's perhaps not surprising that Queen Kahina has always been something of a political and cultural symbol for the Berbers. In the 1990s, for instance, a sometimes violent cultural uprising rocked Algeria and other parts of the Maghreb and Queen Kahina became one of the symbols of this revolt.

During the past decade, the governments of Algeria and Morocco have made some concessions to the Berbers' demands that their culture be recognized and granted financial support. As a gesture of goodwill, in 2003 the President of the Algerian Republic attended a ceremony in Baghai — the town where Queen Kahina had one of her greatest military successes. What was the highlight of this ceremony? The moment when a huge bronze statue of Queen Kahina was unveiled.

Morocco has also agreed to invest more in Berber culture. Its Royal Institute of Amazigh (Berber) Culture recently developed a comic book whose primary goal is to teach youngsters the Tamazight (Berber) language. As we know, the best way to teach children language skills is to cloak the grammar and vocabulary within an enthralling tale. Therefore, the story they chose to use for this new educational tool was, of course, the story of Dehiya, Al-Kahina, Queen of the Berbers.

—September 2007

Is There a Doctor in the House?

It's common knowledge that women have worked as healers and midwives throughout the ages. What's less well known is that when a sick person living in medieval Europe went to see a physician, the "doctor in the house" just might have been a Jewish woman.

"For brightening the light of the eyes: Take calamine that is similar to a white stone of a weight of half a zekuk and take from it five or six pieces and burn them. Remove it with tongs and put it into a jar of strong vinegar. Do it nine times to soften the calamine. Afterwards pound the calamine in a mortar well until it is a fine powder and sift the powder through a thin cloth. Every night take a palm's worth and dilute it with a bit of wine or saliva and put it around the eye when you go to sleep. And it will brighten the eyes. This is a tested and proven remedy." — *Doctors: Medieval*, Cheryl Tallen, Jewish Women's Archive

To be honest, when I first read this "tested and proven remedy" for red eye and other eye ailments offered by Marat Yuskah, a Jewish woman who worked as an oculist (eye doctor) in the early 1200s in Germany, I was leery. Isn't it a big no-no to put calamine lotion anywhere near the eyes? Was this just an old wives' tale, and one that did more harm than good?

Apparently not. Six hundred years later, in the early 1800s, *The London Medical Dictionary* gave a recipe for an ointment that was very similar to Marat Yuskah's to treat discharges from the eye and cloudiness of the cornea. Chinese medicine has also recommended a similar mixture for many long years.

Marat Yuskah was therefore in good company—one that knew, unlike me, that calamine lotion and this remedy are two very different things. But at a time when Jews were barred from so many professions, how did she obtain her medical knowledge? Who were her patients? And, the six-million-dollar question, could a medieval physician who happened to be both Jewish and a woman make a decent living?

The Doctor Is In

Jewish doctors have always been in demand. Even during the Middle Ages, a period when Jews were barred from most professions in most European countries, medicine was often the exception. One reason is that Jews served as a bridge between the Arab lands—where medical knowledge was at a higher level—and medieval Europe. Just as Jewish doctors had translated Greek medical treatises for their Arab colleagues during the Golden Age of Spain, a time when relations between Jews and Muslim were, on the whole, good, Jewish doctors who later fled from the Iberian Peninsula and settled on the European continent translated these medical works into Latin, the vernacular of Europe's scholarly class. They also brought with them their own expertise and skill, culled from Jewish sources such as the Talmud, medical works written in Hebrew, and knowledge that was handed down throughout the generations from father to son.

And, sometimes, to daughters.

This partially explains how Jewish women received their medical education—and anyone who called themselves a physician or doctor did need to be educated. Despite the fact that much of medieval medicine would be considered primitive by today's standards, and many of the treatments for serious ailments were horrifically painful, not just anyone could hang a shingle that said "The Doctor Is In." All professions were heavily regulated during the Middle Ages, and the medical profession was no exception.

Medical practitioners were divided into four main categories. At the top were the university-trained physicians, who made diagnoses and suggested remedies. Next came the surgeons/barbers; as their names suggest, they offered hands-on treatments. After them came the apothecaries, who would whip up a plant- or herb-based powder or potion for common complaints. Finally, there were the midwives.

There was another class, which Jewish physicians sometimes fell into, that was known as "empirics." These doctors hadn't received a university education; instead, their medical knowledge came from practical experience. But why would a Jewish young person choose to be an empiric, when it lacked the status of being a full-fledged physician?

The answer, of course, had to do with discrimination. There were times and places when Jews were welcomed into the medical field with open arms. For instance, the medical school at Italy's University of Salerno, which had its glory days between the tenth and thirteenth centuries, not only trained Jewish physicians, but also had Jewish doctors on the faculty. The medical school was also one of the few places that allowed women to enroll and receive a degree. But this was the exception, and it was much more common for European universities, which were governed by the Catholic Church, to exclude all Jews and most women.

Jewish women therefore would learn their profession by becoming an apprentice to an experienced physician. For modesty reasons, this would usually be a father or husband. The teacher might also be the woman's mother, although this was rarer.

Practicing medicine without a university-recognized license did have its drawbacks. For instance, when Parisian authorities decided to crack down on unlicensed physicians in 1322, a doctor named Belota the Jewess was one of the doctors hauled before the court. Interestingly, the charge that was made against the accused, which were mainly women but did include some non-Jewish male physicians as well, wasn't that their treatments were inferior. Instead, it was an open attempt by doctors trained at the University of Paris to put the competition out of business.

The Doctor Is Out

Belota the Jewess, like the others who were put on trial, was barred from ever again practicing medicine. But that wasn't the end of Jewish women physicians. During the Middle Ages, European cities grew at a fast pace, and the need for qualified doctors far exceeded the number who had been university trained. Therefore, a doctor's reputation often counted for more than a diploma, and women doctors were usually held in high regard by their grateful patients.

However, practicing medicine wasn't always a full-time job. In addition to her duties as a wife and mother, a typical medieval Jewish woman might have several professions, which she worked at from her home on a part-time basis. For instance, Mayrona of Manosque, who lived in Provence during the 1300s, was renowned as a skillful physician but she also had a successful career as a moneylender.

Other Jewish women physicians looked upon their profession as a way to do *chesed* (acts of kindness), as opposed to make money. Virdimura, for instance, told the physicians of the Sicilian Royal Court who examined her that she wished to become a doctor in order to provide treatment to poor people who couldn't afford to pay the high fees that most doctors charged. Apparently, the royal doctors didn't mind this sort of "competition," since Virdimura received permission to practice medicine in the Kingdom of Sicily in 1376.

The Eyes Have It

Although Jewish women practiced all sorts of medicine, and had both Jewish and non-Jewish patients, many of them specialized in treating eye problems. The study of eye diseases had always had a prominent place in Arab countries, suggesting that eye problems were more prevalent there than in Europe. It was therefore natural that Jewish doctors took this knowledge with them when they settled in other countries. But no one knows why Jewish women tended to specialize in this particular area.

Historian Amnon Cohen posits that since women also worked as cosmeticians, work that included preparing cosmetics for the eyes, they were already familiar with many eye ailments. Others suggest that women had a more delicate touch and so they were better at treating the delicate eye area. It might also have had to do with modesty issues; since a physician treated both men and women, eye problems posed less problems for a Jewish woman.

Although Jewish women physicians were only a small segment of the medieval medical community, they were generally held in high regard. That regard is perhaps best expressed by Rabbi Yehudah ben Asher, the brother of the *Ba'al HaTurim*, who had this to say about an unknown thirteenth-century woman oculist living in Cologne:

When I was an infant about three months old, my eyes were affected and were never completely restored. A certain woman tried to cure me when I was about three years of age but she added to my blindness to such an extent that I remained confined to the house for a year, being unable to see the road on which to walk. Then a Jewess, a skilled oculist, appeared on the scene. She treated me for about two months and then died. Had she lived another month, I might have recovered my sight fully. As it was, but for the two months' attention from her, I might never have been able to see at all.

* * *

She's on the Health Fund

It shouldn't happen, but if you should find yourself time-traveling back to medieval Europe and you need a doctor, here's a list of a few other Jewish women physicians, by country, courtesy of Cheryl Tallen's article for the Jewish Women's Archive on medieval doctors.

France and Provence
Sarre of Paris might sound like a fashion house, but it's actually the name of one of the first Jewish women physicians on record. She lived toward the end of the 1200s. Her daughter Florian was also a doctor.

Sara of Saint Gilles (early 1300s) both practiced medicine and taught it. A contract found in the Marseilles archives, dated August 28, 1326, states that she agreed to teach one Salvetus de Burgonoro, an inhabitant of Salon in Provence, *"artem medicine et phisice"* for the period of seven months.

Germany

Serlin, a Jewish doctor who lived during the fifteenth century in Frankfurt-am-Main, seems to have been an astute businesswoman as well as a good doctor. She petitioned the local authorities for a tax break in 1428, due to her competence and popularity, but her request was denied. She may be the "Serlin" mentioned in 1431, who was forbidden to lend money on interest (to non-Jews) since she earned enough income through her work as an eye doctor.

Sara of Wurtzburg was practicing medicine around the same time. For the price of two florins for the permission and ten florins for taxes and a contribution, she received permission from Bishop Johann II of Braun on May 2, 1419, to practice medicine.

Italy

Monna Antonia di maestro Daniele, a resident of Florence, earned the title "my daughter the doctor" sometime between 1386 and 1408, after studying at The Guild of Doctors, Apothecaries, and Grocers.

Manuela and her son Angelo were noteworthy physicians for several reasons. Residents of Rome, they were personal physicians to Pope Bonifacius IX, who liked them enough to get them an exemption from paying taxes in 1399. But they were also well known for their work with the poor, whom they treated without requesting payment.

Spain

Floreta ca Noga (late 1300s) underwent a three-year course of study to receive her medical license. The investment paid off handsomely since she was often called to the royal palace to treat Sibila, Queen of Aragon.

Eastern Europe

To date, only one Jewish woman physician has been discovered: Slawa of Warsaw. A 1435 agreement stated that her patient didn't have to pay if the woman wasn't cured, suggesting either that Slawa was very sure of herself or that the medical profession wasn't as lucrative in medieval Poland as elsewhere.

Israel, Egypt, and Turkey

A document found in the Cairo *Genizah* (a synagogue storeroom where more than 200,000 ancient Jewish documents were found) makes mention of a Jewish woman oculist, and it's known that there were several women eye doctors in sixteenth-century Jerusalem. A century later, Bula Ikschati, the widow of Salomon Ashkenazi, a renowned statesman and physician, cured the young Sultan Achmed I of smallpox.

* * *

Would You Like a Haircut with That Operation?

If a young doctor today were to say that she received her medical license from The Guild of Doctors, Apothecaries, and Grocers, most people would insist on going elsewhere for a second opinion. Yet in the medieval world, lumping doctors with grocers wouldn't have been considered odd at all.

The reason had to do with the guild system, which regulated all the professions in an attempt to ensure a high standard of performance. But rather than group together professions by their purpose, the medieval guild was organized according to the tools and materials that the various professions used. Thus surgeons and barbers were in the same guild, since they both made use of cutting instruments. Physicians, on the other hand, were grouped with apothecaries, grocers, and even artists, presumably because they all made use of powders and scales.

—January 2013

Making a Living, One Letter at a Time

The Talmud tells us that making a living is as difficult as splitting the Red Sea. But the "Ink Sea" — the world of printing and publishing — has provided a livelihood for the Jewish people ever since the printing industry began. And Jewish women were often the ones setting the type and managing the business.

Wanted: Women to work in brand new industry. Good eye for detail and an excellent knowledge of Hebrew required. Great earning potential for the right person.

Although this "Help Wanted" advertisement probably never appeared in print during the fifteenth century, it could have. Because just a few decades after Johannes Gutenberg invented his moveable type printing press, a woman by the name of Estellina Conat printed a book called *Bechinas Olam* and became the first Jewish woman printer that we know of.

In the six hundred years since then, Jewish women printers have supplied the Jewish world with *siddurim* (prayer books), *Chumashim* (Torah with commentary), sets of the Talmud and, of course, Passover *haggados*. And even though the industry has changed immensely since the early days when the mechanical printing press was the newest technology on the block, one thing has remained the same. It has always given Jewish women a steady salary, allowing them to support their families in an honorable way.

Welcome to Ye Olde Print Shoppe

Johannes Gutenberg invented his mechanical printing press around the year 1440. Immigrants from Germany brought the printing press to Italy in the 1460s, where the Jewish community enthusiastically embraced the new technology. By the year 1469, books were being printed in Hebrew — which was a year before the printing press arrived in France, and 20 years before it arrived on English shores.

Although the printing press certainly speeded up the bookmaking process, it was still slow work that needed a careful eye. Typesetters had to manually assemble each line of text using individual metal "slugs," which had one letter on each slug. The typesetter would also have to manually adjust the spaces between the letters and words, so that the margins would be justified. The task was even more challenging for Jewish typesetters, since most of the books printed required different sized blocks of text on the same page: one size for the main text, a smaller size for the commentary, and an even smaller size for the commentary on the commentary.

At first printing houses were family affairs, and printing remained a cottage industry until the nineteenth century. It was typical for the family to live above the printing areas and for the whole family to help out with the various tasks involved with running the press, although professional proofreaders and scholars were also employed to oversee the accuracy of the work. Women therefore learned the ins and outs of how to run a printing business from an early age, but they usually only took over the helm of a family-run business after their husband had passed away.

For both men and women, printing was considered to be "holy work." Below we mention a few of the more well-known Jewish women printers, many of whose books have survived in limited quantities and can still be found in auction house catalogues. But they represent just a small fraction of the women who have been engaged throughout the ages in this holy work of supplying the People of the Book with their cherished holy books.

Estellina Conat, Italy, 1470s

"I, Estellina, the wife of my worthy husband Avraham Conat, wrote this book *Bechinas Olam* with the aid of Yaakov Levi of Tarascon."

Scholars will raise their eyebrows at this quote. Yedaiah ben Avraham Bedersi was actually the author of the fourteenth-century ethical work called *Bechinas Olam*. But Estellina Conat, a Jewish woman who lived in Mantua, wasn't a plagiarizer trying to claim the book as her own. She just had a problem. Her husband had opened up a … a … you know, a …

No, people didn't. The technology was so new that no one had yet invented a Hebrew word for it, and so the Conats didn't know how to describe the work that Estellina had done. Avraham Conat therefore wrote that his wife "wrote" the book "with many pens, without the aid of a miracle." In other words, she printed the book on a mechanical printing press. Since she did it in the year 1477, she is the first Jewish woman to print a book that we have on record.

Juan de Lucena and His Four Daughters, Spain, pre-1480s

Although none of his books survive, it is thought that Juan de Lucena, one of the *anusim* who was forced to convert to Christianity, was the first printer of Hebrew books on the Iberian Peninsula. The evidence is based upon records from the Inquisition. De Lucena and his daughters were accused of printing books in two towns: Montalban and Toledo.

There is a danger in relying upon the Inquisition's records, since the confessions were obtained under duress. However, one of the daughters did confess, in 1485, "I accuse myself of having been delinquent by helping my father to write in Hebrew with type, which sin I committed while a girl in my father's house." Approximately 50 years later, another one of de Lucena's daughters was accused of the same crime and sentenced to life imprisonment.

Dona Reyna Mendes, Constantinople (Istanbul), late 1500s

Dona Reyna was the daughter of Dona Gracia and the wife of Don Josef Nasi — two of the wealthiest and most influential *anusim* of the sixteenth century. After a long journey that took the family from their native Portugal to Amsterdam and then to Italy, they found a safe haven in the Ottoman Empire, where they finally were able to practice Judaism openly.

Dona Gracia had supported many Torah scholars and paid for the printing of their books, but she wasn't involved in the actual process, which was done in other countries. The reason for sending the books abroad to be printed was because there weren't any printing presses in Constantinople in any language, and the first book printed in Turkish didn't appear until 1729.

Therefore, the printing press that Dona Reyna established in Constantinople in the 1580s, after her husband passed away and the sultan confiscated most of the family's wealth, was not only the first Hebrew printing press in Constantinople—it was the only printing press in the entire city. Her press printed at least 15 books, including prayer books and a tractate of the Talmud. After she passed away in the year 1599, the press was closed and it would take 40 years until another Hebrew printing press opened in Constantinople.

Ella and Gela, Northern Europe, late 1500s

"These Yiddish letters I set with my own hands, Ella, daughter of Moshe of Holland. My years number no more than nine, the only girl of six children. If you find an error, please remember that it was set by a child."

These words, which rhyme in the original Yiddish, are found on the title page of a Yiddish book printed in Dessau in the year 1696. "Moshe of Holland" was a convert to Judaism who had printing houses in several cities, including Amsterdam, Dessau, Berlin, Frankfurt an der Oder, and Halle. It was most definitely a family business, and most certainly the father employed older and more learned members of the family to work as proofreaders and check his daughter's work. But Ella must have been quite a talented typesetter since in 1697 she moved to Frankfurt an der Oder to work with her older brother on a bigger and more exciting project: a new edition of the Talmud.

Although Ella was the only girl in the family in 1696, soon afterward the family was blessed with another daughter, Gela, who also joined the family business at a young age. Gela worked at the family press located in Halle, where she set the type for two books during the years 1709-1710. Not to be outdone by her older sister, Gela wrote in a prayer book printed in 1710:

"Of this beautiful prayer book from beginning to end, I set all the letters in type with my own hands. I, Gela, the daughter of Moshe the printer, whose mother was Freida … She bore me among ten children. I am a maiden still under twelve years."

Reichel and others, Northern Europe, late 1500s

Although printing presses located on the Italian Peninsula had dominated Hebrew printing during the 1500s, the next century saw the ascendancy of Amsterdam and other parts of northern and central Europe. Hebrew printers in Amsterdam benefited from the influx of Spanish and Portuguese *anusim* fleeing from the Inquisition, who used their wealth to support the flourishing industry. *Defus Amsterdam* — "Printed in Amsterdam" (by then there was a Hebrew word for what printers were doing) — became a byword for excellence in printing.

Furth also became a major center of Hebrew printing during the early 1700s, although it was better known for the quantity of books produced than their quality. The town had many women typesetters, including a woman named Reichel bas Yitzchak Jutels of Wilmersdorf, who was the head typesetter for a Hebrew printing press owned by Tzvi Hirsch HaLevi and his son-in-law Mordechai Model.

Dyhernfurth, located close to the Polish border and near the thriving Jewish community of Breslau, became a center of Hebrew book printing when Shabbetai Bass, author of *Sifsei Chachamim*, saw a business opportunity and opened his press in 1689. Until then, Lithuanian-Polish scholars had to go to either Amsterdam or Prague to publish their books. Bass had gone to learn in Prague after his parents were murdered in a pogrom, and he might have bought a book or two at the printing establishment of Gutel bas Leib Setzer. But he correctly assumed that Polish scholars would be happy to use a printing press closer to home.

The business was partially destroyed by fire in 1708, and then Bass ran into trouble with the non-Jewish authorities. After Bass passed away the press was bought by Yissachar Cohen, a relative by marriage. When Cohen passed away in 1729, his widow took over the management of the company.

Widow and Orphans of Yaakov Proops, Amsterdam, 1780s-1820s

Today the term "widow and orphans" refers to a typesetting problem. A widow is the last line of a paragraph that is "widowed" from the rest of the paragraph when it is placed alone at the top of the following column or page. An orphan is either the first line of a paragraph that appears by itself at the bottom of a page or column, or a very short line of text that appears at the end of a paragraph. But the "widow and orphans" of Yaakov Proops weren't his typesetting errors — they really were his wife and children.

Proops is one of the most famous names in Hebrew printing. The business was founded by Shlomo ben Yosef, a bookseller, in the year 1704. During his career he printed all sorts of books, including prayer books and works of *halacha* (Jewish law), *mussar* (ethics), and *Kabbalah*. He also printed a *Haggadah shel Pesach* in 1712 that is today known as the *Second Amsterdam Haggadah*. This famous *haggadah* features commentary by the Abrabanel, instructions in both Ladino and Yiddish, and a beautiful folding map of the Holy Land written in Hebrew. A well-preserved copy of this *haggadah* was offered for auction by Kestenbaum & Company in 2005, with an asking price of $15,000-$20,000.

Shlomo Proops's sons carried on with the business after he passed away in 1734. When Yaakov Proops, the middle son, passed away in 1779, his widow and sons carried on with their share of the business, first alone and later in partnership with Yaakov Proops's nephew, Shlomo Proops.

The line "Printed by the Widow and Orphans of Yaakov Proops" appeared on a variety of publications, including a holiday prayer book printed in 1793 (which was recently on sale at an auction house), an *Achashverus Drama* for *Purim* printed in 1780, and *takanos* (communal legal enactments) and various other announcements for the Amsterdam Jewish community.

Widow Proops and her sons also printed a third edition of the *Amsterdam Haggadah* in 1781. A copy of the *haggadah* was sold for about $1,400 in 1995 at an auction held by Christie's. However, a Sotheby's auction held about a decade later, in 2004, saw a copy of the *haggadah* sell for $3,000.

Yehudis Rosanes, Lemberg (Lvov), 1700s

Printing was definitely in the blood of Yehudis Rosanes, who was a great-granddaughter of the renowned printer Uri Phoebus HaLevi. Uri Phoebus opened his Amsterdam printing house in 1658. During a career that spanned four decades, he printed deluxe editions of the prayer book, inexpensive books for impoverished scholars, an edition of what was then a new bestseller, a Yiddish anthology of Torah lore and *Midrashic* commentary called *Tzena Urena*, a Yiddish translation of the *Tanach* (Torah, Prophets, and Writings), and even a monogram on the then recently discovered Jews of Cochin, India. When he was in his 60s, he relocated to Zolkiew and set up a printing press there.

It was in Zolkiew that Yehudis Rosanes began her printing career. After her first husband died, she moved to Lemberg and married Rav Tzvi Hirsch Rosanes, who was Lemberg's chief rabbi. Yehudis Rosanes printed at least 50 books during a career that spanned a quarter of a century. Assisted by her son from her first marriage, Naftali Hertz Grossman, she supervised a staff of 24 workers. Her name was so famous that when government authorities banned the publication of new chassidic and Yiddish books in the mid-nineteenth century—some 50 years after she had passed away—printers used her name on the title pages of their newly published books to suggest that the books had been printed much earlier. The authorities never caught on to the ruse, even though the authors of these books would have been children at the time that their books were supposedly published.

The Lemberg Ladies Printing Circle, Lemberg, 1800s

Lemberg became a prominent center for Hebrew printing after the Austrian authorities ordered all of Zolkiew's Jewish printers to move there in 1782. Books printed in Lemberg were distributed all over Eastern Europe and the Balkans, and there were quite a few Jewish women involved in this thriving industry.

Chave Grossman, a daughter-in-law of Yehudis Rosanes, and her daughter Feige ran a printing press during the first half of the 1800s. There are some scholars who believe that the books falsely ascribed to Yehudis Rosanes were printed by Chave and Feige.

Two cousins of Rosanes—Chaya Taube, the wife of the aptly named printer Aharon Madpis, and Tsharni Letteris, the wife of

Ze'ev Wolf Letteris—also had their own printing presses. However, the most famous Jewish woman printer in Lemberg during the second half of the nineteenth century was Pessel Balaban.

The Balaban printing dynasty began in 1830, when Yehudah Loeb Balaban opened the doors to his new printing press. From the start, the Balabans were committed to printing only Torah literature, leaving the printing of modern Jewish literature and works of scientific thought to other printing houses. When Yehudah Loeb Balaban passed away in the year 1848, his son Pinchas Moshe, the husband of Pessel, inherited the business. Pessel worked alongside her husband until his death in 1860. Pessel expanded the business, and eventually it became famous throughout Galicia, Poland, and Russia. Some of the firm's most famous works were the printing of the *Shulchan Aruch* (Code of Jewish Law) in the early 1880s and a *Mikro'os Gedolos* (Torah with commentaries) in 1885 that had 18 commentaries.

Widow and Brothers Romm, Vilna, 1800s

The Romm family was another venerable family with a long history of Hebrew printing, which began in Grodno in 1789. Established by Baruch ben Yosef Romm, the printing press was the first Hebrew printing press in Lithuania. Baruch opened a second printing press in Vilna in 1799. After he passed away in 1803, his son Menachem Man Romm inherited the business. Menachem formed a partnership with Simcha Zimmel of Grodno and the two embarked on a project that is the high point of a Jewish printer's career—the publication of a new edition of the Talmud, which would become known as the *Vilna Shas*. It was a huge venture, and since the goal was to correct many of the printing errors and omissions of previous editions the company employed the best proofreaders and top scholars who were experts in deciphering manuscripts. The project took almost 20 years, and Menachem didn't live to see it completed.

After Menachem's death the firm passed to his son Yosef Reuven, and the *Shas* was completed in 1854 under his direction. When he passed away, his son David took over. When David died in 1860, his wife Devorah assumed the leadership position of the family business. Devorah Romm was only 29 years old when her husband passed away, and she was the mother of six children and stepmother to a child from her husband's previous marriage. Yet she managed to successfully expand the business, which she did in partnership with her two brothers-in-law, Chaim Yaakov and Menachem Gavriel, and with the assistance of her literary director, Shmuel Shraga Feigensohn.

By the end of the nineteenth century, the Romm printing house was the largest and most important one in Russia, and possibly in the entire Jewish world. The most famous work produced by the company under Devorah Romm's direction was a new edition of the *Vilna Shas*, which was printed during the years 1880-1886 and became the model for all later editions.

The twentieth century was not kind to Hebrew printing houses, and the story of the demise of the Romm family's press is perhaps representative of what happened during that era. Devorah Romm passed away in 1903. Her three sons had moved to the United States. One of them, Iga, founded an American branch of the company, which he called Widow and Brothers Romm and Company. An article in the August 24, 1904 edition of the *Jewish Chronicle* announced that the company was looking for collaborators on several upcoming projects, including an English edition of the Talmud, but nothing came of the project.

The family business back in the Old Country was sold to outsiders in 1910, although the new owners continued to use the name "Widow and Brothers Romm." The company remained in business until 1940, when the Soviets occupied Vilna and destroyed the press.

Today tour guides in Vilna will point out to their Jewish visitors the building that once housed the Widow and Brothers Romm printing house. The presses are long gone, of course, as are the pages and pages of Torah that once flowed from them. The one bright note is that plates and templates for the *Vilna Shas* were taken out of Vilna before the press was destroyed and transferred to both the United States and Israel. And so even though this great Jewish printing house is no more, somewhere in the world, at every moment of the day, someone is learning Talmud using the *Vilna Shas* of Widow and Brothers Romm.

—February 2010

Borrowed Lives:
Medieval Jewish Women Moneylenders

Although when most people think of Jewish moneylenders it's the image of Shakespeare's Shylock that they see, moneylending wasn't an exclusively male profession. It wasn't always a despicable profession either, as the lives of these three Jewish women who lived during the Middle Ages show.

Who was the breadwinner in European Jewish homes of yore? Like today, many Jewish women worked so that their husbands and children could learn Torah full time. And although women engaged in a variety of businesses during the medieval period—ranging from doing embroidery work in the home to engaging in trade—one of the most popular and lucrative jobs for women was to work as a moneylender.

Yes, you read right. While Jewish men certainly did do this kind of work, the court and tax records that have come down to us show that women were surprisingly well-represented in this profession. But if the profits were high so were the dangers, as three moneylenders from the medieval era—Minna of Worms, Pulcelina of Blois, and Dulcea of Worms—found out.

Women's Work?

Many modern Jews cringe at the thought of the Jewish medieval moneylender, who was often accused of charging ruinous interest rates. To soften the sting of the historical record, it became common to say that the Jews were forced to take up this unsavory business; unable to own land or join a workers' guild, lending money was one of the few professions that were open to them.

But as historical scholars have delved more deeply into the court and tax records, it's become clear that the medieval breadwinner wasn't limited to being either a farmer or a skilled artisan, which required membership in a guild. Many, including many Jews, were engaged in what we would today call a "cottage industry," where they made a product in their homes and then took their wares to the central market to sell.

Yet at the same time as people were producing their rounds of cheese or sewing cloaks on a small scale, the economy of medieval Europe was developing at a rapid rate and a new business opportunity opened up: providing the ready cash necessary to keep the wheels of commerce turning. The Jews took note. As Mordecai ben Hillel of Germany (b. 1298) wrote, no form of commerce produced better profits than lending money.

Still, the lure of high profits wasn't the only reason why many Jews became moneylenders. Often Jews were allowed to live in a place only because they had been invited to do so by the local ruler, who usually extended the first invitation to a few moneylenders and their families. Afterward, when the economy was booming, the ruler would become greedy and place an exorbitant tax burden on the Jewish community — and thereby start a vicious circle. The ruler, feeling that the Jews had become too wealthy, taxed the community even higher, which forced the community to seek out business opportunities that would bring even higher profits so that they could pay the taxes and escape expulsion. Lending money was the surest way to meet the tax bill.

Since it was common for the entire family to help out with the family business, Jewish women who grew up in a family that lent money, or married into one, could learn the ropes on the job. Should they become widows — and the women who appear most frequently in the commercial records were widows — they could support themselves by continuing to work in the family business.

Jewish businesswomen were so central to a Jewish community's economy that they were even able to swear in a Jewish court of law concerning their business dealings. The reason for this is given by Rabbi Eliezer ben Nathan of Mainz (c. 1090 - c. 1170), who wrote in his book *Even ha-Ezer*, "… and certainly in these days when women are legal guardians and vendors and dealers and lenders and borrowers and they pay and collect and withdraw and deposit money, and if we say they cannot swear or affirm their business negotiations, then you will forsake these women and people will begin to avoid doing business with them."

Not surprisingly the wealthy moneylender was often one of the most prominent members of the community. And so the woman moneylender not only provided for her own family, but she was often the largest contributor to the community's synagogues and schools.

But who were these women? Can we put a human face on what was so often portrayed as a heartless profession? First, let's take a look at a woman who was one of the earliest known businesswomen in northwestern Europe: Minna of Worms.

"A Worthy Woman"

Like Mayence and Cologne, Worms was one of the oldest Jewish communities in Germany. Although there is a legend that the first Jews arrived there during the era of the Romans, the first recorded mentions of Jews living in the city occur in the eleventh century. A 1090 edict by Emperor Henry IV, for example, granted the Jewish community the privileges of free commerce and exemption from taxation, showing the importance that the ruler attached to their economic activities. But in the year 1096, the time of the First Crusade, the good times came to an end. On May 18, and again on May 25, Crusaders rampaged through the Jewish quarter and murdered practically the entire community, which numbered some 800 souls.

One of the members of the Jewish community was a woman named Minna, a powerful moneylender who was apparently respected and well-liked by both the Jewish community and the non-Jewish authorities, with whom she often did business. When the pogroms spread to Worms, her non-Jewish business associates gave her a cruel choice: convert or die. Her story appears in *Mainz Anonymous,* a chronicle of the First Crusade written by an anonymous Jew:

A worthy woman lived [in Worms] and her name was Madame Minna. She hid in the cellar in a house outside the city. And there gathered unto her all the people of the city and said to her, "Behold, you are a woman of valor—know now that God no longer wishes to save you. The dead lie naked in the streets, and there is no one to bury them. Baptize yourself."

They fell on the ground before her, as they did not wish to slay her since her name was known far and wide, since at her house were found all the great ones of the city and the nobles of the country. And she answered and said, "Far be it for me to deny God in Heaven. For His Sake and for His sacred Torah slay me. Delay no more."

A Tragic Mistake

Despite her wealth and position, which would have enabled her to live a comfortable life as a non-Jew, Minna of Worms chose to die sanctifying God's Holy Name. It was an act that would be repeated 75 years later, this time in France, by another Jewish woman who gained wealth and prominence as a moneylender: Pulcelina of Blois.

Blois, which is situated in France's Loire Valley, is today a postcard-pretty city. The showpiece is the Chateau de Blois, a fairy-tale-like palace that dates back to the thirteenth century. The city's Old Town, with it winding cobblestone streets and steep staircases, has retained much of its medieval flavor. But this superficial charm hides a dark and tragic past.

Toward the end of the twelfth century, Blois was home to about 40 Jews. Included among them were Torah scholars who were *talmidim* (students) of Rabbeinu Yaakov Tam and Rabbeinu Shmuel ben Meir, grandsons of the great medieval commentator on the Torah Rabbi Shlomo Yitzchaki, better known as Rashi. Another member of the community was a woman named Pulcelina, a widow who worked as a moneylender and who was a trusted financial advisor of the town's ruler, Count Thibaut.

According to the records that have come down to us, Pulcelina's wealth and power may have gone to her head, since it says that "she acted proudly." On the other hand, it could be that the rest of Count Thibaut's court disliked her because they owed her significant sums of money and because she had considerable influence over the Count. Whatever the reason, certain members of the nobility were given an opportunity to take their revenge upon Pulcelina in the year 1171, when a tragic error was made.

The event initially had nothing to do with her. What happened was this: During Passover of that year a Jewish resident of Blois,

Yitzchak ben Eleazer, road up to the river to water his horse. A servant of a nobleman rode up to the river at the same time. The meeting happened at dusk, when the light was fading, and the servant mistook an animal's untreated hide that belonged to Yitzchak ben Eleazar for the body of a dead Christian child.

The servant, who had become convinced that Yitzchak had thrown the "body" into the river, ran to tell his master. The nobleman happened to be one of those who hated Pulcelina, and the other Jews as well. He went to the Count — and by this time the Jews of Blois had been accused of using blood from the "dead child" to bake their matzos — and the Count ordered that all the Jews of Blois should be seized and thrown into prison.

Pulcelina was jailed along with the others, but because of her business relationship with the Count she was spared the hardship of being chained in irons. Pulcelina was sure that she could use her influence with the Count to get her fellow Jews released. Indeed, Count Thibaut would have released the Jews — for a large ransom. But the Count's wife made sure the meeting never happened. And when the Bishop arrived in Blois soon afterward, the fate of the Jews was sealed. Since no body had been found, and so the only evidence against the Jews was the servant's testimony, the priest arranged that the servant be "tested" to determine if the man was telling the truth. Of course, the test was rigged and so the servant passed the test with flying colors. The Jews were condemned to be burned at the stake.

The Count informed the Jews that they could save their lives if they converted, but the entire community, including Pulcelina, refused. On the 20th of the Jewish month of *Sivan* they died *al Kiddush Hashem*, sanctifying the Divine Name. Their martyrdom was witnessed by Rabbi Baruch ben David HaKohein, who had tried, unsuccessfully, to ransom the community. His account was written down and sent to Rabbeinu Yaakov Tam.

In the letter it was reported that as the flames soared, the martyrs began to sing, first softly and then louder and louder.

The Christians asked us, "What kind of a song is this, for we have never heard such a sweet melody?" We knew it well, for it was the hymn Aleinu: *"It is our duty to praise the L-rd of all... for He has not made us like the nations of the lands ..."*

French Jewry was so shocked by the incident—this was the first time that a Jewish community on the European continent had been accused of ritual murder—that Rabbeinu Tam, who passed away a few weeks later, declared the 20th of *Sivan* a day of mourning and fasting. Pulcelina's sad ending became an early cautionary tale of the rise and fall of a court Jew.

"She Fed and Clothed Him in Dignity"

Although there were several Jewish women moneylenders who became financial advisors to noblemen and kings, the majority of them worked on a more modest scale. They made small loans to Christian small businesswomen engaged in weaving or some other craft—in the early medieval era Jews weren't consigned to a ghetto and so there was freedom of movement between the two groups—or to Christian merchants and traders. But even on this smaller scale, she could make a nice living; she could support her husband and children in dignity and contribute to the communal charitable fund.

Perhaps the most famous Jewish woman moneylender of the Middle Ages was Dulcea of Worms, the wife of Rabbi Eleazer of Worms, known as the Rokeach. Much of what we know about Dulcea's accomplishments as a Jewish wife and mother comes from the elegy written by Rabbi Eleazer after her tragic death, which is based upon the "Woman of Valor" verses found in the *Book of Proverbs*. For instance, we know that Dulcea spun cords that were used for sewing together the pieces of parchment of Torah scrolls, *tefillin*, and *megillos*. She made wicks for the candles that were used in synagogues and the *yeshivos*. She taught prayers to the women in her own and in neighboring towns, and helped poor brides get married. But her primary source of income came from lending money, and as Rabbi Eleazar wrote, "Her husband trusted her implicitly, she fed and clothed him in dignity so he could sit among the elders of the land and provide Torah study and good deeds."

From Rabbi Eleazer's words, and from knowledge that has come down from other sources, it is assumed that Dulcea's business worked in the following way: Her neighbors would give her their spare cash, which she would pool together into a sizeable sum. She would then lend the money to a non-Jew, taking a commission as her payment for the transaction.

Such work might have lacked the glamor that came with doing business with kings and counts, but the quiet life suited the family, whose world revolved around Torah study and doing *mitzvos*. However, their world came crashing down in November of the year 1196, when two armed men entered the family's home and killed Dulcea and the family's two daughters, Bellette and Hannah. Rabbi Eleazer who was also in the house, along with a son and some students, were unharmed. Dulcea had managed to raise the alarm, before she died from her wounds, and the attackers — who were most likely robbers that knew Dulcea kept large sums of money in the home because of her business — fled.

It is Rabbi Eleazar who perhaps gives us the clearest, and brightest, image of the Jewish woman moneylender of those times. Writing about his wife, he reveals the eternal link between Jewish "gelt" and Torah study:

Before her murder, she purchased parchment for the writing of books. She supported me and my sons and my daughters by [lending] other people's money. Because of my great sins she was killed, and my daughters. As Hashem *(God) is my witness, she was put to much trouble so that I and my son might study.*

Dulcea's dedication to Torah learning and her community served as a shining example to the many women who came after her, whose names we don't know, but whose similar dedication helped preserve the light of Torah during those often dark and turbulent times.

* * *

Easy Money?

Before there were banks, people had to hide their money in their homes or places of business, which were often located in the same building. That made moneylenders an easy target for dangerous characters who didn't mind killing people to steal their money and property. Licoricia of Winchester, a very wealthy and influential English moneylender, ended her long and successful life at the hands of armed robbers, who had broken into her home, as did Kandlein of Regensburg (Germany). But obviously there were many moneylenders who died peacefully in their beds—otherwise Jews wouldn't have continued in that line of business.

Chaile Raphael Kualla, the matriarch of a large and influential family, had a thriving business as a court factor in Württemberg during the eighteenth century. A court factor was a type of moneylender. When a member of the nobility or the royal court needed money, they went to the court factor for the funds. The court factor was paid back with interest and, sometimes, with increased privileges.

Madame Kaulla, as she was known in the non-Jewish records, eventually became the richest woman in Germany. In addition to lending money to the royal family, she headed Stuttgart's stock exchange and trading house. Towards the end of her long life—a painted portrait of her shows a kind-looking woman with gray eyebrows and a gently wrinkled face—she was a co-founder of the Royal Württemberg Hofbank, which after several mergers became the Deutsche Bank.

But despite her frequent dealings with counts and emperors, she remained loyally connected to her community. The same record that lauds her many business accomplishments notes that she was also praised for her considerable charitable work on behalf of the poor.

—November 2010

A Lovely Prayer To Say (Not Too Quickly): The World of Women's *Tekhines*

Tekhines, *prayers of supplication and praise, were written in Yiddish for Jewish women living in towns and* shtetls *throughout Eastern and Central Europe. Some of them were written by women, who used their own experiences to put into words the often unspoken thoughts and hopes hidden inside a Jewish woman's heart.*

It can happen at any time—before a family celebration, or after a sorrow; after lighting the Shabbos candles, or before bringing a new *neshamah* (soul) into the world. Suddenly, you want to pour out everything that is in your heart and speak to Hashem (God). You want to thank Him for all His goodness; you want to plead with Him to unlock the Gates of Mercy. You want to express your gratitude for the beautiful holiday of *Sukkos*; you want to admit that you feel a little lost during the celebration of *Simchas Torah*.

Yes, you want to speak to Hashem. But you feel silly. You search, but you can't find the words. How, you wonder, can your words compare with the concise eloquence of the *Amidah* prayer written by the Sages of the Talmud, or the lofty poetry of King David's *Psalms*?

A few hundred years ago, Jewish women knew exactly where to turn during times like these. Sitting alongside the *siddur* (prayer book) and their *Book of Psalms* was a little volume written in Yiddish. This book was filled with *tekhines*, prayers that spoke to the daily concerns and the spiritual aspirations of the typical Jewish woman.

And even though these *tekhines* were written hundreds of years ago, they still speak to us today.

A Pretty *Tekhine* to Say with Great Devotion

The Yiddish word *tekhine* has its origins in the Hebrew word *techinah*, which means "supplication." Small and anonymous collections of *tekhines* began to appear in the late 1500s. However, the first major collection, which had 36 prayers, was published in 1648 in Amsterdam.

As historian Devra Kay, author of the book *Seyder Tkhines: The Forgotten Book of Common Prayer for Jewish Women*, points out, 1648 was also the year when Bogdan Chmielnicki and his Cossack hordes began their two-year reign of terror in Poland and Ukraine. By the time their rampage ended, approximately 100,000 Jews had been massacred and tens of thousands more fled west to Amsterdam and Prague.

Devra Kay suggests that the turbulence of these times could have led to the printing of the Amsterdam edition. Many refugees had fled from their homes in a panic, leaving behind most of their Jewish books. Jewish printers had fled with them, and when they re-established their businesses in their adopted cities they began to publish new editions of cherished works. The book that was known simply as *Tekhines* was published soon after the refugees arrived in Amsterdam and it was reprinted many times during the following years. Several other volumes of *tekhines* were also published, and the genre remained popular well into the nineteenth century.

The fact that these books of women's supplications were published and republished so often shows the deep place that the prayers had in women's hearts. Yet it would be a mistake to think that the supplications only had to do with sad topics, such as death and bereavement. *Tekhines* were written for all occasions: Shabbos, *Rosh Chodesh* (New Moon), and the holidays; *mitzvos* such as separating *challah*; and life passage events such as marriage, birth, a child's first tooth, his first day in *cheder* (Jewish school), and his *bar mitzvah*. *Tekhines* also addressed the issues of childlessness, making a good livelihood, and warding off the evil eye.

There is some debate as to whether or not these prayers were meant to replace the traditional liturgy — many women couldn't read

Hebrew — or whether they were meant to supplement the daily prayers. What can be said is that *tekhines* were definitely written in a more intimate style. A *tekhine* is usually written in the first person singular, and not in the plural, as is customary with the traditional prayer service — and is often prefaced with a written instruction, such as: "A pretty *tekhine* to say on Shabbos with great devotion," or "A confession to say with devotion, not too quickly. It is good for the soul."

Although the language of some *tekhines* recalls a simpler time and place — such as one author's prayer to give birth as easily as a chicken — others demonstrate a high level of sophistication. In a *tekhine* to be said before lighting the candles of *Yom Tov Sukkos* (see below), for instance, the author makes a moving comparison between the body, which is a temporary "house" for the soul, and the sukkah — our temporary home during the holiday.

Who wrote these *tekhines*? Some volumes were written by men — such as the 1718 book *Seyder Tekhines*, which was authored by Rabbi Matthias ben Meir, the former rabbi of Sobota. However, many books were comprised of prayers written by women. And even though some of these women chose to remain anonymous, the names of a few of them have been preserved for us.

From Sarah to Sarah

Perhaps the best-known author of *tekhines* is Sarah bas Tovim. Although there are some scholars who doubt that she really existed, there are others who tell us that she was born in a little Ukrainian town called Satanov in the late 1600s and may have been descended from Rabbi Mordechai of Brisk. Two works that are attributed to her are *Shloshe She'arim* (*Three Gates*), which was the most widely circulated volume of *tekhines*, and *Sheker haChen* (*Beauty Is Deceptive*).

According to tradition, she wrote *Shloshe She'arim* when she was already an older woman and was looking back on her life. In her youth, she tells us, she was a vain and flippant young woman who came to synagogue wearing jewels and gossiped and joked throughout the prayer service. She goes on to write that she was later punished for this behavior when she was forced to become a wanderer.

If there is uncertainty about the truth of Sarah bas Tovim's existence, we stand on surer ground when we come to other women authors of popular volumes. Many of these women came from distinguished rabbinical families, whose existence can be verified. In addition, their family lineage can perhaps explain why their prayers are able to draw upon such a wide variety of sources and ideas from the Jewish tradition, including *Chumash*, *Midrash*, the traditional liturgy, and even *Kabbalah*.

Tekhine Imahos Fun Rosh Chodesh Elul (*Supplications of the Matriarchs for the New Moon of the Month of Elul*), for example, was written by a woman called Serl bas Yaakov ben Wolf Kranz. If the name Yaakov ben Wolf Kranz doesn't ring any bells, perhaps his other title will—he is none other than the renowned Maggid of Dubno, whose profound and pithy parables inspired an entire generation and which continue to be widely quoted even today.

Another volume that was written for *Elul* and the High Holidays was *Tekhine Teshuvah U'Tefilah U'Tzedakah* (*Supplication of Repentance and Prayer and Charity*) by Mamael, the daughter of Rabbi Tzvi Hirsch and the wife of the head of the Beis Din of Belz, Rabbi Yitzchak.

Sarah Rivka Rachel Leah Horowitz, a daughter of Rabbi Yaakov Yokl of Brody, authored a well- known volume of *tekhines* that also took as its topic the Shabbos before Rosh Chodesh and was called *Tekhine Imahos*. And finally there is Rivka Tiktiner, a daughter of Rabbi Meir Tiktiner who lived in the first half of the sixteenth century and who is considered to be the first woman author to write in Yiddish. She penned a prayer for the holiday *Simchas Torah* called *Simchas Torah Lied* (*A Song for Simchas Torah*), amongst other well-respected works.

In both their scope and their depth of expression, these *tekhines* show that Jewish women always had a rich spiritual life. They were always in conversation with Hashem, they were always striving to attach themselves to the holiness of Shabbos and the Jewish holidays, and they were always searching for the deeper meaning of the *mitzvos* that had been entrusted to them in their roles as wives and mothers. Fortunately for us, many of these *tekhines* have recently been translated into English and Hebrew, so that we too can take inspiration from them and borrow their authors' eloquent words whenever we wish to speak to Hashem.

* * *

Tekhine for the First Night of Sukkos, Before Lighting the Candles

A *tekhine* found in holy books, to be said at the time of lighting the candles in the *sukkah*. And every woman who will say this *tekhine* with crying and great concentration will certainly be helped from Hashem, May He Be Blessed.

Master of the Universe, Who holds the life of every creature
In Your hand. You created all the bodies,
Which are made like a *sukkah*
For the souls that You created—
Because the body is temporary
And like a *sukkah*,
Which is a temporary tent.
All the time that You, Blessed Be Your Name,
Desire the life of the person,
The body covers the soul,
To hold on to it.

We find that the soul
Is compared to a candle,
As it is written: "The candle of Hashem
Is the soul of the person."
The *mitzvah* is also
Compared to a candle,
As it is written:
"A *mitzvah* is a candle,
And the Torah is light."
One who guards well the light
Of the *mitzvah* will have
The light of his soul protected.
And in particular for us, the women,
We need to be careful about
The three *mitzvos* that we
Were commanded to fulfill.

May Your Holy Name Be Blessed,
May we merit to have You accept
This holy holiday, the holiday of *Sukkos*.
And I, the woman (the woman's Hebrew name),
Have come to the holy *sukkah* to fulfill
The *mitzvah* of lighting the candles.
Therefore, I will make a request of You, Hashem,
Who is merciful and compassionate,
That in the merit of the light I shed
With the kindling of the candles
In honor of the *Sukkos* holiday,
Shed light on my soul,
And do not extinguish my candle, God forbid.

And as Rachel Our Mother cried and pleaded
For her children, so do I cry and plead
For my husband and my offspring,
That we will have a holiday
Filled with light and a good year.
Just as the *sukkah* protects us,
As well as the light of the *mitzvah*,
May it also protect our bodies
And our souls, so that we shouldn't
Pass away, God forbid, before our time.
And just as this holy holiday is called
The time of our happiness,
May our hearts be glad, for the good.
May we have a joyous holiday
And a happy year, a year of life and
Blessing, a year of good livelihood
And success, a year when we will
Announce the Final Redemption.
Amen.

My translation, from a Hebrew version of traditional tekhines *written in Yiddish.*

—September 2007

"Dear Esteemed Pious Women ...":
A Sixteenth-Century Yiddish Authoress Finds a New Audience

It's not every author who gets a second chance at finding a new audience, especially when the author has been dead for four centuries and her biggest bestseller was a book of moral instruction written in Yiddish. Yet in the year 2009 Rivkah bas Meir Tiktiner returned to life, so to speak, with the re-publication of her book Meneket Rivkah *(Rivkah's Nurse), a sixteenth-century book of advice that still has something to say to us today.*

"Who has ever heard of or seen such a novelty; has it ever happened in countless years, that a woman has written something of her accord?"

These words appeared in the original introduction to *Meneket Rivkah*, a book of *mussar* (ethical instruction) for women that was printed in Prague in the year 1609 by the famed Gersonides family of printers. And apparently the unknown person who penned those words was right. According to modern historians the book's author, Rivkah bas Meir Tiktiner, a member of Prague's Jewish community and a contemporary of the Maharal of Prague, was the first Jewish woman to write a book in Yiddish.

But if Rivkah Tiktiner's name or the name of her book doesn't ring any bells, don't feel badly. Although *Meneket Rivkah* was popular enough to receive a second printing in 1618 and it continued to be referred to during the eighteenth century, by the nineteenth century it had disappeared from the Jewish bookshelf. It was only during the 1970s that the book was "rediscovered." And it was only this year—four hundred years after its first printing—that *Meneket Rivkah* received a first-class reissue, courtesy of the Jewish Publication Society, complete with a new introduction and commentary by Frauke von Rohden, a lecturer in Jewish history and literature at the Free University of Berlin, and a translation into English by Samuel Spinner.

But who was Rivkah bas Meir Tiktiner, and why did she decide to publish her lessons of moral instruction? And why was her book "lost" for so many years? The truth is that the information we have about her is sketchy. Yet there's just enough to make an excursion to medieval Prague worthwhile.

A Clue in a Cemetery

For the person who is interested in the history of Prague's Jewish community, there are two indispensable places to visit: the Old Jewish Cemetery and the Altneuschul (Old-New Synagogue). It's therefore not surprising that the two tangible clues about Rivkah's existence that still remain, other than her book, can be found in these two places.

Her gravestone informs us that Rivkah, who passed away on the 25th of *Nisan*, 1605, was the daughter of Rabbi Meir Tiktin. It also tells us that she was given the title *"Rabbanit"* (a title given to a wife of a rabbi who is also a communal leader and teacher in her own right), and that she "preached day and night to the women." Although the epitaph praises her as an *aishes chayil*, a woman of valor, and a lecturer, there is no mention of her being a mother.

That omission can also be found in the *Sefer Hazkaros* (*Memorial Book*) found inside the Altnueschul. This memorial book recorded the names of deceased members of the synagogue whose family had made a contribution to the synagogue in their name. There is a record for Rivkah, and we once again learn that her father was Rabbi Meir. We also learn that she lived to a ripe old age and that the contribution to the synagogue was made by her husband—whose name may have been Rabbi Bezalel Baruch, but many of the letters are so faded that it's impossible to decipher the exact name. Like the epitaph on her gravestone, this inscription confers upon her the title of *Rabbanit* and refers to her "preaching." And like the epitaph, there is no mention of children.

But according to Dr. von Rohden, the evidence is inconclusive. She points out that in the text of *Meneket Rivkah*, the author expresses the wish that she should merit to see "her children's children" do good deeds. It could therefore be that Rivkah's children passed away before she did.

Yet even if she didn't have children of her own, it is certain that she did have someone to whom she could pass on her wisdom — the many women she instructed in the correct way to behave. What led her to take on a public role? And from where did she receive the qualifications to instruct others? To answer these questions, we must try to reconstruct the social milieu of Jewish communities in Bohemia during the late 1500s.

A Golden Age of Money and *Mussar*

A popular stop on many Jewish tours to Poland is the tiny town of Tykocin, population 1,800. Although Tykocin's Jewish population of approximately 1,500 souls was murdered during the Holocaust, the community's synagogue, built in 1642, is still standing. In fact, it's one of the best preserved in Poland, and it is now a museum. One of the town's other claims to fame is that it is also, perhaps, the birthplace of Rivkah bas Meir. Like so much of Rivkah's life, it's impossible to know for sure. But scholars assume that her father, Rabbi Meir Tiktiner, was from Tykocin — or Tiktin, as the town is called in some Jewish sources.

Tykocin was a flourishing center of Jewish life during the 1500s. Did Rivkah's father sit among the circle of Talmudic sages who gave Tykocin a reputation as a place of Torah? We don't know. But even if he was one of the wealthy merchants who supported the town's scholars, one thing is certain: He must have imparted his deep love of learning to Rivkah and provided her with access to a wide range of Torah literature, because in her own book she shows that she was knowledgeable about *Tanach* (Torah and the commentaries) and the *Midrash*, read books of *mussar*, and was familiar with the medical writings of the Rambam (Maimonides).

When and why Rivkah came to Prague is a mystery, but when she arrived she surely wasn't disappointed with the Torah community that she found. Rabbi Yehudah Loew, the Maharal, made his home in Prague for at least some of the time that Rivkah lived in the city. Rabbi Mordecai ben Avraham Jaffe (the Levush), Rabbi Shlomo Ephraim ben Aaron Luntschitz (the Kli Yakar), and Rabbi Yom Tov Lipmann Heller (the Tosofos Yom Tov) are just a few of the illustrious rabbis who were also living in Prague at various times during the mid to late sixteenth century.

Yet despite the high caliber of its Torah scholars, all was not well in Prague. The community had always had its share of ups and down—or, rather, its cyclical periods of settlement, exile, and resettlement. But by the late 1500s a new and dangerous wind was blowing.

When Emperor Rudolf II moved his residence from Vienna to Prague in the year 1584, Prague quickly became a major financial and intellectual center. The Catholic emperor, who was surprisingly tolerant for the times, issued a protective edict for the Jews, hoping that their financial expertise would further increase his wealth. The Jews responded by flocking to the city, until its Jewish population swelled to some 3,000 souls, making it the second largest Jewish community in Europe.

Although most members of the Jewish community were poor, the new climate of tolerance led to the creation of many well-to-do merchants, tradesmen, and doctors. A few became fabulously wealthy. Mordecai Meisel, for example, served as the emperor's banker and amassed a fortune, which he used to help the Jewish community. Two Jewish goldsmiths, Yosef de Cerui and Yaakov Goldscheider, were granted lucrative royal privileges that included being able to practice their craft in districts outside the Jewish Quarter. Emperor Rudolf also created a class of Jew called the *Hofbefreiter Jude*, Jews who were attached to the imperial court and enjoyed privileges such as being exempt from paying taxes and wearing the Jewish badge.

The ease with which the wealthier Jews could interact with their non-Jewish business associates resulted, in some cases, in increased assimilation. Czech became the everyday language, some Jews adopted Czech names, and there were some who went so far as to disregard the prohibition against drinking non-Jewish wine. In addition to the threat of assimilation, the *emunah* (faith) of the Jewish community was also coming under attack. Throughout Europe the new religion of science was on the ascendancy, and its advocates were publicly denying the existence of basic tenets of religious faith, such as the immortality of the soul and divine providence.

We know that the Maharal fought to strengthen both the community's *emunah* and strict adherence to *halachah* (Jewish law), and that one of his "battlegrounds" was the field of education. The Maharal called for a new system of study that would both build a person's character and add depth and meaning to the person's religious observance. On a practical level, he established study groups in *Mishnah* for the less learned members of the community.

Was there a similar call to the women, not to formally learn texts but to strengthen their *emunah* and refine their character? Is this why Rivkah bas Meir began to speak to the women and write her book?

For readers who have read thus far, you probably already know the answer: We don't know. Yet we do know that *mussar* books were very popular during this era. *Orchos Tzaddikim* (*Ways of the Righteous*), for example, which was first published in the year 1581, was very well received. *Reishis Chochmah* (*Beginning of Wisdom*), the sixteenth-century *mussar* work written by Rabbi Eliyahu de Vidas, was another popular work. New books of moral instruction were also being written in Yiddish, such as *Brantshpigl*, a widely read book that was written for women.

However, most of these books, which were written by men, were quite encyclopedic in scope. Rivkah, being a woman, may therefore have noticed a flaw that needed remedying: Women who were busy with raising their children and managing a household didn't have time to read multi-volume works. They needed something short and practical. In other words, they needed something like *Meneket Rivkah*.

"Dear Women ..."

And so, dear women, do not take amiss what I have written or that I have admonished you ... most women are truly righteous ... They know everything ten times better than what I have written; rather, my intention is to find the one among these thousands who does not. – Meneket Rivkah

Women teachers were not unusual during medieval times. For instance, Dulcea, the wife of Rabbi Eleazar of Worms, was eulogized by Rabbi Eleazar as being a teacher and spiritual model for the women in her community. He also mentions that she translated the Hebrew prayers into the everyday vernacular of their twelfth-century community.

The women who performed the task of translating the prayers had their own name: *firzogerin* or *zogerkeh* (sayer). Women also began to compose prayers for other women during this time, which were called *tekhines*. However, it's unclear when women began to take on the role of teaching other women moral instruction, and where the lectures were held.

Dr. von Rohden surmises that the introduction of a *mussar* talk given in Yiddish by a woman was a direct result of the increased popularity of the rabbi's sermon given in Hebrew. But whereas the rabbi's sermon given in synagogue would have been on a more learned subject, the sermons for women would have been on topics closer to home: cultivating modest behavior and dress, honoring one's parents, raising one's children, creating *shalom bayis* (marital harmony) with one's husband, developing a good relationship with the in-laws, and fulfilling one's *chesed* (charitable) obligations.

Rivkah Tiktner's book *Meneket Rivkah*, which covers all of the above topics, was most certainly based upon lectures she gave to the women of Prague. And since her intended audience was the financially well-off married woman who was responsible for both managing her home and fulfilling her charitable obligations to the community, Rivkah must have been a respected member of her community and come from a similar social class. But even if we can assume that becoming a *darhanis* (lecturer) was a natural step for an educated woman in Prague, what made Rivkah take a further step and write down her lectures and publish them in a book?

The reason might be quite simple: She did it because she could. The printing press had been invented a century earlier, and during Rivkah's day Prague was an important center for printing Hebrew and Yiddish books. Moreover, *Meneket Rivkah* was not her first printed work. She was also the author of the poem *Simkhes Toyre Lied,* a Yiddish poem for *Simchas Torah* that enjoyed great popularity during the sixteenth century and was reprinted many times. Therefore, she was no stranger to the written word or the world of the printing press.

However, like many aspiring authors, she may have discovered that writing a book was easier than getting it published. In the book's introduction she thanks a certain Reb Azariah ben Shmuel, who helped to pay for the printing costs. Yet even with this assistance the book did not appear until five years after she passed away. Did she ask that the book, although written, not be published until after her death? Or were financial obstacles the cause of the delay? The reader already knows the answer. We don't know.

Lost and Found

Although we don't know how many copies of *Meneket Rivkah* were printed and sold, we can gauge the impact of the book by the influence that it had on later writers. Rivkah's use of examples from traditional sources combined with contemporary anecdotes taken from everyday life was something new at the time, but it was a literary style that caught on quickly and is still being used today.

But even though the book was very popular in its day, it wasn't reprinted after 1618. By 1879 the historian Meyer Kayserling confidently proclaimed that the book had been lost. Another nineteenth-century scholar, Gustav Karpeles, made the claim that Rivkah's true importance was due to her translation of *Chovos HaLevavos* (*Duties of the Heart*) into Yiddish—something that she didn't do, as far as we know.

The twentieth century wasn't much kinder to Rivkah and her book. In the 1970s an incomplete copy of the 1618 Krakow edition was discovered in the library of New York City's Jewish Theological Seminary. A few years later another copy of the work was discovered in the library of the University of Erlangen, located in Nuremberg. Then in 1992 Rabbi Meir Wunder, a *chareidi* historian based in Israel, included a facsimile of the incomplete Krakow manuscript in his book *The Crown of Rivkah: Four Women's Tehinot with Translation into Hebrew and the Moral Book Meineket Rivkah*. But modern scholars weren't particularly interested.

According to Dr. von Rohden, the lack of interest was due to several reasons. By the 1900s *Meneket Rivkah* had been reduced to a "women's book" on childcare and other mundane topics, in the minds of modern scholars. Furthermore, *mussar* books written in Old Yiddish, which carried a stigma of being "popular literature," didn't generate the same scholarly excitement as more serious books written in Hebrew.

Will this change, now that a new edition of the book has been published, especially one that has the complete text in both Yiddish and English? It's doubtful that *Meneket Rivkah* will make the best seller list of the *New York Times* or Amazon. Yet despite the passage of time, this pious and learned woman from Prague does still have some valuable knowledge to share—not with those of us who already know everything, of course, but with that "one in a thousand" woman who is wise enough to know that she still has room for improvement.

* * *

Excerpts from *Meneket Rivkah: A Manual of Wisdom and Piety for Jewish Women*

By Rivkah bas Meir Tiktiner; edited with an introduction and commentary by Frauke von Rohden; translated by Samuel Spinner, published by the Jewish Publication Society in May 2009.

Chapter Two

This is the next chapter, which will speak of how a woman should relate to her husband, if they want to grow old with each other with respect.

She should not tell him everything that goes wrong in the house—she should excuse him from (involvement) since nothing good comes from a fight ... [a fight] begins with a quarrel over one little word, and later a big fight grows out of it. This is why the verse says, "Before a dispute flares up, drop it." In Yiddish this means, before the fight begins, give it up. This means that one should quickly cut it off.

Chapter Three

How a woman and her husband should spend time with their father and mother, so that God, blessed be His name, should lengthen their years in this world and the world to come.

... one should not deny one's father or mother a favor. But, due to our many transgressions, it is all too common not to value one's parents, as the proverb says, "A mother can raise ten children, but ten children cannot support one mother." Everything is too much:

whatever they do, or eat, or say is disagreeable. They laugh and mock them, and don't consider that when they grow old, they will be measured by the same standard that they used to measure their parents.

Chapter Six

How a mother-in-law should behave toward her daughter-in-law and her [son-in-law], and should avoid quarrelling and fighting in her house, and God, blessed be He, will bestow His blessing on her house, on both of them.

Now, every woman should be aware and make sure that she does not sin against her son- or daughter-in-law, God forbid. As we see regarding King Saul, peace be upon him, who hated his son-in-law, King David, peace be upon him, much bad came from that—he caused himself and his children to sin. Nothing good comes from conflict, only jealousy and hatred. Even if a daughter- or son-in-law does not always do the right thing, one should judge them favorably. One should also remember, it is because of their [youth]—we were also once young, and "Wisdom comes with age." If they had as much experience as we do, they would probably change.

—March 2009

Blossoms in the Rubble:
In Search of Dona Gracia's Tiveria

During the early days of the Ottoman Empire, two wealthy anusim *fleeing from the Spanish Inquisition — Dona Gracia and her nephew Don Yosef Nasi — were given permission to rebuild the city of Tiveria, located on the banks of the Kinneret (Sea of Galilee), and create an independent Jewish city-state. What remains today of that early re-blossoming of Jewish life in the Land of Israel? In February 2010 I paid a visit to Tiveria to find out.*

At the end of time, the Talmud tells us, in the tractate *Rosh Hashanah* 31b, the redemption of the Jewish people will begin not in the holy city of Jerusalem or to the north, in the *Kabbalah*-renowned city of Tzfas, but in the city of Tiveria. And so it isn't difficult to imagine the excitement that must have spread throughout the Jewish world some 450 years ago, when an amazing thing happened: Sultan Suleiman, the mighty ruler of the Ottoman Empire, gave permission to a wealthy Jewish woman named Dona Gracia to buy Tiveria, rebuild it, and establish there a quasi-autonomous Jewish state.

Who was Dona Gracia, and why would a Muslim ruler grant her permission to establish a Jewish state within his empire? What happened to this early attempt to create a flourishing Jewish community in Tiveria? And several earthquakes and one flood later, is there anything left of Dona Gracia's Tiveria to see?

As is often the case with Jewish history, it depends upon who you ask.

A Life on the Run

The weatherman promised that it would be sunny. But after my Egged bus pulled out of Afula's central bus station and began its ascent to Tiveria, the dark clouds that had been chasing us ever since we left Jerusalem finally caught us. As big drops of rain splattered against the windshield, I reminded myself that rain is a blessing — even if my photographs came out all dark and gloomy. Because gloomy or not, I was still lucky. I was in Eretz Yisrael, the Land of Israel. In another half hour I would reach my destination, the city of Tiveria. The same could not be said for two of the central characters in this story Dona Gracia and her nephew Don Yosef.

But that's the end of the story. To start at the beginning, we must turn around and go not to the Kinneret, but across the Mediterranean Sea to Spain. We must also go back in time to the year 1492, the year when Spain's Jews were expelled from the country they had lived and prospered in for almost 1,000 years.

While many of these Jews fled eastward — to countries in Europe or lands within the Ottoman Empire — some families tried to rebuild their lives in nearby Portugal. One of them was the Nasi family, who had been one of Spanish Jewry's most illustrious families. When the Portuguese king decreed that all Jews living in his land had to convert — this time exile was not an option — the Nasi family, like many others, were forced to become *anusim*. On the outside they pretended to be Christians. But within the privacy of their homes, and in the even more private recesses of their hearts, they remained loyal to their Jewish faith.

In the year 1510 a daughter was born to the Nasis, whom they named Beatrice. But that was for the outside. Her real name was Gracia, which was Spanish for Chanah. When she grew up, Gracia married another secret Jew, Francesco Mendez, who came from a family of wealthy bankers.

Just six years after they were married, Francesco passed away. King John III of Portugal, sensing an opportunity to get his hands on the Mendez fortune, demanded that the young widow hand over her two-year-old daughter, Reyna, and have the child raised at court — an "honor" that came with a hefty price tag. Dona Gracia took her daughter, along with a few other family members who were dependent upon her — including the orphaned son of her deceased brother, who later became known as Don Yosef Nasi — and fled. Her destination was Antwerp, where her husband's brother had already established a branch office of the family bank, as well as a successful business trading in spices, which was one of the most lucrative businesses of the time. But tragedy struck once again when her brother-in-law also passed away.

By now her nephew had grown up and so Dona Gracia and Don Yosef jointly took over the management of the Mendez financial empire. The Almighty blessed their efforts, and they became two of the wealthiest people in Europe. However, it is not their great wealth that won them an esteemed place in the annals of Jewish history. Rather, it is what they did with that wealth to help their unfortunate brethren. For instance, they employed hundreds of secret agents who ran an "underground railroad" system that transported *anusim* fleeing from the Spanish Inquisition to safe havens. They also used their banking empire to help *anusim* either transfer their assets to more hospitable countries or provide financial assistance to those who had been forced to flee with only the clothes on their backs.

Yet despite their great wealth, they were also the victims of evil plots that were devised against them by jealous and greedy rulers. Charles V of Spain and his sister Queen Marie, Regent of the Netherlands, for instance, decided to make a match for Reyna with an elderly Spanish nobleman of dubious character. For their efforts, the rulers expected the Spaniard to pay them a hefty "*shadchanas*" (matchmaking) fee, which would come from the bride's dowry money. Dona Gracia, of course, looked upon the proposed match with horror. When Queen Marie demanded that the stubborn businesswoman give her consent to the match, Dona Gracia's reply was brief and to the point: she would rather see her daughter dead.

It was a brave answer, but it meant that Dona Gracia and her family once again had to flee, this time to Venice. But a few years after they arrived, Dona Gracia was arrested for "Judaizing" and a freeze was put on her assets.

The rest of the family managed to flee to Ferrara. Don Yosef used his contacts to request help from Sultan Suleiman, the powerful ruler of the Ottoman Empire. The sultan saw the value of having Dona Gracia and Don Yosef move their financial empire to Turkey, and so he threatened Venice with military action if she wasn't released. The Venetians let her go.

The family moved to Constantinople, the magnificent capital of the Ottoman Empire, in the year 1553, and their 15-year flight from the Spanish Inquisition finally came to an end. For the first time in their lives, they were able to live openly as Jews and go by their Jewish names—and Reyna was finally safely married to a Jewish man, her cousin Don Yosef. But no sooner had one adventure-filled chapter in their story ended than an even more exciting one began.

The Senora, the Don, and the Holy Land

The sultan encouraged Dona Gracia and Don Yosef to carry on with their vast trading empire, and their wealth continued to increase. But for Dona Gracia, her greatest satisfaction still came from helping her fellow Jews, which she could now do openly. From her magnificent palace located on the shores of the Bosporus, she supported *yeshivos*, hospitals, and other institutions. She also sponsored the printing and publication of thousands of manuscripts. And it is said that every day 80 poor people dined at her table. Her generosity was so legendary that she became known by the honorary title *"La Senora"* — The Lady.

Yet Dona Gracia had one dream that still remained unfilled: she longed to end her days in Eretz Yisrael. That was not such an impossible dream, since the Holy Land had come under Ottoman rule in the year 1516. Former *anusim* were settling in Jerusalem, Tzfas, and elsewhere, many of them through her assistance. So why shouldn't she follow their example?

For reasons that remain unknown she decided to settle in Tiveria, which at the time was in ruins. Tiveria's beginnings were humble—it was founded by a son of King Herod in the year 20 CE—but after the Bar Kochba Revolt and the expulsion of the Jews from Jerusalem by the Romans, Tiveria became the final location of the *Sanhedrin* (high court of law). By the end of the second century, Tiveria had become an important center of Jewish learning, and it's believed that both the *Mishnah* and the Jerusalem Talmud were compiled there. The city once again experienced a decline after the tenth century, and by the beginning of the twelfth century only about 50 Jewish families called it home. A traveler who visited the place in 1522 wrote: "Tiveria was formerly a great city ... but now it is desolate and waste, heaps of black stones, as though it had burned by fire."

All that began to change in the year 1558, when Dona Gracia made a deal with the sultan to lease the city for a yearly fee of 1,000 ducats. Her dream was to establish a community of Torah scholars and to return the city to its former glory. However, she didn't act alone. As always, she consulted with her nephew Don Yosef.

Don Yosef had his own ideas about what to do with the city. For years his dream had been to create an independent, economically viable safe haven for any Jew who needed a place of refuge. When a war broke out between the sultan's two sons—and Don Yosef supported the victorious elder son, Prince Selim—Don Yosef finally got his chance to put his dream into action. Prince Selim convinced his father to grant Don Yosef ruling authority over Tiveria and seven neighboring villages. Although the residents of the territory would have to pay taxes to the sultan, Eretz Yisrael would now have something that it hadn't had for some 1500 years—a quasi-independent Jewish city-state ruled by a Jewish leader.

The Building Begins

Don Yosef never visited his new "empire." In Turkish politics, absence did not make the heart grow fonder. It only gave your enemies an opportunity to plot to destroy you. Don Yosef therefore entrusted the rebuilding of Tiveria to a trusted friend, Yosef ben Adereth, who was a descendent of the illustrious Catalan rabbi known as the Rashba, Rav Shlomo ben Adereth.

The first task was to rebuild the city's walls, to protect the future residents from the marauding Arabs who roamed freely throughout the countryside. Ben Adereth hired a crew of Arab workers and at first the work went smoothly. But when an unhappy Arab sheik started a rumor that the new Jewish settlement would spell the end of Islam the workers revolted and fled.

European leaders also voiced their complaints. However, by this time Don Yosef had become one of the sultan's most skilled and indispensable diplomats. The sultan therefore ignored the Europeans, threatened the Arabs, and the work continued. The walls were rebuilt, and houses and a synagogue were constructed. Don Yosef, having decided that silk manufacturing would be the community's principal means of support, shipped mulberry trees to the Holy Land. Only one thing was lacking: Jews.

Don Yosef sent out a call, which was soon answered. By the 1560s it wasn't just the *anusim* who needed a place of refuge. A spirit of religious intolerance had swept across the Italian peninsula and so many Italian Jews were eager to join the new project. However, most of them never made it to the Holy Land. In some cases, their cruel rulers refused to let them leave. Others succeeded in fleeing, only to fall into the hands of Barbary Pirates or the ransom-hungry Knights of Malta.

However, some Jews did reach Tiveria, including some 70 important scholars, and for a few short years the fledging community rivaled the city of Tzfas. But the Torah community suffered a severe blow in the year 1569, when Dona Gracia passed away.

Despite her great fame during her lifetime, the events surrounding Dona Gracia's death are shrouded in mystery. Although she supposedly made plans to travel to Eretz Yisrael in the year 1565, it's not known if she ever reached its shores. It's also not known where she is buried. All that is certain is that she was greatly mourned by the common people and the great Torah leaders of her generation alike.

After the death of his aunt, it seems that Don Yosef gradually lost interest in the community he had helped to found in Tiveria. Although he continued to use his wealth to support *yeshivos* and help Jews fleeing persecution, international political intrigues consumed more and more of his time. Then Sultan Selim II, who had become the sultan in the year 1566, passed away in 1574, and one of Don Yosef's bitterest enemies ascended to the throne. This new sultan, who was biased against the Jews, informed the aging Jewish diplomat that his services were no longer needed.

Don Yosef's personal troubles affected Tiveria's Jewish population, which began to be attacked by its Arab neighbors with alarming frequency. The community suffered another severe blow when Don Yosef passed away in the year 1579. He was buried in Constantinople, in the cemetery at Cassim Pasha, but oddly, like his aunt Dona Gracia, there is no record of where his grave is located or what was inscribed on his gravestone.

Even though Tiveria had lost its two patrons, the community didn't immediately disband. However, by the mid-1600s, Tiveria once again languished in a state of ruin and desolation. It did experience yet another revival when Rav Chaim Abulafia and Rebbe Menachem Mendel of Vitebsk both established communities there in the 1700s. But that's another story.

If the Walls Could Speak

Tiveria may be small, but there is a fair amount of history tucked away in its streets. In the center of town a few Roman ruins lie not too far away from the remains of a Crusader-era gate, which are just a few steps away from a late Ottoman-era governor's residence. Tiveria is also the location of the final resting place of some of the Jewish people's most illustrious scholars and leaders — including Rabbi Akiva and his pious wife Rachel, the Rambam, the Ramchal, Rav Chaim Abulafia, and Rebbe Menachem Mendel of Vitebsk. But what remains of the city that was built by Dona Gracia and Don Yosef?

According to some opinions, nothing. Others, however, claim that traces do still remain, if we know where and how to look.

I decide that a logical place to begin my search is the street bearing Dona Gracia's name. But even though it's scenic, thanks to the remains of an eighteenth-century fortress that is located there, a lonely street sign is the only thing that links it with *La Senora*. I therefore head across town to the next site on my list, Tiveria's famous southern wall.

After an earthquake destroyed the walls built by Don Yosef's emissary, the walls were rebuilt in the 1720s by a popular Bedouin leader named Dhaher al-Omer, who also encouraged the rebuilding of Tiveria's Jewish community by inviting Rav Abulafia to settle there. A few years ago, an Israeli archeologist named Dr. Yosef Stepansky conducted an excavation of Dhaher al-Omer's southern wall, at a section located between HaBonim and HaGalil Streets, on behalf of the Israel Antiquities Authority, and the remains of an earlier wall were discovered. When was this earlier wall built, and by whom?

In his report Dr. Stepansky cautiously suggests that this wall might have been part of the rebuilding commissioned by Dona

Gracia and Don Yosef. Or maybe not. The findings are too inconclusive.

Disappointed, I next go to the Jewish Courtyard — which is just a few steps away from the Promenade overlooking the Sea of Galilee. On the southern side of the square stand the Etz Chaim Synagogue that was founded by Rav Abulafia, the Karlin-Stolin synagogue built on the site of the synagogue founded by Rebbe Menachem Mendel of Vitebsk, a Chabad synagogue, and a Sephardic synagogue. I'm sure they all have interesting stories, but since they were established later I continue my search until I see a dilapidated building sitting by itself on the other side of the square, nestled modestly between a few touristy *tchotchke* stalls and the towering Caesar Hotel.

A closer look reveals that this seemingly abandoned building is actually "The Senor" Synagogue. According to the Ninio family, who are currently restoring it, the synagogue was founded by an ancestor of theirs, Rav Chaim Shmuel Hacohen Konorti. Rav Konorti came to Tiveria from Spain in the year 1837 — the year that an earthquake devastated the city. The synagogue was part of the community's efforts to rebuild.

While the Anglo-Jewish historian Cecil Roth doesn't disagree with this assessment of the synagogue's post-1837 history, he wasn't at all certain that the "Senor" being referred to was the nineteenth-century rabbi who built the present structure. Recalling that synagogues supported by Dona Gracia were known as *Kahal de la Senora*, Roth wondered if the present-day synagogue is in fact sitting upon the remains of an earlier one, which was built with funds donated by Don Yosef and therefore named after Tiveria's illustrious sixteenth-century patron.

If Cecil Roth's hunch is true, "The Senor" synagogue is presently the only tangible, albeit tenuous, remnant that links modern Tiveria to Dona Gracia and Don Yosef. But even if there's no connection, one thing is certain: wherever a synagogue in Tiveria is being rebuilt and wherever a renewal of Jewish life is blossoming, from their abode up above Dona Gracia and Don Yosef are surely smiling.

— February 2010

Riches amongst the Ruins:
The Women of the Old Yishuv

They came from many countries, but they came to settle in Eretz Yisrael *for only one reason: spiritual elevation. And despite the poverty, hunger, and disease, they found it – the amazing women of the "Old Yishuv," who lived in Jerusalem during the final years of the Ottoman Empire.*

"I wish to record now what I heard in my parents' home and what I have seen with my own eyes.

"When in the year 5601 (1841) my grandmother's father, the saintly *mekubal* (*kabbalist*) Rabbi Abdullah ben Rabbi Moses Chaim, of blessed memory, went up to the Holy Land, my grandmother's mother, the old wife of the Rabbi, used to go every Friday noon, summer and winter, to the *Kosel Maaravi* (Western Wall) and remain there to read the entire *Book of Psalms* and the *Song of Songs*, till it was time to kindle the Sabbath lights."

Thus writes a resident of Jerusalem's Old Yishuv, Reb Yitzchak Yechezkiel Yehudah, in a 1930 document prepared by leaders of Jerusalem's Jewish community for a Special Commission of the League of Nations. (The term "Old Yishuv" refers to Jews who immigrated to the Land of Israel before Zionist-inspired immigration began in the late 1800s.)

Today, when there are daily flights to Israel in abundance and the hardest thing about getting to the *Kosel* is finding a seat on an Egged bus, it may be difficult to appreciate what was so astounding about this old woman's weekly vigil, except for the fact that she must have been an incredibly organized housewife to find time to visit the Western Wall before Shabbos.

However, our writer clarifies the significance of his ancestor's act, when he continues: "In those days the city was forsaken and desolate. Not a single Jew was found there at noon. However, from early afternoon people would come for the Inauguration of the Sabbath. So she would be there alone many hours."

Forsaken. Desolate. Alone. Words like these wouldn't usually entice a person to pack up her belongings, leave her family and friends behind, and embark on a dangerous journey to begin a new life — even if the destination was the holy city of Jerusalem, and she made the journey with her husband.

However, by the mid-1800s more and more Jews were doing just that. What caused this new wave of immigration, and who were these Jews who came to live in Jerusalem and Eretz Yisrael (Land of Israel)? And how did the women manage to thrive in such harsh conditions? To answer these questions, we first need to know something about the times that led to the development of the Old Yishuv.

The Crimean War Connection

When most people think of the Crimean War — if they think about it at all — two things come to mind: The Charge of the Light Brigade, the disastrous cavalry charge that was immortalized in verse by the British poet Alfred, Lord Tennyson, and the work of Florence Nightingale, the selfless British nurse who became known as the "Lady with the Lamp." However, anyone familiar with Jewish history will know that there has to be a Jewish connection somewhere to this war that involved most of that era's great powers and, indeed, they won't have to look far.

The Crimean War began in 1853 when Russia objected to France's declaration that France, with the agreement of the Ottoman Empire, was the "sovereign authority" in the Holy Land. The war involved Russia on one side, with England, France, Prussia, and Austria joining up with the Ottoman Empire on the other side. Russia lost, but the Muslim Ottoman Empire also had to pay a price for the help it received from its European allies. The Paris Treaty of 1858 stipulated that both Jews and Christians had the right to settle in what was then called Palestine. Furthermore, people from European countries didn't have to become a citizen of the Ottoman Empire to do so. They could retain their foreign passports and receive protection from their home country's consulate in Jerusalem. The result was that it became more feasible for Jews from Europe to move to Eretz Yisrael.

Another result of the Crimean War was that it improved living conditions in Eretz Yisrael, at least a little. The reason was relatively simple. The Holy Land became a popular tourist destination for European and American travelers, and these tourists demanded "luxuries" such as beds to sleep on and wardrobes for their clothes, as opposed to the mattresses on the floor and niches in the wall that had been the standard furnishings of a Jerusalem dwelling before the 1850s.

But whereas non-Jewish visitors mainly came to tour the land and then go home, when the Jews came they were coming home and so they stayed. The nineteenth century was therefore a period of great growth for the Jewish population of Eretz Yisrael. For instance, in 1840, about the time that Reb Yitzchak Yechezkiel Yehudah's great-grandmother was making her weekly pre-Shabbos visits to the *Kosel*, about 5,500 Jews lived in Jerusalem, out of a total population of approximately 13,000. By the time of the outbreak of World War I in 1914, the Jewish population had grown to some 47,000 souls, and the city's total population was 70,000.

The composition of Jerusalem's Jewish community also changed drastically during the nineteenth century. In the early 1800s, most of the Jews were Sephardic. Then a wave of *chassidim* from Europe arrived and they became the dominant group. After the *chassidim*, came the *misnagim*, also known as the *Perushim*, who formed the majority of Jerusalem's Jewish residents by the end of the century. Yet even as the city became increasingly Ashkenazic, Jerusalem remained a fascinating mosaic of Jewish cultures from around the world. Yiddish mingled with Ladino and English in the courtyards and narrow streets, since each group clung to its language and customs.

Of course, the astounding growth of Jerusalem's Jewish population during the nineteenth century wasn't due only to the Crimean War, or to new-fangled means of transportation, such as railroads and steamships. Living in Eretz Yisrael has been a cherished dream of the Jewish people since the destruction of the *Beis HaMikdash* (Holy Temple) and our exile from our Land. The events and inventions of the nineteenth century just made it easier to turn that dream into a reality.

The Long Journey Home

What was it like for these new immigrants to Eretz Yisrael? Syla Bergman, a German-speaking woman who lost all her possessions in a storm off the coast of Jaffa – and this was a time when there was no such thing as travel insurance—wrote in *Se'u Harim Shalom*, "I console myself … with the thought that I am now in Jerusalem. For that is a great privilege … Nevertheless, I would not advise anyone not strong enough to attempt this. One must suffer a great deal."

Rivkah Lipa Anikshter, who immigrated to Eretz Yisrael in 1862 with her husband, Rabbi Meir Anikshter, wrote in her booklet *Zekher Olam*, "You should know, my beloved children, that our journey to the Holy City of Jerusalem was very difficult; it was a test like the binding of Yitzchak Avinu (the Patriarch Isaac)."

Many women considered the physically and emotionally arduous journey to be a sacrifice, and yet it was a sacrifice that most were happy to make. Some women came with their families because they hoped to escape the influences of the Enlightenment movement that was gaining strength in Europe and raise their children in the spiritually pure air of Jerusalem. Other women, who were childless, came with their husbands with the hope that their sacrifice of material comforts would make them worthy of having children. And then there were the widows—both rich and poor—who arrived alone and with the wish to end their days in doing *mitzvos* in the Holy Land.

What seemed to unite them all was that they came filled with a strong spiritual purpose—a striving for holiness that could only be achieved in the Holy Land. And it was this purpose that helped them to meet the challenge when they caught their first glimpse of their new home.

Home Sweet Home

Many of us have heard stories about how the previous generation managed to raise a large and beautiful family in a Jerusalem apartment that consisted of just two rooms. What many of us haven't heard is that in the Jerusalem of the nineteenth century, two rooms would have been considered to be a palace. A typical Jerusalem apartment for a family consisted of just one room, and it was usually a dark and dreary one. The rent for this room — which was usually owned by an Arab landlord — was exorbitant. So how did families manage?

If the ceiling was high, the family might build a wooden roof and separate the room into two floors. If the room was long or wide, part of the room could be partitioned with a curtain. The family didn't have to worry about where to put all their furniture, since furniture was scarce. A typical Ashkenazic home might have a few beds — which were made from two iron bases and a plank of wood — a second-hand table and a few chairs, and perhaps a chest to store clothes and bedding.

Very little was thrown out and families learned to recycle long before there was such a thing as the Green Movement. For instance, the Old Yishuv Museum in Jerusalem's Jewish Quarter has on display an unusual copper table. It's actually the upside-down lid of a big copper pot that became too battered to use. Someone affixed metal legs to the lid, and some lucky family became the proud owners of a "new" table.

There were a few comforts, of course. For instance, when a woman was about to give birth, the husband would rent one of the community's famous *Himmel* (Heavenly) Beds. This comfortable canopy bed made the new mother feel, if not in heaven, at least like an earthly queen.

One reason families could survive in such cramped quarters was because of the shared courtyard, which served multiple purposes. It was the kitchen — each family stored its own stove there — laundry room, and lavatory. However, there was no oven in the courtyard and so bread was baked in a neighborhood's communal oven, which also kept the *cholent* (stew) warm on Shabbos.

The shared courtyard also served a social function, since it allowed women to form close bonds with each other and give one other support. Although the women might have come to Jerusalem to raise their spiritual level, there was no question but that the grinding poverty dampened their spirits from time to time—especially since this was a time when infant mortality was devastatingly high. Therefore, women often needed an encouraging word, and *Rosh Chodesh* (New Moon) and *Motzei* Shabbos (Saturday night, after Shabbos) were traditional times for women to get together to share a meal, sing, and strengthen one another.

Home-Based Businesses

Although there were some wealthy families and rich widows, the vast majority of the Jewish population was poor. Most families were dependent upon their stipend from the communal charitable fund, which was funded by contributions from Jews living in the Diaspora. However, when this wasn't enough to support the family and enable the husband to continue to learn Torah, women engaged in professions similar to what they might have done back in the Old Country.

Some women opened shops, where they sold flour, wine, coffee, or milk, or items to make clothing, such as cloth or thread. However, one difference between the shops of today and the shops of the 1800s was that the shopkeeper often had to manufacture the items she sold. Malka Yadler, for instance, churned the butter that she sold in her small grocery store. Others ground their shop's flour or spun their shop's yarn and thread.

From these humble beginnings an occasional Jerusalem landmark business was born. Krisha Berman, who arrived in Eretz Yisrael in 1874, supported her family by baking rolls for tourists. She would probably be both surprised and happy to know that from those few rolls sprouted Jerusalem's Berman Bakery, which provides a livelihood for many workers today and whose cinnamon *rugelach* sustained this author during the writing of this article.

Not every woman had the means to open a shop, though. Poorer women would hire themselves out to do domestic labor, such as clean houses, cook or bake, or do laundry. Women also worked as midwives, although these were usually older women who had both experience with delivering babies and knowledge about the correct amulets and charms to use to ward off evil spirits.

Although one might have expected that women would have worked as seamstresses or did needlework to earn a living, during the first half of the nineteenth century people were too poor to buy clothing made by others. It was only after the textile industry was mechanized—and, ironically, there was a longing for handmade items among wealthy residents and tourists—that producing handicrafts such as embroidered tablecloths or lace curtains brought income to Jewish women.

Charity Begins at Home

Like today, the nineteenth-century Jerusalem woman had to juggle many roles, but she had to raise the children and earn a living while churning her own butter and sewing her family's clothes. Yet she still found the time to help those who were less fortunate, inspired by the knowledge that each act of *chesed* (kindness) she did in the Holy Land would hasten the *Geulah* (Redemption).

Sometimes women banded together to cook meals for the sick or elderly, raise funds to marry off penniless brides, or organize visits to the sick. Some, however, created their own one-woman charities. Malka the washerwoman, for instance, took it upon herself to do laundry for orphans, the sick, and the elderly. A woman named Rivkah made it her mission to buy clothes in the market and then distribute them to the poor. Another woman, Tzipa, took on a similar mission only her unique *chesed* was to provide people with shoes.

Although some visitors to Jerusalem saw only the miserable living conditions of the residents of the Old Yishuv, and therefore judged the community with a critical eye, there were others who were able to look beyond the poverty and hardship that existed on the physical plane and see the nobility of these women's lives. One of them was Dr. Bernhard Neumann, a Jewish physician who worked in Jerusalem during the late 1800s, who wrote: "No one who observes the life of the Jews of Jerusalem … can deny that the motives that brought them there and their willingness to live lives of self-sacrifice are admirable."

A Taste of the World to Come

Since Jews came to live in Eretz Yisrael for spiritual reasons, it's perhaps not surprising that women frequently visited and poured out their hearts at our holiest sites. Rachel's Tomb obviously had a special place in women's hearts, and the traditional time to visit the tomb was on Rosh Chodesh. Hebron and the burial site of the prophet Samuel were also popular. However, there is no question that for the women of Jerusalem a spiritual highlight of their week occurred on Friday afternoons, when they would go to the *Kosel* and say psalms until it was time to light the Shabbos candles.

An eye-witness account quoted in the document prepared for the League of Nations, gives us an idea of what this special time in the Old Yishuv was like towards the end of the nineteenth century:

"Every Friday, immediately after noon, crowds of our brethren, men, women and children, hasten to the *Kosel Maaravi* of the Temple Mount, to pour forth supplication that God have mercy upon the remnant and scattered ones of Judah, etc., and also for the welfare of our brethren in exile who support them, etc. In every house in the city where we are passing, tumuli and haste are noticed. Everyone hastens to finish his work so as to manage to be at the *Kosel Maaravi*. As we walk through the streets we see in every direction and corner a crowd of men running, dressed in holiday attire, carrying holy books. Old men and women supporting themselves on crutches, tender babes carried by their parents, all are moving eastward. Scorching heat or cold and wind, storm and snow and drenching rain, do not prevent them."

And so we conclude our brief visit here, in the narrow streets of the Jewish Quarter, as the women of the Old Yishuv rush to the *Kosel* to pray for the welfare of Jews everywhere and for the rebuilding of the Beis HaMikdash—may it be speedily and in our days.

—February 2009

PEOPLE OF THE BOOK

Boker Tov (Good Morning), America!

It's a well-known fact that the United States and the State of Israel have a special relationship. Did that relationship almost include having a common official language, namely the Hebrew language? We investigate a popular rumor that is as old as the United States of America, itself.

The hour was late, and tensions were running high. The statesmen who had gathered in Philadelphia for the Continental Congress were well aware of the importance of their mission. After all, it wasn't every day that one had the opportunity to create a new nation.

What form of government would the new country have? What would be its laws? And how would the lofty vision of the Founding Fathers be preserved for future generations? What language would best express the principles of liberty and equality that had led to "the shot heard around the world" and the creation of a new country called the United States of America?

"Down with English!" yelled out a young firebrand. "Down with the language of the oppressors! The language used to create the oppressive Stamp Act and Sugar Act has no place in our legislatures and homes."

"Let us speak Greek in our new land," called out a delegate from Virginia. "Let us create a new Athens on our shores."

"No, we must speak Latin," suggested a statesman from Connecticut. "Latin is the basis of European civilization. Let us build upon the good of our common past to create an even better future for our children."

"Fellow Patriots, listen to my words," said a distinguished delegate from Massachusetts. "There is only one language that is the language of liberty and sound government. It is the language of the Hebrew Bible, the book that our forefathers, the founders of these colonies, looked to for inspiration and guidance. If we must speak at all, let us speak Hebrew!"

A faction within the Congress eagerly seized upon the suggestion and a passionate debate broke out. On one side stood the idealists, who wanted to make a complete break with the old world. On the other side stood the pragmatists, who saw no reason to discard a language that was capable of coining the phrases "No taxation without representation" and "Give me liberty, or give me death."

After all the arguments had been presented, the motion to make Hebrew the official language of the United States was put to a vote. As the President of the Congress went down the list of names, the tension mounted. With only one more name to be called upon, the vote was evenly divided. Half of the delegates were for, half were against.

"George Wythe!" called out the President. All eyes looked to the delegate from Virginia, whose name appeared at the end of the list. "How do you vote?"

"Against!" Wythe called out.

The motion to make Hebrew the official language of the United States had lost by just one vote.

The Making of a Rumor

Versions of the above story have appeared in various books and newspaper articles ever since the incident supposedly took place. But even though it makes for a good tale, it's highly unlikely that the vote ever happened. For one thing, there's no record of the vote in the annals of the Continental Congress. In addition, the issue of the United States having an official language isn't addressed anywhere in the U.S. Constitution. This omission has led historians to surmise that the Founding Fathers always assumed that English would be the *lingua franca* of the new country. However, like most rumors that stand the test of time, there is actually a kernel of truth in this one.

When the American colonists declared war against Great Britain, it wasn't just because of political and economic grievances. They declared an intellectual and cultural war, as well. Anti-British sentiment was therefore everywhere and, according to one eye-witness, that hatred for anything British included hostility toward the language that the British spoke.

Francois Jean de Beauvoir, Marquis de Chastellux, was a French general who helped the American rebel army win the war. He was also a linguist, a member of the Academie Francaise, and the author of the book *Voyages de M. le marquis de Chastellux dans l'Amérique septentrionale* (Travels of the Marquis de Chastellux in North America), which was published in 1786 in Paris.

The book was displayed at the New York Public Library, Dorot Jewish Division, in the Fall of 2004, as part of the exhibition *Jewes in America: Conquistadors. Knickerbockers, Pilgrims, and the Hope of Israel.* The exhibition's accompanying notes make mention of some of de Beauvoir's impressions concerning the "English problem."

According to de Beauvoir, there were many colonists who felt that English was the language of oppressors. Therefore, when he spoke to them using excellent English, the people wouldn't say, "You speak good English." Instead, the patriotic Patriots would comment, "You speak good American." Or, "American is not hard to understand."

In addition, de Beauvoir writes, "Not long ago, it was seriously proposed to introduce a new language and a number of people desired that, in the public interest, Hebrew should take the place of English. It was to be taught in the schools and used in all aspects of public life. It will be evident that this project did not materialize; nevertheless, the Americans' aversion to the English could hardly have expressed itself in more visceral form."

It may be de Beauvoir's comments that provide the source for the words of Dr. Abraham I. Katsh, who writes in his 1977 book *The Biblical Heritage of American Democracy*:

"At the time of the American Revolution, the interest in the knowledge of Hebrew was so widespread as to allow the circulation of the story that 'certain members of Congress proposed that the use of English be formally prohibited in the United States, and Hebrew substituted for it.'"

Unfortunately, de Beauvoir didn't specify who made the proposal to replace English with Hebrew, and his reticence has allowed modern scholars such as Katsh to regulate the story to the tall-tale bin. It might have stayed there, except for one thing: there were people in the colonies who thought that Hebrew should be the language of the new land, and some of them even left a written record of why they thought the way they did.

Wanted: a Replacement for the "Heathenish Language"

Hebrew has been studied by the Jews throughout the millennia, but the language's fortunes amongst the gentiles has waxed and waned. In his book *God's Sacred Tongue: Hebrew and the American Imagination,* Shalom L. Goldman, an associate professor of Hebrew and Middle Eastern at Emory University, writes that although there was some interest in studying the language during the twelfth and thirteenth centuries in England, the real surge of interest occurred during the sixteen and seventeenth centuries, the time of the Renaissance and Reformation.

During those two centuries, a mastery of Greek, Latin, and Hebrew became the hallmark of a truly educated man throughout Europe. However, Hebrew found its greatest champions in England. By order of King Henry VIII, Hebrew began to be taught at Oxford and Cambridge. Cambridge, in particular, was responsible for educating the Puritan leaders who arrived on the shores of North America in the early 1600s.

Part of the non-Jewish world's interest in Hebrew can be attributed to their belief in Hebrew's status as the world's original language. (Whereas most Jewish scholars also believe this, there are some opinions in the Talmud which state that *Adam Harishon* [Adam, the first man] spoke Aramaic in the Garden of Eden.) Yet in an era where religious and political beliefs were derived from the same source, namely the Hebrew Bible, the interest in the language wasn't just a scholarly one. It also had political ramifications.

The British fascination with Hebrew can perhaps be partially attributed to the fanciful belief, in some quarters, that the word "British" was formed from the Hebrew words *brit ish* (man of the covenant). This linguistic sleight of hand fit in nicely with England's view of itself as being an "elect nation." Having supposedly replaced ancient Israel in that role, Englishmen saw themselves as being the true inheritors of the Covenant with the Al-mighty and having a unique role to play in world history.

The British were not alone in their fascination with the idea of elect nations and new covenants. Winds of change were blowing all across Europe and during the 1600s "millennium fever" was in the air. Gentiles and Jews, alike, were convinced that the messianic era was about to begin, spurring a renewed interest in the Hebrew language and the Hebrew Bible.

At the forefront of the millennial movement in England was a Puritan sect known as the "Fifth Monarchy Men." They took their name from the prophecy found in the *Book of Daniel*, where Daniel foretold that after the fall of the four kingdoms — Babylonia, Persia, Greece, and Rome — there would be a fifth kingdom, the utopian kingdom of the messianic era, that would never be destroyed. Central to the sect's belief system were two historical developments that would herald the beginning of the messianic era: the Jews would be returned to their homeland and the Ten Lost Tribes would be restored to the House of Israel.

When these two things happened, the Jews would regain their importance as a people and the Hebrew language would be restored to its original supremacy. Since the new era was about to begin, there were those who reasoned that it behooved men of learning to master the language that would eventually be the spoken language of the entire world.

Although Jewish calculations foretold that the messianic era would begin in the year 1648, the Fifth Monarchy Men proclaimed that 1666 would be the year that the Jews would be returned to their homeland. In certain circles, therefore, non-Jews followed the spectacular career of the false messiah Shabbatai Tzvi as closely as the Jews. When entire Jewish communities began to sell off their property and pack their bags, in anticipation of their imminent transport to the Land of Israel, as promised by Shabbatai Tzvi, there seemed to be ample proof that the first step toward the Final Redemption soon would be fulfilled.

Other hopes had been fueled a few years earlier by the testimony of Antonio Montezinos, a Spanish explorer of Jewish ancestry also known as Aaron Levi, who arrived in Amsterdam in 1644. He supposedly told Rabbi Menasseh Ben Israel, author of the influential millennialist tract *The Hope of Israel*, that during his explorations of what is today part of eastern Colombia, in South America, he discovered a "remnant of the tribe of Reuven." According to the report that later circulated throughout much of Europe, the Indians, who spoke an archaic version of Hebrew, had greeted Montezinos by saying, "*Shema Yisrael!*" — the first words of a prayer said by Jews twice daily.

In truth, what Montezinos had said was that he had discovered a few lost Jews living among the Indian tribes. However, because the second step in the Final Redemption was the reunification of the Ten Lost Tribes with the rest of the House of Israel, the news quickly spread that the Lost Tribes had been found. Subsequent "studies" of the language and culture of the Indians living in North America revealed that they too were descendants of the Ten Tribes, further "confirming" the exciting news.

The year 1648 did turn out to be a pivotal year — for the Puritans. Civil war broke out in England, leading to the beheading of King Charles I on January 30, 1649, and the establishment of the Puritan Reformation under Oliver Cromwell. (Puritans were called by that name because they wished to "purify" the Church of England from what they perceived to be vestiges of the Roman Catholic religion.) The 1650s therefore was a heady time for all Puritans. They had free rein to put their religious beliefs into practice and create what they believed to be a utopian society based upon the model found in the Hebrew Bible. With things going so well for the millennialists, it is perhaps no wonder that the Hebrew language was studied with such zeal.

However, the English Puritan bubble burst in the year 1660, when the monarchy was restored. Millennialist hopes were further dashed in the year 1666, the year the Jews were supposed to return to the Land of Israel. Instead, on September 16, 1666, Shabbatai Tzvi converted to Islam and his Jewish followers were forced to tearfully unpack their bags.

Although the Puritans in the New England colonies were also affected by these developments, their physical distance from England gave them space to hold on to their dreams. The delay of the messianic era was unfortunate, but it didn't mean that they couldn't put into action their vision of creating a utopian society on American soil.

From the very first, the American Puritans, especially those who settled in the Massachusetts Bay Colony, viewed themselves as being the new "children of Israel" who had "crossed the Red Sea" to arrive on the shores of the new "Promised Land."

Their identification with the story of the Exodus was not just metaphorical. They took their perceived role, and their Bible, so seriously that John Cotton, for instance, proposed in 1641 that the government of the Massachusetts Bay Colony should be based upon the laws of the Torah.

He was not alone. A few years earlier, John Davenport had told the New Haven assembly that, "Scriptures do hold forth a perfect rule for the direction and government of all men ..." His words were apparently accepted, since 38 of 79 statutes in the New Haven Code of 1665 derived their authority from the Hebrew Bible.

Men like John Cotton and John Davenport didn't have to rely on translations to develop their ideas for a legal code based on Torah law. Like many of the leaders of the New England colonies, they were fluent in Hebrew and could read the Scriptures in their original language. The importance of Hebrew to John Davenport and others was mentioned by President Calvin Coolidge in a May 3, 1925 speech he gave about Jewish contributions to the American Revolution:

"The founders of the New Haven, John Davenport and Theophilus Eaton, were expert Hebrew scholars. The extent to which they leaned upon the moral and administrative system, laid down by the Hebrew lawgivers, was responsible for their conviction that the Hebrew language and literature ought to be made as familiar as possible to all the people. So it was that John Davenport arranged that in the first public school in New Haven the Hebrew language should be taught."

In addition, to the colonial leaders' interest in teaching Hebrew as an academic subject, there was a movement brewing—fueled by the millennialist aspirations of the Fifth Monarchy Men living in New England—to gradually replace the everyday usage of the "heathenish language" with Hebrew. For example, when Massachusetts resident Josiah Flint printed his Almanack in the year 1666, he proposed that Hebrew names be used for the months, writing:

"It hath been the zealous desire of many famous men that heathenish language might be laid aside, forgotten and unnam'd ... In imitation of which I have ventured to make a beginning, and shall leave the progress to the wise disposal of Divine Providence, and the discretion of those that shall succeed."

William Aspinwall, a leader of the Fifth Monarchy Men in Massachusetts who later returned to England, also gave voice to this vision of Hebrew one day becoming the language of the world in his 1653 work *A Brief Description of the Fifth Monarchy or Kingdome That Shortly is to Come into the World*:

"As for the names of Parliaments and Dyets, etc., though there be no evil in the names, yet I suppose they will be laid aside in the time of this Fifth Monarchy, when men begin to affect more the language of Canaan than the imitation of idolatrous nations."

The Harvard Connection

The Fifth Monarchy Men were no dreamers. They were activists who planned to bring about the Final Redemption by their own hands, rather than wait for Divine Providence to choose the moment for ushering in the new era. Although their movement failed, and many of their members were hanged after King Charles II assumed the English throne, their desire to firmly plant the Hebrew language on American soil had more success.

To ensure that their Puritan values would be transmitted to future generations, the early colonists living in New England made education a priority. Harvard College, for example, was established in the year 1636 — just six years after the Puritans arrived in Massachusetts — in order to train future clergymen and statesmen.

Although not all Puritans were millennialists, the Hebrew Bible was at the center of all Puritan intellectual and religious thought. Therefore, Harvard's founders demanded that upperclassmen learn Hebrew, along with the Bible, Latin, and Greek, making Harvard the first university in the world where Hebrew was a required subject. The university's first presidents, Henry Dunster, Charles Chauncey, and Increase Mather, were all fluent in the language, and an oration in Hebrew was an integral part of Harvard's commencement exercises until 1817.

Yale University, founded in 1701, followed the Harvard model and also required the study of Hebrew. Ezra Stiles, Yale's president from 1778-1795, was an avid Hebraist who was responsible for including the Hebrew words "Urim" and "Thummin" on the Yale seal. Hebrew was also diligently studied at colonial universities such as Brown, Princeton, and King's College (today known as Columbia University).

Yet despite the fact that men such as Harvard president Increase Mather were so fluent in Hebrew that they could quote the Talmud and classic Jewish commentators such as Rashi and Rambam, all was not rosy in those Ivy League halls. In his 1946 article *The Teaching of Hebrew in American Universities*, Dr. Abraham I. Katsh, comments that almost from the beginning students at Harvard complained about learning the language.

A touching example of this clash between educators and students is the sorrowful lament expressed in the August 29, 1653 diary entry of Michael Wigglesworth, an early Hebrew tutor at Harvard: "My pupils all came to me this day to desire they might cease learning Hebrew; I withstood it with all the reason I could, yet all will not satisfy them. Thus am I requited for my love, and thus little fruit of all my prayers and tears for their good."

Cotton Mather, a well-known Puritan minister and scholar from Massachusetts who was also one of the guiding spirits behind the founding of Yale, once commented, "I promise that those who spend as much time morning and evening in Hebrew studies as they do in smoking tobacco, would quickly make excellent progress in the language." Unfortunately, his words went unheeded.

By 1782, Harvard students were allowed to substitute French for Hebrew, provided they received approval, and things weren't going much better at Yale. A Yale student, Class of 1788, recorded for posterity that although he and his fellow classmates managed to learn the Hebrew alphabet and could struggle through a few of the psalms, that was the extent of their knowledge. In 1790, Edward Stiles was forced to admit defeat and change Yale's Hebrew language requirements, as he records in his diary:

"From my first accession to the Presidency ... I have obliged all the Freshmen to study Hebrew. This has proved very disagreeable to a Number of the Students. This year I have determined to instruct only those who offer themselves voluntarily."

To his great satisfaction, the majority of Yale's freshmen did sign up for Hebrew instruction and the valedictorian of Yale Class of 1792 delivered his speech in Hebrew. However, the winds of change were blowing once again. By the end of the eighteenth century, "millennium fever" was just a memory and Puritanism had lost its dominance over America's intellectual imagination.

The dream of creating a utopian theocracy based upon the laws of the Hebrew Bible had been replaced by the reality of the formation of a democratic system of government that looked to both religious and non-religious sources for inspiration. Although Hebrew continued to be associated with the language of liberty — and the Torah was acknowledged as the source for the Declaration of Independence's statement that "all men are created equal" — with the erection of the wall between church and state, Hebrew found itself on the wrong side of the divider.

True, Hebrew continued to be taught at the divinity schools associated with universities, such as Harvard and Yale, but it was no longer a part of the regular curriculum. It did remain a subject of interest for the new nation's intellectual elite, including James Madison, Noah Webster, and Alexander Hamilton. However, there were other Founding Fathers, the most famous being Thomas Jefferson, who were not familiar with the language. And as for regular American citizens, it seemed that they were happy to make do with speaking the "heathenish language," after all.

Let Them Speak Greek!

So even though that cliff-hanging vote in the Continental Congress never occurred, the idea of Hebrew becoming the language spoken in the United States is not as totally far-fetched as it may sound. Although they were few in number, there were some Americans who would have cast a vote in favor of the proposal, whether for pro-millennialist or anti-British reasons.

However, the attitude of the majority of the colonists can perhaps best be summed up by the supposed words of Roger Sherman, a delegate to the Continental Congress. As the story goes, when Sherman was asked his opinion about replacing English with some other language, he wryly replied, "It would be more convenient for us to keep the language as it was and make the English speak Greek."

* * *

A Trip to the Rumor Mill

Hebrew isn't the only language that was supposedly just one vote away from becoming the official language of the United States. Greek, Latin, and French have also been cast in the role. However, the most famous version of the story involves the German language and is known as the "Muhlenberg Legend." Here's how an historical event made the journey from fact to fiction, in just three easy steps.

First, the real story:

By the late 1700s there were many German-speaking people living in the colonies, and the Germans living in Virginia drew up a petition asking the Continental Congress to print all federal laws in both English and German. The proposal was debated by the Continental Congress on January 13, 1795.

At one point in the discussion, it was suggested to adjourn and continue the debate at a later time. The vote to adjourn was defeated by just one vote. No decision was made about the translation proposal, however, and a month later the proposal was debated again. This time the proposal was soundly defeated.

Frederick Augustus Muhlenberg, a Federalist from an assimilated German family who could barely speak German, was the Speaker of the House of Representatives at the time of the vote to adjourn. Tradition has it that he stepped down from his role as Speaker to cast the deciding—and negative—vote, but there is no evidence that this is what happened. There is evidence, however, that it was Muhlenberg who cast the deciding vote in favor of ratifying the Jay Treaty during the Fourth Congress, a move that was highly unpopular with the Germans living in the U.S.

Now, for the rumor:

Turn the petition to translate U.S. federal law into German into a petition to make German the official language of the United States of America.

Turn the vote to adjourn, which loses by just one vote, into the vote on the German language, and make it also lose by just one vote.

Attach a real name to the story to give the rumor credibility — pay no attention to the fact that Muhlenberg cast the deciding vote on an issue that had absolutely nothing to do with the German language — and *voila*!

A version of the "new and improved" story appeared in 1847 in Franz Löher's book *History and Achievements of the Germans in America*. Since then, the story has enjoyed a long and happy life. *Zeit gezunt!*

Source: The Legendary English-only Vote of 1795, by Dennis Baron, professor of English and linguistics at the University of Illinois at Urbana-Champaign.

* * *

The Lad Who Laughed at the Idea (in Hebrew)

Although Hebrew never did become the official language of the United States of America, there are some scholars who believe that Hebrew has contributed more to the English language than is commonly recognized.

In his 1989 book *The Word* (Shapolsky Publishers, New York), Isaac E. Mozeson has complied a list of thousands of English words whose roots have been attributed to Latin, Greek, Anglo-Saxon, Old Norse, Old French, Old and Middle English, German, obscure origin, etc., but whose roots may actually lie in the Hebrew language. Here are three examples, as quoted from the book, with the English word followed by the Hebrew word:

LAD/ *YEHLED*
Roots: The *Oxford English Dictionary* states "of obscure origin" for LAD. Noah Webster's eighteenth-century dictionary, scorned by the O.E.D. and the linguistic establishment, cites Chaldaic and Syriac sources for LAD.

Yehled (YEH)-LED, the Hebrew word for "boy" is mentioned in *Genesis* 21:8.

LAUG(H)/ *LAH-AG*

Roots: LAUGH is from Anglo-Saxon *hleahhan*; akin to the German *lachen* ... Both are to mean "to cry out, sound" ...

A better entymon is *lah'ag*, which means to jest, to laugh at or to mock.

IDEA/(Y)ID-EE-AH

Roots: Greek *idea* means idea (as well as appearance and form – those these last two definitions may be confused with Greek *eidos*).

Yide'ah is knowledge or information. From the same root in the Hebrew are *hoda*, means brought to one's knowledge (*Leviticus* 4:23); *yoda*, to know or be aware of something (*Genesis* 31:32); and the two-letter root word *da*, which is "Know!" in the imperative.

Although not everyone accepts Mozeson's work, the idea is intriguing that millions of English-speakers may actually be speaking a post-Tower of Babel, scrambled form of Hebrew, after all.

—September 2006

You Must Remember This:
A Short History of Early Jewish Memoirs

Often, our most cherished possessions aren't things. They are the family stories that get passed down from generation to generation. And when the memoir-writer is someone like Gluckel of Hameln, those family stories allow future generations to get a glimpse of what Jewish life was like in long-ago eras.

In my parents' home there is an old photograph of my great-grandmother. Dressed in what are probably her Shabbos clothes, she sits staring into the camera with a stern look on her face, tightly clutching a small pocketbook. It is not a happy image.

What's more, this photographer's depiction of my great-grandmother is my only image of her, an "ordinary" Jew who grew up in Vilna and made the long trek to Kansas City, Missouri, after the First World War. As with my other great-grandparents, there are no written eulogies that recount her praises. The stories that might have been told about her around a holiday table have vanished long ago, along with the food, the table, and the storytellers. And there is no account, written in her own words, to tell me who she really was, when she wasn't sitting in a photographer's studio.

And so whenever I hear that someone has in their possession a personal account written by an ancestor from a few generations ago, I feel a twinge of envy. Suddenly, formulaic phrases, such as "a link in the chain of our golden tradition," come alive. The "link" no longer conjures up an image of cold metal, or even faded photographs, but of living people clasping the hands of others across the centuries. Jewish history is no longer a sad litany of pogroms and expulsions, but an inspiring tale of how real people – one's ancestors! — drew upon deep reservoirs of faith to overcome seemingly impossible challenges.

Yet despite the obvious advantages of having a family memoir or two sitting on a shelf in the bookcase, apparently my memoir-less family is not alone. These sorts of documents — personal accounts told by ordinary Jews in their own words — appear to be rare, at least before the Holocaust. And so as I contemplated the image of my tight-lipped great-grandmother, I began to wonder about the silence of previous generations versus the talkative generation of today, which has made memoir-writing a popular — and sometimes even profitable — pastime.

Has this change come about merely because of today's new computer technology, which makes it so much easier to write one's life story? Or has our attitude about preserving that story also changed? And why do some people feel compelled to write down their personal history, while others prefer to remain silent?

As these and other questions began to tumble out of my keyboard and spread all over the page, I confess that I began to feel more than a little overwhelmed. And so I decided to take a few steps back and begin at the beginning, which is to first ask the most basic question of them all: What is a memoir, anyway?

Paging Mr. Merriam-Webster

The coffee mug is filled. The clean sheet of paper is prepared. You're all ready to begin your big project and the first thing to do is give it a title. But what should that title be?

"The Diary of …"?

"The Autobiography of …"?

"The Memoirs of …"?

All three of those words could be used to describe a life story written in the first person. However, they are not interchangeable terms, as a visit to a dictionary such as Merriam-Webster's shows. A diary is a record of events or transactions or feelings that are written down daily or at some other frequent interval. It records single moments, without attempting to "connect the dots." On the other side of the life story spectrum is the autobiography, which is written as a chronological narrative that attempts to faithfully record the facts of a person's life.

Somewhere in the middle of those two genres is the memoir. More similar to an Impressionist painting than a digital photograph, a memoir, in today's publishing parlance, is a narrative that presents selected events from a person's life and attempts to find meaning in those events. A memoir could be about a person's childhood or the way a person coped with a traumatic event. Or it might be focused on lessons learned from the person's professional life, such as the memoirs of a teacher or congregational rabbi looking back on their career.

So now that we've defined our terms (and pointed out that both "memoir" and "memoirs" are acceptable ways to describe this particular type of life story), it's time to move on to the next question: What makes some people feel compelled to write one?

Dutch Lives

Since one of the most famous first-person accounts ever written was penned in Amsterdam — Anne Frank's diary — it is perhaps not entirely surprising that Holland is a major center of research on this topic.

A few years ago historian Rudolf M. Dekker conducted a study of 1,121 Dutch "egodocuments" — an inclusive term used by academics to describe the full range of first-person accounts, including autobiographies, memoirs, diaries, personal letters, etc. — that were written between the years 1500 to 1814 to answer a question similar to my own: Why do people write them?

Professor Dekker discovered that the most popular reason mentioned — and it is mentioned by 80 percent of the authors who give one — is to relay information to one's children. Other authors state that they are writing as a way to respond to a crisis, such as the loss of a loved one or the outbreak of war. Still others write that they wish to keep track of their spiritual or intellectual development, while a few authors openly declare that they hope their writing will reach a general readership. Finally, the study also mentions the desire of some immigrants, including Jewish memoirists, to use a family history as a forum for urging their descendents to adhere to their faith.

Since this short list of motives seems to have a rather timeless and universal ring to it, I wondered if these same motivations could be applied to the Jewish memoirist. If so, then with our emphasis on education and our crisis-filled history, surely we, of all the nations, should win the prize for the people with the most memoirs ever written.

But then the image of my great-grandmother once again appeared to me. She had lived through a crisis. She was surely concerned about what would become of her children's connection to Judaism in Kansas City. So why didn't she feel compelled to write down her story? Was there something unique about the attitude of previous generations of Jews that still has ramifications for today?

Jewish Memoirs Before the Modern Era: A Selective History

As I was pondering this question, I recalled a conversation I once had with a woman who is a well-known teacher and lecturer in the *chareidi* community. I was trying to convince her to grant me an interview, since I was sure that her life story would inspire this magazine's readers. Her eloquent answer was brief and to the point: "*Acharei mos, kedoshim.*"

"Huh?" I not so eloquently replied. I recognized that *Acharei Mos* and *Kedoshim* were the names of two portions of the Torah that are often read together on the same Shabbos, but surely she was referring to something else.

She was, and she graciously explained that after a person has passed away (*acharei mos*) is the time to speak of their greatness and their accomplishments (*kedoshim*). Not while the person is still alive.

This conversation comforted me after I researched the history of Jewish memoirs and discovered an interesting fact: There aren't any—at least not until the Renaissance (circa 1350 - 1600), when the modern concept of the individual self began to emerge. True, we have the Ramban's personal account of the Disputation and the travel diaries of Benjamin of Tudela. However, in these documents the author acts as a faithful recorder of events that are of interest to the public. They are not meant to give the reader a glimpse into the author's private life and his inner world.

Some historians explain this inner silence by suggesting that for the pre-modern Jew, meaning was found solely in the "four cubits" of Jewish law, the communal experience, and the Jewish people's relationship to Hashem (God). Although a person knew that he was responsible for his actions, the thought that the mundane activities of his individual life were worthy of being examined, recorded, and recounted was utterly foreign.

The average Torah-observant Jew might add a few other reasons for the reticence, which would still apply today. The *chareidi* world is one of the last places on earth where modesty is valued and privacy is scrupulously guarded. And, of course, who wants to be singled out for attention and possibly attract the evil eye in this world or increased scrutiny by the Heavenly Court?

However, as convincing as these arguments may be, at least one historian disagrees with all of them. In his book *Autobiographical Jews: Essays in Jewish Self-Fashioning*, Michael Stanislawski points out that a diary written by a medieval German Jew was discovered in Oxford University's Bodleian Library a few decades ago. Although the diary is very brief, it does show that at least one medieval Jew viewed himself as an individual who felt there was something about his life that was worthwhile to record. And, according to Stanislawski, this diary's existence suggests that there could be others gathering dust on European library shelves or hidden away in private family collections.

Yet even if writing a full-fledged memoir wasn't on the agenda of a typical pre-Renaissance Jew, an element of individual expression can sometimes be found in the personal documents that Jews did write, such as the *zava'ah*, or ethical will, which began to develop as a genre around the tenth century. Yehudah ibn Tibbon, translator of the classic twelfth-century *mussar* (ethical) work *Duties of the Heart* and one of the genres first practitioners, wrote a famous ethical will for his son, Shmuel, which is still studied today.

In addition to advising Shmuel to devote his time to Torah study and to honor his wife, the worried father warns his only son — who had been dangerously ill — to be more careful about his diet ("And not slay me before my time!"). The famed translator also admonishes his son to improve his Hebrew and Arabic handwriting ("Do not swallow up the *yud* [the tenth letter of the Hebrew alphabet] between the other letters, as you always do.") and to take better care of his book collection ("If you lend a volume, make a memorandum before it leaves your house, and when it is returned, draw your pen over the entry.").

Yehudah's many admonishments show us that bringing up children was never easy. But since Shmuel became a renowned translator in his own right—he translated the Rambam's *Guide for the Perplexed*—it is assumed that the son did mend his ways, perhaps by doing as his father, and many a writer of ethical wills, instructed: "... read this, my testament, once daily, at morn or at eve. Apply your heart to the fulfillment of its behests, and to the performance of all therein written. Then will you make your ways prosperous, then shall you have good success."

Ethical wills reached the height of their popularity during a 200-year period that began in the seventeenth century. While most were private documents that remained within the family, some of the wills written by renowned rabbinic figures were publically circulated. For instance, the three generations of ethical wills written by the Horowitz family—Rabbi Avraham's *Yesh Nochalin*, Rabbi Yaakov's emendations to his father's will, and the ethical will of the grandson, Rabbi Shabsai Sheftil—were published together in the early 1700s and reprinted dozens of times.

In addition to the ethical will, there's another type of document that can be considered a forerunner of the Jewish memoir: the *megillah* (scroll or account). Like the *megillos* in the biblical canon, a family's personal *megillah* was a scroll where the family would write down the details of a tragedy that had befallen them—or, more happily, the story of their deliverance from tragedy.

An example of this genre that continues to inspire today is *Megillas Eivah*, a brief personal account by Rabbi Yom Tov Lipmann Heller (also known as Tosafos Yom Tov) of his fall from eminence due to false accusations, his imprisonment, and his subsequent deliverance. Set against the backdrop of Europe's Thirty Years War, *Megillas Eivah*, which has been translated into English under the title *A Chronicle of Hardship and Hope*, gives the modern reader a glimpse into the precarious situation of the Jews of that time. For as Rabbi Heller says in the beginning of his account, after giving an overview of his illustrious career, "I am not relating all of these things in order to boast about my achievements. Rather, my purpose is to demonstrate how, within a mere blink of an eye, all my glory and grandeur vanished into oblivion. ..."

Both Rabbi Heller and his son, Rabbi Shmuel — whose *Supplementary Chronicle* adds the son's perspective to the events — demonstrate considerable skill as memoir writers. The action is fast-paced, the dialogue is lively, and they draw in the reader by sharing with us their emotional state. For instance, after Rabbi Heller is told that he will be publically flogged if he doesn't pay the Emperor the fantastic sum of 12,000 *thalers*, he reveals his anguish:

"I, the Chief Rabbi of the foremost community in the world, was to be humiliated in front of my community, something that has not happened since the destruction of the *Bais HaMikdash* (Holy Temple)!"

Of course, Rabbi Heller doesn't give into despair. With the help of his supporters, he manages to raise the money and he is restored to a rabbinical position. Peace is also restored between Rabbi Heller and the man who falsely accused him, a wealthy Jew named Raphael. In Rabbi Shmuel's supplementary *megillah*, the son dramatizes the meeting between his father and Raphael, who has fallen ill:

[Raphael:] "...Please, Rabbi, have mercy on me and my soul. Forgive me and pray to Hashem that He heal me, so that I may be able to repair the wrong I have committed."

"Raphael, I forgive you with all my heart," my father replied, gently holding his hand. "And I will pray to Hashem that He restore your health."

On that note of forgiveness, Rabbi Heller's *megillah* comes to an end. However the Thirty Years War continued to wreck havoc for another 16 years, and two years before the war ended a Jewish girl was born in Germany who would grow up to write what is considered to be one of the best known book of memoirs of modern Jewish history.

Gluckel of Hameln

Gluckel, the wife of Chaim Hameln, didn't write the first Jewish memoir. That honor, as far as we know, goes to Yehudah Aryeh (Leon) Modena, a Venetian rabbi who began writing his *Chayei Yehudah* (*Life of Yehudah*) in 1617. However, Gluckel's book, which was written about 300 years ago and is still selling strong on Amazon.com, is thought to be the first Jewish memoir to be written in Yiddish—and it's one of the earliest examples that we have of an autobiographical account written by an "ordinary" Jew.

Gluckel and her family were pious Jews who belonged to Germany's merchant class. Her memoirs are filled with vividly described accounts of an ordinary person's lifecycle events: family births, beginning with her own, which occurred in the year 1646; her own marriage and the marriages of her children (she had 14, 12 of whom survived to adulthood); and deaths, including the early death of Chaim, her beloved first husband. And she describes, in great detail, the business deals that reaped a terrific profit, as well as the deals that went sour.

Although the modern feminist movement has tried to cast Gluckel in the role of marginalized Jewish woman who used writing as a means to express her supposedly suppressed spirituality, all one has to do is read Gluckel's own words to see how far off the mark that assessment is. In fact, her close relationship with Hashem, whose Name is constantly on her lips, is one of the most prominent recurring themes of the book, as the following passage about her becoming seasick shows:

"… how I fell sick – as though I were suddenly thrust at death's door. I thought my end had come and I began to recite the confession for my sins as well as I could and as much as I remembered by heart. My husband continued to lie quietly on his bench, knowing well it was no mortal illness and that once I set foot on dry land it would pass. When he heard me confess my sins and turn my thoughts to God, he began to laugh. I heard him and I thought to myself, "Here I am at death's door, and my husband lies there and laughs." Although I was mighty angry, still this was not the time to quarrel with your husband; moreover, I hadn't the strength to say a word. So I had to remain lying in my agony until, in about a half an hour, we touched land and left the ship. And our sickness, God be praised, vanished at once."

However, if Gluckel wasn't a feminist pioneer, she was a literary trailblazer. To write her memoirs, she took the dominant characteristic of three literary genres and fused them into one: the event-filled drama of the family *megillah*; the lofty *mussar* message of the traditional ethical will; and the personal, homey tone of the

Tekhenes prayers — special prayers for women that were known during Gluckel's time but only first began to be published a few years after Gluckel was born.

The result is a memoir that remains poignantly alive some 300 years after it was written. And her three ingredients for writing a readable memoir — a story with a universal theme, an inspiring and instructive message, and an engaging writing style — are still the "recipe" for writing a successful Jewish memoir.

Go West, Young Memorist

Gluckel's memoirs, which were meant for just her family members, weren't published until the early 1900s, when a descendant decided to make them public. By then, the idea of writing — and publishing — one's life story had become commonplace, at least in secular circles. The Enlightenment in Europe had made it fashionable to write a memoir about one's flight from the Torah-observant world to the supposed Promised Land of socialism, Zionism, or academia.

Across the ocean the same story was repeated, but with a New York accent. Even memoirs that describe a Torah-observant family's attempts to hold on to their traditions in the American hinterland — such as Sophie Trupin's *Dakota Diaspora: Memoirs of a Jewish Homesteader* — are bittersweet. Despite the fervent hopes of Sophie's mother that her children would remain Torah-observant, Sophie eventually left both North Dakota and Torah observance in pursuit of the American dream.

Until the Holocaust, memoirs written by a Torah-observant Jew who remained firmly within the Orthodox camp are few and far between. During the first few decades after the war, most Orthodox survivors were too busy rebuilding their families and communities to think about the past. It has only been more recently that they have started to record their wartime experiences, so that future generations will have a better understanding of the spiritual battles that were fought — and often won — in addition to the battle for physical survival.

Perhaps my great-grandmother was also much too busy with trying to build a life in Kansas City to set down her thoughts on paper. And perhaps she knew that even without pen and paper she was already writing her book of memoirs—the book in Heaven where we record our good deeds and transgressions every night, and which will be read to us when we reach the age of one hundred and twenty years.

—September 2008

Etched in Blood and Fire: America's First Jewish Author

When Luis de Carvajal stood trial in an Inquisition chamber, his own diary sealed his fate.

On February 1, 1595, Luis de Carvajal the Younger was arrested by the Mexican Inquisition for the second time. He was searched. Found in his possession was a leather bag containing three contraband items: a book of *Psalms,* a book containing *Nevi'im* (Prophets) and another book containing *Berashis* (Genesis). If the searchers would have looked under Luis's hat, they also would have found a small version of the Ten Commandments sewn into its rim.

As a relapsed Judaizer, Luis knew that only a miracle would save him from the fires of the auto-de-fé. Yet he still clung to the hope that at least his mother and sisters would be spared from the same fate. That hope crumbled when he was brought to the inquisitors' audience chambers. During the questioning, one of his interrogators produced the Inquisition's most potent weapon against Luis and his family: a diary written in Luis's own hand.

Within the pages of the small black leather book was Luis's life story, the tale of his transformation from a Christian boy in Spain to the leader of the "Judaizing" community in New Spain. Along with an account of the events that brought him across the ocean to the New World, Luis revealed his hopes, his fears, his frustrations and his dreams, as well as his belief in Hashem and the truth of the Jewish faith.

The Inquisition, of course, viewed the memoir as a book of heresy, evidence that Luis had committed the ultimate crime. It was attached to Luis's file, where it remained until the early 1930s, when it disappeared under mysterious circumstances.

For us today, it reads as a remarkable testimony to Luis's unshakeable *emunah*—a faith made even more remarkable by the fact that if Luis had chosen differently, his path might have led not to the stake, but to the leadership of a kingdom in New Spain.

The Secret

Luis Rodriguez Carvajal was born in 1566 in Spain to Francisco Rodriguez de Matos and Francisca de Carvajal, respected members of the Catholic Church. He received an education that was typical for bright Catholic boys of the time. In addition to learning how to read and write in Spanish, he learned Latin and studied the works of classical authors such as Virgil and Cicero. Instruction in mathematics and the Catholic credo and prayers rounded out his education.

Although Luis knew nothing about his father's ancestors, he could point with pride to his mother's family. The Carvajals were high achievers: one uncle served the Portuguese crown in the Guineas, while several others were wealthy and powerful businessmen. Perhaps most famous of all was his mother's brother Luis de Carvajal, a *conquistador* who had proven his worth to the Spanish crown through his exploits in the untamed lands called New Spain, which is today part of Mexico. With such powerful connections, the young Luis could look forward to a successful and prosperous future.

That all changed on September 10, 1579, when Luis was thirteen. His older brother Baltasar took Luis aside and explained that their family wasn't descended from Old Christians, as Luis had been led to believe. They were New Christians. They were descended from Jews.

It was standard for *anusim* families to wait until a child was bar or bas mitzvah to reveal their great secret. The Spanish Inquisition was already a century old by the time Luis turned thirteen, and it was still at the height of its power. An older sibling was often given the task of breaking the news to the younger child; the child would feel freer to ask questions of a sibling than a parent. In fact, such questions were encouraged, because in this way the family could determine if the child was ready to be entrusted with more secrets — such as the fact that September 10 was the Day of Pardon, when Jews like them fasted and were cleansed of their sins. If instead the child reacted with horror and insisted he was a Catholic, the older sibling let the matter drop, joking he had just been testing the child's faithfulness to their Catholic religion. The Inquisition insisted even family members betray one another, so it was too dangerous to let an unreliable child in on the family secret.

Luis passed the test. He quickly learned to become adept at leading a double life. He continued to attend his Jesuit school, but he also was introduced to the circle of Judaizers — as the *anusim* were called by agents of the Inquisition — who were friends of his family. One of the most prominent members of this circle was a physician named Licentiate Manuel de Morales, who taught Luis and the others everything he knew.

That wasn't much. After the Expulsion from Spain in 1492, those who had converted to save their lives were left without rabbis, Jewish books, and even a Jewish calendar. As the decades progressed the *anusim*'s knowledge of Judaism became condensed to a few principles: the unity of Hashem, the immutability of His Torah, the chosenness of the Jewish people, a belief in the coming of Mashiach and the eternity of the soul. In many *anusim* communities only four special times were observed: Shabbos; the three-day Fast of Esther, which was observed in mid-February; Passover, which was observed a month later, in March; and the Day of Pardon, or Yom Kippur, which was observed on the 10th of September. They also observed many individual fasts throughout the year.

The year 1579 was an eventful one for Luis for yet another reason. His father had decided to try to flee to France, which was often a first stop for *anusim* on their way to countries where Jews could openly practice their religion, such as Italy and the Ottoman Empire. But this plan was put aside when Luis's uncle, Luis de Carvajal, arrived on the scene and convinced the family to come instead to New Spain. The elder Carvajal had received a grant from the king that enabled him to establish and govern a colony in a wild and not-yet-settled territory, which Carvajal named Nuevo Leon, or the New Kingdom of Leon (today a region in Mexico). In addition to a promise of riches in the new land, which was famed for its seemingly endless supply of silver and fertile farmland, the childless

Carvajal promised to make young Luis his heir to this vast kingdom. The family agreed. Luis took on the last name of his benefactor and also became known as Luis de Carvajal.

The family, along with about 100 others the Governor had handpicked to colonize his lands, left Spain in June 1580. Three months later those who had survived the sea-tossed, illness-wracked passage across the ocean straggled onto shore, where they were greeted not by fine palaces and pleasant squares but by dingy hovels and hordes of mosquitoes.

The First Arrest

Historians are still debating why the Governor insisted his sister's family come with him to New Spain. He, more than anyone, knew it would take years to establish towns, locate profitable silver mines, set up self-sustaining farms, and subjugate the mostly hostile Indian population. Until then, it would be rough going. Most historians therefore think his actions were governed by one thing: fear.

Although the elder Carvajal knew his ancestors were New Christians, and he was even married to a Judaizer, he had spent a lifetime successfully hiding that fact. If his sister's family fled to France, the Inquisition's interest in the Carvajal family would be aroused. Once that happened, he too might get caught in the net. It therefore was better to hide his family in the wilds of Nuevo Leon, where either they would shed their Judaizing or at least escape the notice of the Mexican Inquisition.

To his dismay neither happened. In their new land, his family became the center of a group of Judaizers. And young Luis, whom he had named as his heir, disappointed the Governor most of all. While the Governor had been right about his nephew's leadership qualities, when forced to choose between life as a Catholic *conquistador* and life as a Judaizer, the young man chose the latter.

Luis's faith in the path he had chosen was strengthened by several near escapes from death, which he deemed miraculous and later recorded in his memoir: a house where he had taken shelter during a hurricane collapsed just moments after he fled from it, and twice he was saved from rampaging Indians.

There were also miracles of a happier kind: his uncle's plans to marry off two of Luis's sisters to Old Christians was thwarted when two wealthy New Christians appeared on the scene and married the girls; when Luis and Baltasar went to visit an old Jewish cripple, their good deed was rewarded when the cripple gave them a book composed by Dr. Morales, which included a translation into Spanish of *Devarim* (Numbers) and several prayers; a Jewish merchant from Italy gave the brothers a prayer book, before he returned to Europe.

The Enlightener

Luis was still in his early twenties when he was arrested in April 1589, along with his mother and two unmarried sisters. During the long months of his imprisonment, Luis began to have vivid dreams, which gave him both comfort and courage. As he reflected on the meaning and purpose of his life, he came to the conclusion that Hashem had placed him in his particular circumstances for a reason: His role was to be a leader of the Judaizers, not only within his own family circle but within the wider community. He began to closely identify with the biblical Joseph, who had also been imprisoned and who had sustained his family and his people. After this first brush with the Inquisition—Luis and his family escaped death by pretending to be reconciled to the Church—he therefore took on a new name: Joseph Lumbroso, or Joseph the Enlightener.

Although the family was released from prison, they still had a heavy sentence to pay, which included wearing special clothes which marked them as former "heretics" and having to work at menial jobs. It was during this period that Luis was sentenced to work in a Catholic school for Indians, where he had access to a library. He used his free time to study the *Nevi'im*. He also came across a book that included the Rambam's Thirteen Principles of Faith, although he didn't know who the author was.

From his notes, Luis compiled several booklets in Latin and Spanish, which he distributed to other Judaizers. He also translated the Book of Psalms into Spanish and composed a version of the Ten Commandments in Portuguese. He composed original works as well, where he explained the core beliefs of the Judaizers. Thus, through the written word and through private conversations, he attempted to both strengthen the faith of present Judaizers and convince other New Christians to shed their Catholic identity and adopt the "Law of Moses."

Sometime in late 1591 or early 1592 Luis began to write his memoir as yet another means to help Judaizers remain true to their faith. In the memoir, which is mostly written in the third person, Luis refers to himself as Joseph. Thus, when he describes the day he bought a Bible for six pesos and read for the first time the verses concerning Avraham's circumcision, he writes*:

> The words which say "The soul which is uncircumcised shall be blotted out from the Book of the Living" caught Joseph's eye and struck his heart with terror. Without delay and with the inspiration of the Most High and His good angel, he got up, put the Bible down without even stopping to close it, left the hall in his house where he had been reading, took a pair of blunted and worn shears and went to the ravine at the Panuco River.

There he circumcised himself, and he would later convince his brother Baltasar to do the same.

One of the visions that Luis-Joseph describes in his journal is the one that came to him in prison after he heard the cries of his mother, while she was being tortured to make her confess:

> In the midst of the day of affliction, the L-rd permitted him to doze off by the door of his cell. On other days, if he fell asleep for a moment, he awoke melancholy and faint, but not that day.
>
> As soon as he fell asleep, he saw the L-rd sending him a man who was a paragon of virtue and patience. He was a fearer of G-d, one of his own people. In his hands he carried a large and beautiful yam. He showed it to Joseph and said, "Look! What a handsome and beautiful fruit!"
>
> To this Joseph replied, "Indeed."
>
> He gave it to Joseph to smell. Joseph blessed the L-rd, creator of all, and said to the man, "Indeed, it smells good, indeed." The man then cut the yam in two and said to him, "Now it smells better."
>
> The man then gave Joseph the interpretation. He said, "Before being imprisoned and racked with torture, your mother was whole and she smelled sweet; she was a fruit of sweet savor before the L-rd. But now, when she is cut with torture, she exudes the superior fragrance of patience before the L-rd."

With this Joseph awoke and was consoled. May the Most High G-d, who brings consolation to the afflicted, likewise be adored and extolled.

In his memoir, Luis also describes a harrowing incident that occurred when he and two of his sisters were on their way to the home of another Judaizer: along the way, his younger sister lost a prayer book that Luis and his brother Baltasar had pieced together from the few sources available to them.

Joseph and his two sisters returned home and the rest of the family shared their consternation. Their pain and fright were understandable, since at stake for all of them was nothing less than their lives and what they treasured most in life. They began to regard themselves as arrested and even dead. So great was their fright that were it not for the danger of damning their souls they would have taken their own lives rather than risk falling into the cruel hands of their terrible enemies! In short, every hour they fearfully and bitterly expected the moment of their imprisonment. But, blessed and exalted be the infinite and true L-rd G-d, for He helped them in this difficulty with His accustomed kindness.

Whenever anyone knocked, they thought that the Inquisition's nefarious ministers were at the door to arrest them, and as a result they were in a continuous state of anxiety and trepidation. They purchased only half their usual amounts of oil and other necessities, thinking they would not even be able to finish these.

Luis-Joseph recounts several other near escapes from being caught by the Inquisition, while he and his family continued to Judaize. As always, he saw the Hand of Hashem in everything that happened to him. But time was running out. On February 1, 1595, he was rearrested.

Pardon Me, O L-rd

Luis's memoir shows him at the peak of his powers: both confident of his mission and his eventual salvation, whether in this world or the next. Even when he knows that a colleague has denounced him as a Judaizer, in the memoir's final entry Luis writes confidently about his family's experiences:

And because the road along which the Lord G-d has been leading them has been full of mercies, and His rod has been only the soft scourge of fear, He decreed that ... they should suffer a new blow, one of the most severe yet — though they never suffered any from which the L-rd G-d, in His infinite mercy, did not deliver them in two hours.

But this second sojourn within the Inquisition's prison was much more terrible than the first. Although in the beginning Luis remained defiant, this time there was no question that Luis was a Judaizer — the booklets, letters and memoir found in his mother's house all testified against him. Therefore, when he was taken to the torture chamber twice during the period of February 8 - 14, it wasn't to make him confess his own "sins." His torturers wanted to know the names of the other Judaizers in Luis's circle.

The records of the Inquisition are precise. They record every twist of the rope, every cry of pain, every agonized plea of "Pardon me, O L-rd, pardon me, have mercy upon me." In the end, Luis broke. He revealed the names of more than 100 Judaizers, including good friends and members of his family.

We like our heroes to be perfect, to remain steadfast and true until the bitter end. Apparently, Luis felt this way too, and was bitterly disappointed by his own weakness. But Luis knew one of the rules of the Inquisition was that a confession couldn't be regarded as the truth — and used as evidence against others — until the accused had signed it. Therefore, on February 15, Luis retracted all he had said while being tortured. Because he also knew that such a brazen act could only result in another visit to the torture chamber, where he once again was liable to break, on his way back to his cell Luis jumped through a window, in an attempt to commit suicide and cheat the Inquisition of his confession.

Luis survived, although his legs were badly broken. In the end he did sign the confession coerced from him in the torture chamber. But despite efforts to also make him convert, in his Final Testament Luis proudly asserted his commitment to Judaism, "solemnly declaring that I will not change my faith until I die, nor when I die."

On December 8, 1596, which was a Shabbos, Luis, his mother and three of his sisters, along with other prisoners, were marched through the streets of Mexico City to the Great Square. After a "festive ceremony," which was attended by thousands, all those sentenced to be burned at the stake were led to the place where the pyres had been constructed. Along the way, several members of the clergy tried again to convince Luis to convert back to Catholicism. Although conversion wouldn't save Luis from death, it would allow him to be strangled before his body was set on fire. It would also be a big victory for the Church if the leader of New Spain's Judaizing community publicly renounced his Judaism before his death.

Did Luis convert, or did he remain a faithful Jew until the end?

According to a clergyman named Father Contreras, he managed to convince Luis of his "error" and Luis died a Catholic. The records of the Inquisition go to great length to say that this was so, because apparently there were other clergymen present who said Luis wasn't sincere when he converted at the last minute; he chose to be garroted only to escape the ordeal of being burned alive. He even uttered words and made gestures used by secret Jews before he was strangled to show that his supposed conversion was a sham.

Yet another version of Luis's final moments comes from Manuel Tavares, a Portuguese Judaizer, who insisted Luis didn't convert, even as a sham. If Luis was indeed garroted, it was done against his will, to give the impression he had renounced his faith.

What really did happen? Only Hashem knows.

All translations are by Martin A. Cohen, whose translation of The Autobiography of Luis de Carvajal, the Younger *originally appeared in* American Jewish Historical Quarterly, *Vol. 55, No. 3 (March 1966).*

* * *

Who's a Judaizer?

Like the Inquisition in Spain, agents of the Mexican Inquisition had a long list of activities that could mark a person as a heretic and a Judaizer (Protestants were also considered heretics) — and therefore a target for arrest and subsequent conviction.

The observance of Shabbos was one of the most common signs. Judaizers would often clean the house and cook on Friday, as well as bathe and put on clean clothes. On Shabbos, they would refrain from work, if they could. Luis de Carvajal's mother and some of his sisters, like other crypto-Jewish women, would light a candle or cruse of oil to usher in Shabbos. The entire family would have a festive meal on Friday night and eat either cholent or cold food on Shabbos day. Luis's family and their guests would also have a communal prayer service on Shabbos, which was usually conducted by Luis or his brother Baltasar. The prayers—which consisted mostly of saying psalms, reading sections from the Vulgate Bible and reciting special prayers written by other crypto-Jews—were said mostly in Latin and Spanish. The only Hebrew they might know would be *Shema Yisrael* and its response.

The "crimes" of observing the fast of Yom Kippur, the Fast of Esther, and eating unleavened bread and bitter herbs on Passover also appeal regularly in the trial records of the Mexican Inquisition. So do the elements of kashrus that continued to be observed, such as not eating pork products, covering the blood of slaughtered poultry and soaking and salting meat.

Jewish mourning rituals were also passed down and observed by Judaizers. Luis was at his father's side when he passed away, and Luis made sure that his father's body was washed, his fingernails were cut, and his father was wrapped in a shroud before the burial. This was Article 2 in the Indictment read to Luis during his first arrest.

The Carvajals were also singled out for their role in converting other New Christians back to the "old Law of Moses and its rites and ceremonies," another serious crime in the eyes of the Inquisition. Thus, when Luis was arrested the first time, he was found guilty of being "a heretic, Judaizer, apostate, supporter, and concealer of heretics."

* * *

Who Stole the Diary?

In the summer of 1932 shock tremors shook Mexico's Archivo General de la Nación (National Archives). Many of the records pertaining to the Inquisition's trial of Mexico's most famous "Judaizer," Luis de Carvajal the Younger, who was burned at the stake on December 8, 1596, at the age of 30, were missing. The lost documents included pages from the official record of his interrogations, some of Luis's letters to his family, and his memoir—

the brief account of his young life that has since qualified him for the title of the New World's first Jewish author.

Jac Nachbin, a respected Jewish scholar from Brazil who had been doing research in the archives, was blamed for the theft and arrested. Three months later, the professor was released due to lack of evidence; he claimed, as he told the *El Paso Herald-Post*, the papers had gone missing before he arrived in Mexico. Dr. Nachbin then went to Illinois's Northwestern University, where he researched a collection of South American manuscripts acquired by the university's library. He died of tuberculosis before his work was completed.

Or did he?

Another narrative identifies "Jac" as Jacob Nachbin, a Yiddish-speaking orphan from a Polish shtetl who moved to Brazil during the early 1900s. In addition to editing the first Yiddish-language newspaper in Rio de Janeiro, he did some research on Brazil's Jewish communities. While working as a journalist, Nachbin traveled to Spain in 1936 to cover that country's civil war. He disappeared there without a trace.

Or did he?

Yet another narrative claims that while Jacob Nachbin was indeed a Yiddish-speaking orphan from a Polish shtetl, he moved to Brazil after World War I, where he reinvented himself as a Jewish historian—and did it well enough to convince academics in both South America and the United States. After he was expelled from Mexico due to the documents he had supposedly purloined from the National Archives, he and his wife moved to Las Vegas, New Mexico, where he taught for a while. He later went back to Europe, where he was killed during the Holocaust.

While we may never know the true story of what happened to Jacob "Jac" Nachbin and his role in the National Archives theft, we do know that at least some of the documents pertaining to Luis de Carvajal the Younger were recovered. A package mailed from Las Vegas, New Mexico, went to New York City, where it was sent back to Mexico, to a person named Mr. Lang of Mexico City. When the package wasn't claimed, it was opened by postal workers, who returned the documents to the National Archives, where they were placed back in Luis's file.

Still missing was the memoir. Although a somewhat garbled version of the memoir had been copied by a member of the Inquisition's staff and attached to Luis's file—which is how we have a copy—the small black book with its tiny script written in Luis's own hand has never been found.

In some ways, though, the convoluted story surrounding the memoir's theft—the multiple identities attributed to Nachbin, the roundabout journey of the documents, and the unsolved mystery of the memoir's whereabouts—is a remarkable mirror of the life of a young man who traveled across both physical and spiritual worlds, exchanging identities as he did so, and whose final moments are still being debated today.

—September 2015

Letters from the Past, Fonts for the Future

All it takes is a quick stroll down a street in Jerusalem to see that Hebrew letters aren't set in stone. Store signs, snacks, and even books all come with interesting letter treatments that are designed to catch the eye. But what goes into the making of a Hebrew typeface? And how has the computer age affected this ancient art? To find out, we've gone into the "teiva" (word) to take an inside look at the world of designing Hebrew letters.

It was a tough job, but somebody had to do it. As part of my research for this article, I emptied my kitchen cabinet of its *nosh* and spread it out on the kitchen table—not with the intention of eating the empty-high-calorie treats, mind you, although that turned out to be an inevitable consequence of the experiment. My real objective was to study the Hebrew letters on the packaging, to see what's new with contemporary Hebrew typeface design.

And so as I munched away at some potato chips, I took a good look at that backwards-spinning letter *peh* on the Elite Tapuchips bag—a *peh* that practically sings out: Eating potato chips is fun! In contrast were the sedate letters on the label of my Berman's *Ugat Sheish* (Marble Cake). Those letters, which have a scribal feel to them, seemed to whisper: *Ess!* Eating a piece of this cake is a *mitzvah!*

Obviously, these typographic signals aren't accidents. Someone had to design these fonts and logos; someone had to commission them. And new fonts aren't being designed just to market products. Magazine, books, and even *sefarim* (Torah books) also get a new look from time to time. So what goes into the creation of a new typeface for Hebrew book publishing? What are the challenges, and what makes a font successful?

Before we hear about what some contemporary experts have to say about the present, let's take a quick look at the art of typography in the past.

From Rashi to FrankReuhl

After the printing press was invented in the 1400s, the letters of the *alef-beis* (Hebrew alphabet) began to be set in "stone." Since it was expensive to make sets of type—each letter had to be painstakingly cut from metal—printers would usually have just a few styles of typeface in their workshops. The typefaces used by famous printers such as the Soncino family and Daniel Bomberg—including the typeface that became known as "Rashi Script" (see below)—therefore became the standard typefaces for the next several hundred years.

During the 1800s Vilna's Romm family, the printers of the famous Vilna Shas (set of the Talmud), set the type style for the Jewish world. The next important names in Hebrew typeface design are those of Raphael Frank and Otto Ruehl, who in 1910 developed a new typeface called FrankRuehl, which ruled until the 1950s. By then the center of Hebrew printing had shifted to Israel, and two important names from that era are Henri Friedlaender and Tzvi Narkis.

Henri Freidlaender, a French-German Jew who moved to Israel after World War II, spent more than 30 years designing the typeface that is known as Hadassah. Based upon a *Megillas Esther* in his possession that dated from the early 1800s, Freidlaender's new font quickly became one of the most widely-used fonts in Hebrew publishing.

Tzvi Narkis, who was born in Romania, came to Israel in 1944, where he studied graphic arts and lettering. The first version of his famous Narkis sans serif typeface appeared in 1958, and its contemporary appearance helped to make the typeface an immediate success. (Serif refers to the tiny horizontal lines found at the tops and bottoms of any straight line of a letter. Those in the know sometimes refer to them as "little feet." Sans serif refers to typefaces that don't have the little feet.)

Eliyahu Koren is another famous name in Hebrew typeface history, thanks to the Koren typefaces he developed for his *Tanach* (Torah, Prophets and Writings) and *siddur* (prayer book). However, it is FrankRuehl, Hadassah, and Narkis that continue to dominate Hebrew printing—at least the printing of books and newspapers—until today.

By the 1980s, though, a new technology was once again shaking up the printing community: computers. Due to a computer screen's low resolution, it's harder to read large blocks of text on a computer screen than on a printed page, and so the font has to be very simple and clean. Microsoft came up with a font called Arial to solve the problem, and the Hebrew version has since become the standard font used on Hebrew-language websites. (The font was actually based upon one of Tzvi Narkis's fonts—a typeface called New Narkis. Narkis took Microsoft to court. After a lengthy legal battle—and two months after Narkis passed away—an Israeli court granted his estate $25,000.)

Computers haven't just affected the way we read Hebrew text; they've also made it much easier to design a new typeface. Today there are hundreds of Hebrew fonts on the market, but that doesn't necessarily mean that all fonts are alike when it comes to quality. In fact, when it comes to books and magazines—printed material that requires long blocks of text—no new font has been able to enter the exalted circle shared by the "big three."

Yet.

See Rutz Run

By his own admission, Oded Ezer is a little crazy. By day he is the owner and creative force behind Oded Ezer Typography, a highly successful design firm located in the Israeli city Givatayim. But when he's not designing high-profile logos and commercial material for some of Israel's best-known companies, he's busy doing what he loves best: designing new Hebrew typefaces. Some of them—such as Alchemist, Meoded, and Ta'agid—are bestsellers. One of them, his latest design, is the fulfillment of a slightly crazy dream to design a typeface that will be a classic for our times, just as

FrankRuehl and Hadassah were classics for the previous era. Recently, I spoke to Oded to find out more about this typeface, which he has named Rutz (Running).

How do you go about designing a Hebrew font? What are your influences?

There are three main sources. The first one is the history of Hebrew writing. You can take a font that existed in the past—anytime from 1000 BCE to yesterday—and decide to design a new font that is either a revival of an older font or a reinterpretation. The second source is other languages, especially Latin. When you see a typeface that you like, you can make a Hebrew version—trying not to lose the soul of the Hebrew letters.

The third possible trigger is everything else. I can be influenced by a building, a door handle, or any other item. If it has a visual language, I can borrow from it to use in a typeface. This isn't a common way to design, but I do think in this manner. Where someone else sees a table, for example, I see letters. I can go to a fruit and vegetable store and look at a cucumber and say, "What an interesting form. Maybe there is a way I can use it."

Is there a particular start point when you design a font? For instance, do you tend to begin with a certain letter?

Usually I design a few letters and then I try to form a word. Then I design a few more letters and try to form another word, until I have all the letters. A typeface isn't just a bunch of individual letters. They have to talk to one another in a pleasant way so that you can easily read the words. There's no point to designing letters if they don't relate to each other.

Do you take into account the commercial aspects when you design a new font? For instance, do you look at English-language fonts that sell well and think that it could be a good idea to do a Hebrew font that is similar?

I'm not a commercial thinker. I work more from the artistic side. When I see a font in another language that I like, I want to investigate it and see what happens. This was the starting point for Rutz. I stumbled upon an article by Rob Keller that talked about a typeface he had designed called Vesper. The font's style looked

"Jewish" to me. I asked him if he would be interested in a Hebrew version, and he gave me his permission to design one.

Some of my colleagues are more commercially oriented. They'll say, "What's a best-selling font in English? Let's make a Hebrew version." That's fine, but it's not my way.

Have computers changed font design? Does reading text on a screen require a different kind of typeface?
Today serif typefaces are no longer the only players for reading long text. That's because when you read text on a computer screen it's easier to read a sans serif type, such as a font called Arial.

I can say that we are entering an era where designers have to rethink the inner truth of type design. What my teachers taught me is completely irrelevant for the computer screen. But this isn't something different from what happened in the past. In the 1950s Henri Freidlaender and others also had to rethink type design because the technology had changed.

Do computers mean the end of the creation of beautiful new typefaces? Will the next generation be as lacking in character and individuality as Arial? Not necessarily, since technology advances all the time. But it could be that Arial will be considered a classic typeface by our children. What we see as a downgrade could become a classic for the next generation.

Speaking of Henri Friedlaender, in the old days it could take a type designer several decades to design a new font. Has computer technology speeded up the process?
It took Friedlaender 30 years to design Hadassah for two reasons. One, he didn't know Hebrew before he started to design his typeface. So he learned Hebrew while he was working on the font. Second, he was trapped in Europe during World War II. He had to move from country to country, which is a horrible, unsettling experience.

In our time, typeface design takes less time because you don't have to draw each letter. Designers do the work on the computer. Rutz took me three years to design, which included all the preparations and the initial sketches. But there are typefaces that take only three months, so it depends.

I understand that when you designed Rutz you hoped to design a classic that would be on a level with classic fonts of the previous generation. How does one go about designing a classic font, and what separates a classic from the others?

A classic font has to be used for books, not just for logos. I can only hope that one day Rutz will be considered a classic, but when I designed it I had in mind that the typeface would be used for a book. Already four books have been printed using this typeface. I've also been approached by some people who manufacture e-readers. They think the font could be very good for books that are read on these devices. I was very pleased to hear this.

But we don't have a menu for how to design a classic item. Classic means that a typeface has a strong personality, but it holds the past inside the letters. It's not trendy. It's here to stay. Nobody can teach a person how to design a classic typeface. You have to try again and again and hope that your wisdom and knowledge will get you there.

The Business of Letters

While I appreciate the need of typeface designers to make their mark on their chosen field, I have to admit that some of my favorite Hebrew letters can be found in a *siddur* that I used as a child. The *siddur* was a gift from my great-uncle Max, who had used it when he was a soldier in the United States Army during World War II. Printed by Ktav Publishing House in New York, it was small enough to fit into a soldier's pocket, even though it had both the Hebrew and an English translation.

I suppose the "fight" between the large amount of text and the book's small size is why the Hebrew was printed with "old-fashioned" letters, a typeface that I believe is the one used by the Romm family in Vilna. The letter *lamed*, for example, sometimes soars upward, proud and straight as a *lulav* (palm branch). Other times its "tower" literally bends over backwards to make room for the vowels sitting underneath the letter above it.

While researching this article, I learned that the "curly" *lamed* was created to make the printed text clearer. As the technology progressed, the "curly" *lamed* all but disappeared. I, for one, am sorry to see it go. Although my Hebrew School taught me nothing about either the *kabbalistic* or typographic reasons for writing and printing the letters in a certain way, I learned whole *mussar* (ethical) lessons from those *lameds*: Yes, sometimes you have to stand your ground proudly and not give in. But other times you need to give way, and let the other letters have their say.

But time marches on, as the saying goes, and its not just typeface designers who see a need to create new fonts for Hebrew letters. Publishers have their reasons, as well. To find out what some of those reasons might be my next conversation was with Rabbi Meir Zlotowitz, a founder and general editor of the Orthodox publishing house ArtScroll Publications, who along with Rabbi Nosson Scherman created a revolution back in the 1970s in the way *sefarim* are produced.

Why did ArtScroll decide to develop a new font for its Torah books?

The first ArtScroll volume was our *Megillas Esther*, which was published in 1976. We wanted a font that was legible and contemporary, but that maintained a connection to traditional typefaces. At that time there were very few fonts available, and so we developed a font of our own, based upon Hadassah.

Can you give an example of what you did?

Many of the fonts from the past, such as Vilna and FrankRuehl, had very strong contrasts between the thick strokes and the thin ones. We tried to strike a balance, so that the letters would be easier to read. I compare book type to a garment. When the garment is made properly, you don't see the seams. The same is with a font. It has to be invisible. It's a vehicle that enables the reader to appreciate the words on the page.

Did it take long to design the font?

It wasn't a long process. But it was a different process than what we have today, since back in the 1970s there wasn't desktop publishing. We were one of the first Torah publishers to use a process called phototype, which was very innovative for its time. We worked with a company called Photon, located in Boston. Galleys were produced in strips, which in a very exacting and skillful manner had to be pasted together to create the finished page. There was a lot of trial and error, and Rabbi Sheah Brander, our designer, spent many long hours to get it right.

More than 30 years have passed since ArtScroll's first Torah book was published. Has the typeface remained the same?

We've kept refining the typeface. Initially, the *lamed*'s flag went to the right. We changed it so that it now goes to the left, which is more in line with the tradition. We also made the *alef* more traditional. There is a clear distinction between the *beis* and the *chaf*, which some fonts don't achieve. And we changed the *nikkud* (vowel marks) from square to round shapes.

For our large-type *siddur* we consulted with ophthalmologists at Baltimore's John Hopkins University to be sure that our font would be easy to read for people who are vision-impaired. We've also made some changes with our Rashi type. When a book is reduced to a pocket-sized book, the type has to be legible. So we've retained the traditional form of the letters, but tried to make them clearer.

Back to the Future

The mention of Rashi's name brings our conversation back to where my research began, the early years of the printing press. One can almost hear the conversation that took place five centuries ago between the printer/publisher and his typeface designer: Can you make the *chaf* a little clearer? Can you make the *lamed* a little shorter?

As if Rabbi Zlotowitz is reading my thoughts, he continues, "Five hundred years ago, each letter was designed by hand. It was a real accomplishment. And the work has withstood the test of time aesthetically. Today we wonder, how did they do it? That's what I would like for our *sefarim*. Five hundred years from now, I'd like for people to look at the technology we have today and wonder, how did ArtScroll manage to produce such beautiful books?"

He then adds, "Buildings crumble, but books are timeless. The written word is forever."

* * *

Who Put the "Rashi" in Rashi Script?

Attention all scholars and amateur historians: There's a 500-year-old printing puzzle that is still waiting to be solved. Most of us know Rashi Script when we see it (it's the Hebrew semi-cursive script used for the commentaries on the Torah and Talmud by Rashi and a few other medieval commentators), but who was the first person who gave the typeface its name and when did they do it?

Here's the problem. As most of us know, the printed typeface that we call Rashi Script wasn't used by Rashi, who passed away more than 300 years before the printing press was invented. It's thought that Rashi wrote his manuscripts using a cursive script called Zarphatic, which was common in France and Ashkenaz (Germany) at the time. The typeface that became known as Rashi Script, on the other hand, is based upon a semi-cursive script used by the Sephardic Jews from Spain.

If you think the typeface got its name from the first printed edition of Rashi's commentary on the Torah, think again. The first printed version that we know of—it was printed in Rome sometime between 1469 and 1472 by the Jewish printers and brothers Ovadiah, Menasseh, and Binyamin—was printed using square cursive letters, which is a very different style of script.

It was only in 1475 that a Jewish printer named Avraham Graton printed Rashi's commentary on the Torah in a semi-cursive typeface that is very similar to the typeface that would one day bear Rashi's name. But it's highly unlikely that Graton called his typeface "Rashi".

During the 1500s Hebrew book printing entered a Golden Age, thanks to the high standards set by the printing presses established by the Jewish Soncino family and the non-Jewish printer Daniel Bomberg. It is also thanks to them that the Sephardic semi-cursive typeface that we know as Rashi Script became the standard typeface for printing commentaries on the Torah. But since the same typeface was used for many commentators, wouldn't it have been more precise to call the typeface Commentators Script or Rabbis Script?

Actually, after Daniel Bomberg printed his "Rabbinic Bibles" (known to Jews as *Mikraos Gedolos*) in the early 1500s, the semi-cursive typeface he used did become known as Rabbinic Script, at least among non-Jews.

The earliest reference to Rashi Script that I could find comes from Rabbi Chaim Yosef David Azulai, known as the Chida. Writing in 1673 in *Birkei Yosef, Yoreh Deah* 282:7, he briefly discusses the difference between a cursive script called Mashket and another one called Provencal. He cites an opinion of the Radbaz (Rabbi David ibn Zimra) that Provencal was "what we call Rashi letters." From those five words, we learn that by the Chida's time the typeface had received its name.

Another reference occurs a few years later, in 1683, by a Jew named Shmuel ibn Nahmias, who unfortunately became an apostate. In one of his works he wrote that older Jewish children learn from books that include Rashi Script, which the Christians call Rabbinic Script.

By the 1700s the term Rashi Script was in such wide use that even non-Jews knew what it was. For instance, in 1734 a Florentine printer by the name of Francesco Moucke was granted the right to print "Hebrew and Rashi characters" in the entire Tuscan state by the Grand Duke of Tuscany.

However, between the 1520s and the Chida's citation in 1673 is a gap of about 150 years. And so the question remains: Who gave this typeface the name Rashi Script, and when was the name first used? The person who can find the answer may not win any prize, but they might win a place in Hebrew printing lore.

—March 2011

To Hold History In Your Hands:
Collecting the Passover Haggadah

I still remember the time I held the Geismar Haggadah *in my hands. The book was not terribly old — it was printed in Berlin in the late 1920s — but its wine-stained pages seemed to glow with a light that was linked with eternity.*

How easy it was to imagine the haggadah's *first owners, who were most likely a prosperous German family, as they sat around the* Seder *table, dressed in their fine holiday clothes. While they progressed through the time-honored stages of the* Seder *ritual, surely their conversation was peppered with the latest news: the startling rise of the Nazi party, and what that might mean for German Jewry.*

What happened to this family? How did their haggadah *eventually find its way to a shop in Jerusalem? I do not know. But at that moment I felt deeply connected to them. And I began to understand why collecting haggados has such an appeal for Jews of all ages and denominations and living in all corners of the world.*

The Search for Connection

The Trionfo antiquarian bookshop, located in Jerusalem's Ben Yehuda pedestrian mall, is a quiet haven in this otherwise bustling shopping area. To step through its front door is to step into another world — a world of old books and maps from Europe and Israel, as well as antique Judaica and other objects. It's not a shop for everyone. But for those who love the touch and smell of things from the past, it's a little Garden of Eden in central Jerusalem.

The shop's proprietor, Avraham Madeisker, has been buying and selling old and rare books for more than 15 years, and it is no accident that he is in this line of business. "I always loved history," he explains, "but not the history that you read about in books. I love the history that you can see and touch — things like artifacts from archeological sites, old letters and books. We live in an age where high-quality reproductions are readily available, but none of them can give a feel for a historical period like an authentic document. There is something in the aged paper that is magical."

Madeisker's *haggadah* collection is housed on just two shelves, and he apologizes that at the moment he doesn't have anything outstanding to show. When he gets in an interesting *haggadah*, Madeisker immediately contacts his list of collectors, who may live on all five continents but are just a telephone call away. The *haggadah* is usually sold before he makes it to the end of the list.

Of course, "interesting" is a relative term. Just as not all *haggados* are alike, neither are all *haggadah* collectors.

"There are basically two kinds of collectors," explains Madeisker. "One kind looks at a book as an object. He appreciates its beauty — the quality of the paper, the design of the page, the illustrations. The other kind of collector is interested in the book's contents."

Since more than 4,000 different versions of the *Haggadah shel Pesach* (Passover Haggadah) have been produced since the Jews left Egypt more than 3,300 years ago, there are definitely more than enough *haggados* around to appeal to both types of collectors.

Hand-illustrated *haggados* that were commissioned hundreds of years ago by wealthy patrons in Europe are magnificent works of art that appeal to modern collectors living in New York and Los Angeles. Other *haggados*, such as the mimeographed ones that were distributed to Holocaust survivors living in DP camps after the war, have practically no aesthetic value. However, their introductions and commentaries, which make reference to what the survivors went through during the Holocaust, appeal to collectors interested in this period of Jewish history.

But according to Henry Hollander of Henry Hollander, Booksellers, an antiquarian Jewish bookshop located in San Francisco's Golden Gate Park neighborhood, the appeal of *haggados* is not limited to only art connoisseurs and historians.

"*Haggados* have a popular appeal that goes across education and age," he comments. "The Pesach Seder is the most exciting and involving of Jewish rituals for the greatest number of Jews, and that makes the *haggadah* accessible to just about everyone. And because the *haggadah* is the primary illustrated Jewish book, people find it interesting to see the great variety of styles."

But whatever the reason for the initial attraction, the world of *haggadah* collecting offers an exciting opportunity to connect with Jewish history — and make it.

Why is this *Haggadah* different from all other *Haggados*?

History was made in April 2001 when the Tel Aviv branch of the famed Sotheby's auction house sold a *Haggadah shel Pesach* for the dazzling sum of $1,017,750 — the highest sum ever paid for a *haggadah* to date.

But before people ransack their cupboards looking for their *zeide*'s old *haggadah* from Europe — hoping that it will help pay off the mortgage, marry off the children and provide for a comfortable retirement — it's important to know that not all *haggados* were created equal.

What determines a *haggadah's* value, and why would someone pay more than a million dollars for one of them?

Age is certainly a factor, since very old, hand-illustrated manuscripts are rare. The *haggadah* that broke the record four years ago at Sotheby's was an illuminated manuscript from the mid-1400s called the *First Nuremberg Haggadah*. Such *haggados* don't come on the market very often, because most of them already belong to museums, libraries, or universities — and the New York collector who purchased the *First Nuremberg Haggadah* immediately donated it to the Israel Museum.

However, according to Avraham Madeisker, once we enter the era of the printing press, age is just one factor involved in determining a *haggadah's* worth.

"Who printed the *haggadah* and where it was published also play a role," says Madeisker, adding that Prague, Amsterdam, Mantua and Darmstadt are examples of European cities that were once home to famous printing houses.

The artistic quality of the illustrations is another important component, as is the book's condition, though it is interesting to note that *haggados* are perhaps the only collectible books where wine stains on the pages are sometimes actually a plus.

One thing that does not contribute to the value of a *haggadah* is the sentimental value it may have for its owner. Like most antiquarian booksellers, Madeisker is happy to appraise *haggados* that people have in their bookcases. But he warns that people who don't understand the market are often disappointed when they find out that their *zeide*'s *haggadah* printed in Vienna in 1929 is worth only $50.

Those who want to learn about the world of collecting *haggados* can easily find answers to all their questions. There are several reference books that catalogue and describe most of the editions published up until the 1960s. Sales catalogues from auction houses such as Sotheby's Tel Aviv, the New York-based Kestenbaum & Company or London's Bloomsbury Auctions can also help the novice *haggadah* collector understand why some *haggados* will sell for $220,000, while others are worth $1,500, $50 or just $3.50. But the first step is to understand the history of the genre, which is in many ways a reflection of the history of the Jewish people since they left Egypt.

In Every Generation

Although the *mitzvah* of telling the story of the Exodus from Egypt dates back to the generation who witnessed the event, as late as the first *Beis HaMikdash* (Holy Temple) there was no one way to do it. Every father told the story in his own words, and every child asked his own questions.

A standard text was formulated during the time of the Men of the Great Assembly. It was called the "*Haggadah*" because of the word's linguistic relationship to the words in the verse, "And thou shalt *tell thy son* ..." (*Shemos* [*Exodus*] 13:8). After the destruction of the second *Beis HaMikdash*, when it was no longer possible to bring a *korban Pesach* (pascal sacrifice), certain changes had to be made in the text. More changes occurred when songs of praise and thanksgiving were added, a process that continued through the early the Middle Ages. Yet even with these changes, the structure of the *haggadah* that was formulated in the second century has remained essentially the same until our own times.

Today it is not unusual for even a very young child to demand his own *haggadah* to peruse during the Passover Seder. However, the practice of everyone having their own copy is a relatively new one.

Until the thirteenth century books, which were produced by hand, were a luxury item that few people could afford to buy. The text of the *haggadah* was therefore usually included in the prayer book, which might have been the only book found in a family's house. When new methods for preparing the parchment, inks, paints, gold leaf, and other materials used in the book-making process were discovered, illuminated manuscripts became more affordable and the market expanded.

It was during this era that the *haggadah* began to appear as a separate illuminated work. Although still out of reach for most Jewish families, merchants and courtiers who had both taste and money began to commission illuminated *haggados* and a new art form was born.

The first known illustrations accompanying the traditional text were humble pictures of a piece of *matzah* (unleavened bread) and a leaf of *maror* (bitter herb). But within a relatively short period of time the illustrations became more numerous and artistically complex. Detailed color illustrations of Pesach rituals such as searching the home for *chametz* (leavened bread) and baking the *matzos* were skillfully rendered, as were pictures depicting scenes from the Torah and the *Midrash*.

When the printing press made its first appearance in Europe in 1436, the book publishing industry was revolutionized. The first printed *haggadah* made its debut in 1482, and by the sixteenth century there were 25 different printed editions.

One of the earliest of these printed editions known to still be in existence is a *haggadah* printed in Constantinople in the year 1505. It featured the Abrabanel's commentary on the *haggadah*, *Zevach Pesach*, which was then a brand new work.

The 1526 *Prague Haggadah* is perhaps the best known of the early printed *haggados*. Many of its 60 woodcut illustrations — such as the depiction of the Four Sons, with the Wicked Son dressed as a soldier — set the standard for the *haggados* that followed and they are still reproduced today.

The Ten Plagues make their printed pictorial debut in the *Venice Haggadah* published in 1609. This *haggadah* featured another important innovation: a Judeo-Italian translation of the Hebrew text that was encased within a classical architectural border. When the printer wanted to sell the *haggadah* to Ashkenazic or Sephardic communities, he simply replaced the Judeo-Italian translation with one in either Yiddish or Ladino.

Yet another first occurred in the year 1695, when the *Amsterdam Haggadah*, which featured the Abrabanel's commentary and a map of the Holy Land, became the first *haggadah* to employ the new technique of copperplate engraving.

The year 1770 saw the debut, in London, of a *haggadah* printed with an English translation. The first American *haggadah* was published in 1837, and by this time most Jewish families certainly owned at least one copy of a printed *haggadah*.

Yet even as *haggados* were becoming more widely available, the forces of assimilation were creating havoc in many Jewish families — and the *haggadah* recorded this turmoil. The *Chicago Haggadah*, printed in 1879, features a famous rendition of the Four Sons seated around the Seder table with their family. While the parents are clearly religiously observant, the Wicked Son is dressed in modern clothes and smoking a cigarette.

By the twentieth century a proliferation of new editions began to appear every year. Just about every modern artist worthy of the name tried his hand at illustrating one, and notable pre-war European *haggados* include the ones illustrated by Arthur Szyk and Otto Geismar.

The 1960s saw the birth of the Op Art illustration era, while the 1970s saw another kind of revolution: a renaissance in Orthodox Jewish book publishing. Publishing houses such as ArtScroll and Feldheim began publishing *haggados* with commentaries written by Torah sages from many different generations, thereby making their timeless wisdom available to every English-speaking Jewish family.

The *haggadah* has become not only a mass-market item during modern times, but also a mass-marketing gimmick. Maxwell House Coffee first started doing a *kosher l'Pesach* (kosher for Passover) run of its popular blend in 1923 and in 1934 the *Maxwell House Haggadah* was born. The company has distributed its own *haggadah* every year since then, making this the longest-running marketing promotion by a major brand in the United States.

More than 40 million copies of the *Maxwell House Haggadah* have been distributed, and it is just one type of *haggadah* among the more than 4,000 different versions. No one knows exactly how many copies of *haggados* are still in existence, but one thing is certain: there are a lot of them.

Thus the collecting paradox: Collecting *haggados* has become a popular modern pastime not because they are rare, but because they are so available. Since more editions of the *haggadah* have been printed than any other Jewish book, there is enough variation to appeal to just about every taste and interest. And a person doesn't need a spare million dollars to start building an interesting collection.

Sold — But Not Completed

Henry Hollander says that he leaves the selling of the older and pricey *haggados* to the auction houses. Instead, he mainly deals in affordable popular editions from the last century, and he takes pleasure in being able to provide his clients with what they want.

"There are people who enjoy collecting less expensive things," he comments. "They do so mainly because that's what they can afford. If you are going to collect, you want to have success and enjoy it. You don't want to always be outbid at auction or be in a situation where the book dealer has what you want but you don't have the money to buy it."

According to both Hollander and Madeisker, there are plenty of ways that a new collector can build up an interesting collection at a reasonable price.

"Some people are keyed into just one aspect of the *haggadah*, such as the depiction of the Four Sons," explains Hollander, "because it's fascinating to see how the styles of the illustrations change over the centuries."

Hollander also mentions the inexpensive paperback series that the Diskin Orphanage began printing in the 1950s, and which many people collect. The series includes reprints of eighteenth-century *haggados*, as well as reprints of *haggados* from lesser-known communities, such as India's Bnei Yisrael.

Although the paperbacks are neither fancy nor valuable, they do give buyers a taste for the wide variety of *haggados* that have been produced throughout the centuries and across the globe.

Madeisker's interest in modern Jewish history has made him something of an expert in *haggados* pertaining to the Holocaust era and the early years of Israel's *kibbutz* movement, categories which are still in reach of most collectors. He also mentions that people can build up a collection that is aesthetically pleasing and still pay off the mortgage by buying facsimile editions of the famous *haggados*.

The first facsimiles appeared in 1920s Germany. Printed in limited editions on deluxe paper and using the latest in color-separation technology, some of them — such as the facsimile of the *Bird's Head Haggadah* — are now collector's items worth $500-$2,000.

Less expensive facsimile editions were mass printed during the decades that followed. Although they may lack the quality of the more expensive editions, they do still convey a feeling of the era and the historical development of the *haggadah*. With so many riches available, it's not surprising that Jews from so many walks of life become interested in collecting *haggados*. Jews everywhere gather on Seder night to transmit the message of the Exodus from Egypt to the next generation, and we all want to make the night as exciting and memorable as possible. A collection of *haggados* with inspiring commentaries and beautiful illustrations can be a wonderful starting point for a lively discussion that will enhance everyone's interest and enjoyment.

But collecting *haggados*, like collecting anything, does have its dangers. There is no end to the collecting possibilities and no such thing as a collection that is complete. It can be all too easy for a person to overindulge and spend more than he can afford — or become over-involved in his hobby at the expense of the more important things in life. Henry Hollander therefore offers a final word of advice on how to put collecting into perspective.

"Collecting is exciting, and it's a great feeling when you get a good deal on a book you really want," he says. "But you have to remember that you will only have the book temporarily. It's yours for now, but the day will come when you, too, will have to pass it on."

— April 2005

Zoom, Rotate, Click:
The Cairo Genizah Goes Digital

Ever since the Cairo Genizah was discovered in 1896, the problem of how to store, catalogue, and retrieve the hundreds of thousands of fragments — some of them almost 1,000 years old — has stumped scholars. But thanks to the Friedberg Genizah Project, that problem has now been solved. From the dusty alleyways of Cairo to the rarefied air of Cambridge, and from the quiet lanes of Toronto to the bustling streets of Jerusalem, we follow the trail to discover how in the world a letter from the Rambam landed on the computer screen of this journalist.

Once upon a time — let's say in the long ago year of 1969 — there was a young man, whom we'll call Polony (the Jewish equivalent of John Doe). This Polony wanted to be a scholar and study medieval Jewish history. When he heard about a treasure trove of ancient Jewish documents that had been discovered in a synagogue in Egypt and taken to a big university in Europe, he boarded an airplane and flew to Europe.

When he got to the university, he wandered around until he found the library. A sign on the door informed him that the library would close in three hours. That was discouraging. But since he had come so far, he took a place in the long line, behind all the other scholars who had come to do research in the university library. One by one, the scholars in line received their nicely bound books and went to sit at a clean and well-lit desk. But when Polony presented his request, the librarian looked at him with surprise.

"What you want isn't here," said the librarian. The librarian then directed Polony where to go to find his documents. When he arrived at the place, it was his turn to be surprised. Instead of being filled with orderly bookshelves, the room was filled with 32 large crates. Lying in each of those crates were heaps upon jumbled heaps of ancient documents, many of them just small fragments, and all of them covered with dirt and grime.

Polony glanced from the crates to his watch. It would take much more than a few hours to sort out the mess, he reckoned. In fact, it would probably take at least 20 years! Polony went home and decided to become an accountant, instead.

Fast forward 40 years, to the year 2009. Polony's grandson is a budding scholar who, like his grandfather, is very interested in medieval Jewish history. But he won't have to fly to Europe to do his research, and he won't have to worry about some library's hours. Any time of the day or night he can sit at his computer — whether it's located in New York or Sydney or Kiev — and with the touch of a few keystrokes retrieve a document from the Cairo Genizah, complete with a photograph, a transcription of the text, a short explanation of what it is, and a list of bibliographical references that details the scholarly books and articles that have mentioned it.

How did this amazing transformation come about? And why were the Cairo Genizah manuscripts neglected for so long? And what is a *genizah*, anyway? We begin with a virtual trip to Cairo to find out.

In Old Cairo

Practically everyone has heard of the Cairo Genizah and knows, vaguely, the story of how it was discovered. Whispers of a treasure trove of ancient Jewish manuscripts found in the Ben Ezra Synagogue, which is located in the "Old Cairo" section of the city, began to circulate throughout Europe during the 1700s. By the mid-1800s, a steady stream of scholars, antiquities dealers, and tourists were coming to Cairo, and the city's Jewish community began to sell them small amounts of the manuscripts. Both private and public libraries in cities such as New York, Philadelphia, Oxford, Manchester, Paris, Strasbourg, Vienna, Petersburg, Kiev, Tel Aviv, Jerusalem, and elsewhere acquired small collections of the manuscripts in this way.

But the pivotal year for the Genizah — a *genizah* is a storage room where no longer usable religious books and old communal records are kept — was 1896. In May of that year, two Scottish sisters, Mrs. A.S. Lewis and Mrs. M.D. Gibson, purchased some of the manuscripts and brought them to Cambridge, where they showed them to Dr. Solomon Schechter, a lecturer at the university. Dr. Schechter identified one of the manuscripts as part of the Hebrew text of *The Wisdom of Ben Sira*, which had been known only in its Latin and Greek translations for centuries. In December of that same year, Dr. Schechter set sail for Cairo to see what else was there. Little did he know that he was about to discover one of the most amazing historical finds in Jewish history. But find it he did in a sealed room located in the women's section of the synagogue. The room, which had been untouched for centuries, contained an estimated 200,000 manuscript fragments — some of them dating back to the eleventh century — which pertained to just about every aspect of medieval Jewish life.

Cairo's Jewish community entrusted Dr. Schechter with almost the entire contents of the Genizah — over 140,000 documents — which he brought back to Cambridge University, the sponsors of his expedition. There was an initial flurry of interest in the manuscripts, as new finds were discovered: manuscripts hand-written by the Rambam (Maimonides), for instance, and a letter from the King of the Khazars to Spanish diplomat Hasdei Ibn Shaprut. But eventually interest waned. Perhaps researchers were overwhelmed by the sheer quantity of the material, or perhaps they were deterred by the sorry state of many of the fragments. There was also a prejudice against the study of "social history" — the daily life of the people, as it is detailed in documents such as *ketubos* (marriage contracts), private letters, and business agreements — since it was deemed of lesser importance than the critical study of scholarly documents such as fragments from the Talmud or the works of the Rambam. And so research began to languish, until another native of Scotland came to the rescue.

Have We Got a Job for You

Professor Stefan Reif, a former member of Edinburgh's Modern Orthodox community, is Emeritus Professor of Medieval Hebrew at the University of Cambridge, Project Consultant at Cambridge University Library, and a Senior Academic Consultant for the

Friedberg Genizah Project. Professor Reif is also the Founder of the Taylor-Schechter Genizah Research Unit, located at Cambridge University, and so we asked him to pick up the story from here:

"I came to Cambridge in 1973. I was totally naive. I had heard about the Genizah from teachers, and so I thought I would just have a nice time doing research and publishing books and articles. Instead I found 32 crates filled with fragments that looked like they had just been dug up from a cemetery. They were covered with dirt and mud. It was a complete mess."

His first job, therefore, was to put together the funds and staff needed to conserve the fragments and have them catalogued and microfilmed, which was the cutting-edge technology of the time. The conservation and cataloguing work alone took almost eight years. Fortunately, he found a wonderfully supportive academic atmosphere at Cambridge, and to his surprise he discovered that the field of manuscript conservation was more interesting than he thought.

"Conservation is actually a very exciting field," he comments. "Conservators are experts who know the proper way to clean vellum versus the way to clean paper. They know what can be repaired and what can't. They know where fragments can be joined and where they can't. They also know where it's fine to straighten a fragment and where it's dangerous to attempt to do so. It's exciting to see a fragment that was so crumpled that a scholar couldn't open it become straight and clean and nicely conserved.

"Once the conservation work has been completed," he adds, "the fragments are placed in a special envelope that is then sealed so that people can't get their fingertips on them or spill a cup of coffee all over the text."

But how did a young Jew from Scotland become interested in old manuscripts from Cairo in the first place?

"My *zeide* was one influence," says Professor Reif, referring to his Torah-observant grandfather who came to Edinburgh from Poland. "Rabbi Yitzchak Cohen, who was then the rav of Edinburgh and later the Chief Rabbi of Ireland, was another great inspiration. I went to Jews' College to study for the rabbinate. But when I realized that the life of a Modern Orthodox rav was filled with solving communal problems and that there would be very little time for scholarship, I decided against it. I was more interested in being a scholar."

The next person who influenced him was Naftali Vider, an expert in *tefilla* (prayer), who introduced Professor Reif to the Genizah manuscripts. "To study the development of *tefilla*, you have to go back to the original manuscripts," he explains. "Right now I'm working on a book about how the word *'shalom'* was used in prayer during the Middle Ages. I have on my computer screen six fragments from the Genizah. The word *'shalom'* is used differently in each one, because each person has something different to say."

The $40,000 Camera

This comment about his current research project — and the six Genizah fragments sitting on Professor Reif's computer screen — brings us to the topic of the Friedberg Genizah Project (FGP), which was founded ten years ago by Mr. Albert (Dov) Friedberg to both facilitate and rejuvenate Genizah research.

At first FGP was primarily concerned with locating and cataloguing the Genizah fragments that were scattered all over the world and reawakening interest in the manuscripts by funding scholarly research projects. But by the year 2005, advances in computer and digital technology had created an opportunity to completely revolutionize the way collections such as the Genizah fragments could be accessed and used by the public. FGP decided to seize the opportunity, and Professor Yaacov Choueka (pronounced Shweka), Professor Emeritus of Computer Science at Israel's Bar Ilan University, one of the developers of Bar Ilan's Responsa Project, and FGP's Chief Computerization Scientist continues the story.

"The computerization project began on January 1, 2006. One of our goals was to develop tools that would help researchers find the source material they need ten times faster than it could be found before."

What was life like for Genizah researchers before the computer age began?

"Their research was very complicated," Professor Choueka replies. "Let's say that your research topic is linguistics and you want to examine glossaries or lists of words found in the Genizah. For this, you would have to go to the university library at

Cambridge, say, or Petersburg. But the process was slow. You could do your research only during the hours that the library was open. You had to stand in line and present your request to the librarian, and sometimes you found out that the material you wanted was already being used by someone else. And how many times can a person travel to these places? I know someone, an important professor, who traveled to Cambridge every summer for ten years to do his work. So we wanted to help researchers by speeding up the process. We also wanted to give them research tools that they didn't have before."

One of those research tools takes advantage of the relatively new digital technology. FGP set for itself the astounding goal of digitally photographing as many of the Genizah fragments that they could find, and then uploading the images on their website at www.genizah.com. However, there were a few obstacles—even though FGP was footing the entire cost of the photography—such as the fact that the fragments are scattered among some 50 libraries located throughout the world. Another problem was that at first some of these libraries weren't thrilled by the thought of images of their fragments appearing on someone else's website. But the legal agreements that FGP needed to move the project forward slowly began to trickle in, and the next phase of the work—the actual photography—began.

Professor Choueka and his staff decided that given the needs of the researchers, the minimum acceptable quality for the photographs would be 600 DPI, which means that for every square inch there are 600 dots. Unfortunately, in the year 2006 there weren't many cameras that could take pictures at that high level of quality.

"We did find one kind of camera that had 22 mega pixels, which allowed us to photograph small fragments at a quality of 600 DPI. But the camera cost $40,000."

"Forty thousand dollars?" I ask, unsure that I've heard correctly. "For one camera?"

Professor Choueka assures me that my ears are, indeed, working fine. "Who bought such a camera?" he continues. "It was mainly used for architecture and fashion photography. But we used it for the Genizah's manuscripts."

The result is that the project's photographs can be enlarged and enlarged, and then enlarged some more, and the quality will still be excellent—as opposed to photographs taken at a lower quality where the image becomes blurry when it's enlarged too much.

To date, there are already 90,000 photographs on the FGP website, which are available to everyone, without having to travel or wait in line. But as I learn from Professor Choueka, the news is about to get even better.

Although the Friedberg Genizah Project has always had a very good working relationship with the Cambridge University Library—for instance the Syndics of Cambridge University Library graciously granted permission to *Mishpacha Magazine* to publish photographs from their collection when this article was published in the magazine—it was initially hard to convince Cambridge to let FGP put images of their Genizah collection on the FGP website. Since Cambridge owns about 60 percent of the Cairo Genizah fragments, their absence would have left serious gaps in the Friedberg digitalization project. Fortunately, the two organizations reached an agreement about six months ago, and over the next three years FGP will be adding 400,000 photographs of the Cambridge collection to the project.

All Together Now

Professor Choueka adds that he hopes that now that Cambridge has signed on, other libraries—such as Oxford University's Bodleian Library, the British Museum Library, and libraries in Manchester, Petersburg, Moscow, and Kiev—will also participate. But this isn't an instance of "the more the merrier." Serious research issues are involved, as he explains.

"In the past, what happened when Professor X was sitting in Cambridge and he came to a missing section of the document he was studying? If he had a good memory, he might have remembered that he once came across a similar document in Vienna, which might be the missing section. But what could he do? Fly to Vienna to look at that document and then fly back to Cambridge?"

To help solve this problem, researchers have been manually searching for "joins"—fragments from the same document—for years, and they've discovered thousands of them. But FGP has taken the search to a new level with software it developed for this purpose. The software program can suggest that fragments now physically located thousands of miles apart might actually come from the same original document by analyzing things like the number of lines on the page, the size of the letters, the size of the space between the lines, etcetera. The human researcher can then analyze this information and decide if this is a true join or not.

But the photographs are just a small portion of the computerization story. There is also a large amount of data connected to the Genizah—such as information about some 120,000 bibliographical references to scholarly books and articles pertaining to Genizah research—that have been added to the database. Why is this helpful?

Let's say, for example, that someone is studying a Genizah fragment of a *piyut* (liturgical poem). He believes that the *piyut* might have been written in the twelfth century. He further believes that it might even have been written by the famous Spanish medieval poet Yehudah HaLevi. But are his hunches correct? He can find out what other scholars think by clicking on the website's "Bibliographies" button. In seconds, he'll get a comprehensive list of the books and articles written during the past 100 years that mention or cite this fragment, including the exact volume and page numbers where the fragment is discussed. He can then track down the books and articles and read what they have to say.

Professor Choueka comments that this wasn't possible before. I take his word for it. I also have no doubt that the transcriptions and translations of each fragment, which is done by researchers and then added to the database, will also be helpful—especially for the many documents that were written in Judeo-Arabic, a dialect where the author wrote in Arabic using Hebrew letters.

But despite all the wonderful things that can now be done—and the Friedberg Genizah Project is considered to be a technological leader in the field of cultural heritage digitalization—I still have a complaint. While doing research for this article, I entered the FGP website and tried to do a little scholarly research of my own. In particular, I wanted to find Genizah fragments relating to the topic of women. But there was no way for me to conduct this type of search. I therefore ask Professor Choueka what is going on. Does a person have to know the shelfmark—the fragment's identification number—before she can do any research? And if that's the case, how is an ordinary person like me supposed to know that sort of specialized information?

"Wait two weeks," he assures me. "That's when the next version of the website is going to be uploaded. You'll be able to conduct a search of the entire database, much like you would do on Google, and see all the fragments pertaining to women, or all the fragments written by Saadya Gaon. You'll be able to ask for all the fragments written in the 1300s, or all the fragments that contain just fourteen lines, if you're trying to find a join."

What else can we expect? According to Professor Choueka, the development of the technical aspects of the computerization project is nearing completion. Of course, images and data will continue to be added to the database, but by the summer of next year his work will be done. That will be a bittersweet moment for him, and not just because he will have spent five years working on the project. Professor Choueka has a special connection to the Genizah, because he himself happens to be from Cairo.

"My great-grandfather was the Chief Rabbi of Halab," he explains, using the Arabic name for the city that many English-speakers know as Aleppo. "My grandfather and my father came to Egypt in 1910. I grew up in Egypt. When I was 20 years old—this was in 1957, after the Sinai Campaign—we moved to Israel.

"It's very interesting that someone from Cairo became the head of this project—particularly since there were others before me who tried to develop a computer database and didn't succeed. Either they were computer professionals and they didn't understand *Yiddishkeit* (Judaism), or they understood the *Yiddishkeit* but they didn't understand computers. Apparently, what was needed was someone who understood both and had experience with these kinds of projects."

You've Got Mail—from the Rambam

But even though Professor Choueka and his staff of programmers will soon be moving on to other projects, the work is just beginning for the more than 600 Genizah researchers who are already using the FGP website. And that number is sure to expand once the Cambridge University Library collection is available online.

"We didn't dream that there were that many researchers interested in the Cairo Genizah," Professor Choueka comments. "We have people from America and Israel and England, of course, but researchers from Australia and Africa and even Cairo are also using the site."

Professor Reif, on the other hand, isn't at all surprised by the numbers. "It's exciting to see how Jews lived their lives hundreds of years ago. The documents from the Genizah are a reflection of the reality of life as it was lived. The Dead Sea scrolls didn't provide that. The people who wrote the Dead Sea scrolls were living in the desert. But the Genizah people are living real lives. They have their business problems and their medical problems. They have their religious questions — and religion does play a major role in their lives — but they also write poetry and letters to loved ones. They are living perfectly ordinary lives, and yet they are interacting with the entire Jewish world and with the non-Jewish world as well.

"And looking at the signature of the Rambam is always exciting — no matter how many times you've seen it."

—June 2009

The Wandering Haggadah

Just as Jews have wandered from country to country during our long exile, so too has the Haggadah Shel Pesach traveled over mountains and across seas. But while almost every vintage haggadah has a story of exile and escape, some are more incredible than others – such as the stories of these four haggados, *which are still making headlines in our own times.*

One commemorated the festival when we eat "dry wheat." One suffered the bitter fate of being forgotten in an Osem soup box. One disappeared not once, but twice. One is "reclining" in an arty prison.

What makes the wanderings of these four *haggados* different from most other *haggados*? We're glad you asked.

From Soup to Matzah: The Manchester Haggadah

It once graced the Seder table of one of Europe's most fabled families, so how did this haggadah end up forgotten in an Osem soup box? That was the question that faced Bill Forrest, a member of the Adam Partridge Auctioneers valuation team, who last July was sent to a Jewish home in Bury, England.

The elderly owner of the home had passed away a few years earlier. When the new owner, a niece (who has chosen to remain anonymous), was ready to dispose of the house's contents, she contacted the locally-based auction house.

Forrest went from room to room. When he reached the garage, he saw some old cardboard cartons. At the bottom of one of them, an Osem soup box, he found a "thin, fairly modest looking manuscript." He began to leaf through the handwritten vellum pages, marveling at the more than 50 colored illustrations. Forrest, who isn't Jewish, had no idea what the book was, but he realized at once that he had stumbled upon an amazing find. That initial hunch was confirmed as the illuminated haggadah's story began to unfold.

According to the title page, the haggadah was written in the year 1726. The *sofer* and illustrator was Aaron Wolff Herlingen, a Jew from Moravia, who has been described as one of the greatest Jewish calligraphers of the 18th century. During his lifetime Herlingen put his pen to miniature prayer books, megillos Esther, circumcision books and several *haggados*. It's thought that about 40 - 60 of his works are still in existence. Herlingen specialist Professor Emile G.L. Schrijver of the University of Amsterdam not only authenticated this haggadah as the *sofer*'s work, but added that it is "a better than average example."

The title page also gives information about the person who commissioned the haggadah: Elias Oppenheimer, "son of the deceased R' Mendel Oppenheimer." Elias was a grandson of Samuel Oppenheimer, Court Jew to the Austrian Emperor and the founder of the famous Oppenheimer banking dynasty. In the evocative words of Professor Yaakov Wise, a historian at the Centre for Jewish Studies at the University of Manchester, who examined the haggadah's wine-stained pages, "It is easy to imagine the wealthy family in Vienna sitting around in their wigs and their buckled shoes, reading it by candlelight."

How did the haggadah get to England?

Although much of the haggadah's history remains shrouded in mystery, according to auctioneer Adam Partridge, by the early 1900s the haggadah had been acquired by a family living in Belgium. When the family fled to England in 1940, ahead of the Nazi invasion of their country, the haggadah went with them.

In England, it seems that the family members began to drift apart. At some point the owners of the haggadah moved to Bury, a city located north of Manchester. Apparently, they packed up an Osem soup carton with various Hebrew *sefarim* (Torah books), including the haggadah, and never unpacked the box. The haggadah's existence was forgotten.

That changed once the story of the "rare haggadah found in a garage" made the newspapers. On the day of the auction, November

22, 2013, Partridge set up a bank of phones to handle the calls from all the expected bidders. But with an opening bid of £100,000 ($167,000), smaller collectors and representatives of libraries and museums soon dropped out—leaving only two determined private bidders to battle it out. When Partridge brought down his gavel for the final time, the price had soared to £210,000 ($350,000).

This wasn't the highest price paid for a Herlingen haggadah; Sotheby's New York auctioned off one that included a map of Eretz Yisrael for more than $800,000 in 2012. But both Partridge and the niece were more than happy with the sale.

Who bought the haggadah? Given the manuscript's secretive past, it's perhaps no surprise that the new owner— a private collector from Vienna—has also chosen to remain anonymous. And so the "Manchester Haggadah" is now back where its story began. But unlike the Austrian Empire, which is no more, the haggadah has survived.

"It is a miracle that it was not thrown out, that it was found and someone realized what it was," Professor Wise told the press. "I would call it divine providence."

War and Peace: The Sarajevo Haggadah

It has survived expulsion, the Inquisition and two world wars, but it may not survive a danger of a very different sort: peace. Welcome to the paradoxical world of the Sarajevo Haggadah, one of the most famous *haggados* in Jewish history.

Despite its name, this richly illustrated haggadah was created in Barcelona in 1350. It was most likely smuggled out of Spain after the Expulsion in 1492, perhaps by crypto-Jews. By the 1500s its owners were living in Italy, but all was not well. A note on one of the pages, which was handwritten by an agent of the Roman Inquisition and dated 1609, declares that the manuscript does not speak negatively against the Church. Although this note apparently saved the haggadah from being destroyed, it points to the fiery fate that awaited many other *sefarim* during that time.

How the haggadah ended up in Bosnia isn't known. However, Sarajevo would have been a wise choice for Jews wishing to escape from Christian Europe. The city, which was under the rule of the Ottoman Empire, was known for its tolerant religious atmosphere.

Indeed, as the Jewish community grew and prospered, the city became known as "Little Jerusalem."

By the late 1800s there was at least one Jew, a man named Joseph Cohen, who had fallen upon hard times. How the haggadah came into his hands is yet another mystery, but in 1894 he sold it to the National Museum of Bosnia and Herzegovina, where it remained for half a century. When the Nazis arrived in Sarajevo, they stormed the museum and demanded that the museum's director, Jozo Petrovic, turn over the famed manuscript.

Petrovic, who had no intention of giving up the haggadah, summoned the museum's chief librarian, Dervis Korkut, and asked the librarian to bring the haggadah. Korkut, full of apologies, informed his boss and the officer that he was unable to comply because another German officer had been there earlier and already taken away the haggadah.

"What is this officer's name?" the German demanded.

"Who am I to ask a German officer for his name?" replied Korkut, with mock humility.

As soon as the Germans left, Petrovic, a Catholic, and Korkut, a Muslim, sprang into action—although as often happens during wartime, there are several accounts of what happened next. The most common version of the story says that Korkut smuggled the haggadah out of the city and hid it either in a village mosque or under the floorboards of a Muslim home. Another theory is that the two men simply hid the haggadah among the hundreds of thousands of other books in the museum's collection.

After the war, the haggadah reappeared in the museum. For another half century it reposed there peacefully. Then Bosnian Serbs besieged the city in 1992, in an effort to make Sarajevo part of Greater Serbia. During the three-year Bosnian war many of the city's buildings were burned to the ground, including the National Library, whose entire collection was destroyed. Uncertain about the fate of the National Museum, its director, Enver Imamovic, who was a Bosnian Muslim, decided to dodge the snipers' bullets to save what had become one of the premier symbols of Sarajevo's rich cultural heritage: the Sarajevo Haggadah. After smuggling the haggadah out of the museum, he deposited it in an underground bank vault.

Once again the haggadah emerged from war unscathed and went back on display at the museum. This time, though, it didn't take 50 years for yet another crisis to occur.

The Bosnian war ended in 1995, when the Dayton Accords, a peace agreement brokered by Western powers, went into effect. Although the military fighting came to an end, the peace agreement failed to resolve the area's longstanding ethnic hostilities. Indeed, the weak central government and constitution created by the Accords have caused numerous problems, one of which has directly affected the safety of the Sarajevo Haggadah. Because there is no provision for a Ministry of Culture, cultural institutions that once received funding from a national government have had to survive on donations from local municipalities and private donors to keep their doors open. Time and money ran out for the National Museum in October of 2012, when the staff, which had worked without pay for a year, locked the museum's doors for the last time.

New York City's Metropolitan Museum of Art offered to host the Sarajevo Haggadah for three years, so that the manuscript, which needs special lighting and a temperature-controlled environment to preserve its fragile pages, could have a safe home while the politicians hammered out an agreement that would restore funding to the museum. But the politicians refused the offer, saying they hadn't the authority to loan out the haggadah while the status of the National Museum remains unresolved. Others say the politicians were afraid that if the haggadah ever left the country, it would never return.

What little money the museum does receive from concerned donors is used to keep the Sarajevo Haggadah safely reclining in its special light-and-moisture-controlled box. But the situation is far from ideal for a manuscript that is truly irreplaceable. For the moment, though, there is nothing to be done. While Bosnians wait for the tense political situation to be resolved, the haggadah remains locked behind the museum's closed doors, a hostage to the political squabbling caused by a hobbled-together peace accord.

Gone! Again! The Wolf Haggadah

The art world isn't immune to shady dealings. But the Wolf Haggadah, which was stolen from museums not once but twice, is certainly in a league of its own.

Although we often know nothing about the medieval Jewish scribes who wrote the *haggados* that are today worth hundreds of thousands of dollars, we do know something about scholar, physician and *sofer* Yaakov ben Shlomo Tzarfati of Avignon. In 1382, he lost three of his children in the space of three months to the plague that was then raging in France. Despite his grief, his deep *emunah* is displayed in his work *Evel Rabbati*, which is about the death of his daughter Esther, and — in quite a different way — in the beautiful 36-page haggadah that he penned toward the end of his life.

What happened to the haggadah during the next 500 years is unknown. But when it turned up at a German auction house in 1889, the winning bid was placed by a Jew from Dresden named Albert Wolf. The haggadah, which before this was called the French Haggadah, subsequently became known by Wolf's name.

By the time of his death in 1907, Wolf, a jeweler by profession, had amassed the largest collection of Jewish art in Germany. He donated it all to the Jewish community of Berlin, where it later formed the nucleus of the city's Jewish Museum.

The timing couldn't have been worse: The museum opened its doors in 1933, the year that the Nazis came to power. On the night of November 8, 1938, Kristallnacht, the Nazis closed the museum and confiscated the haggadah. The stolen manuscript, along with other Jewish treasures, was sent to Glatz, a town that was part of Germany before the war but which subsequently became part of Poland.

When Russian soldiers discovered the haggadah in 1944, they gave it to the Jewish Historical Institute in Warsaw. The Wolf Haggadah remained in Warsaw until 1984, when it was loaned out for an exhibition in the United States. After the exhibition closed, the manuscript disappeared.

Who stole the haggadah? As usual, there are a few versions of the story. According to one, the haggadah never made it back to Warsaw, which means that anyone who handled it during the return journey could have made off with it. According to another version, it did get returned to the Institute, but one day it disappeared from the closet where it was being stored, which suggests the theft was an inside job.

In any event, alarm bells sounded in 1989 when Habsburg-Feldman, a Geneva auction house, announced it would be auctioning the haggadah in June of that year. When questioned, the auction house claimed the seller had a "voluminous legal document covering the legal rights to ownership." The seller later told the press that he had bought the haggadah from a Polish agent who had seemed legitimate.

The World Jewish Congress (WJC), acting on behalf of the Jewish communities of West and East Berlin, filed a lawsuit against the auction house. The Polish government, another party to the lawsuit, challenged both the seller's claim to ownership and that of Berlin's Jews. But it later signed an agreement with the WJC that stated that no matter who won the court case, the haggadah would be donated to the Jewish National and University Library of the Hebrew University.

After the Supreme Court in Geneva ruled conclusively in favor of Berlin's Jewish community, the Wolf Haggadah made aliyah. Today it sits in the Jerusalem-based library, where it will hopefully remain safe and secure for many years to come.

Chopsticks on the Seder Table: The Kaifeng Haggadah

If there were such a thing as a "Frequent Flyer" program for *haggados*, the ones from China would certainly be in the top ranking for most mileage. But who were the Jews who wrote these *haggados*?

Most scholars assume that the first arrivals in China were ninth-century Jewish merchants from Persia, who traded their wares along the fabled Silk Road. This assumption is partially based upon two *haggados* from the Kaifeng community that have come down to us: in both of them, the instructions for conducting the Seder are written in Judeo-Persian.

Kaifeng, the capital city of the Song Dynasty, was host to China's largest and most prosperous Jewish community. Although the community never numbered more than 6,000 souls — a drop in the bucket of the medieval city's approximately 600,000 Chinese residents — their "strange" habits, such as refusing to eat pork, were noted by their neighbors. But the Jews were never discriminated against because of their religious beliefs. Although the Chinese themselves didn't believe in Hashem, they didn't mind if others did. The Jews were therefore free to go about both their material and spiritual business, including celebrating the "Feast of Dry Wheat" — a name the Kaifeng Jews gave to Passover.

However, by the time China closed its borders to foreigners in the early 1500s, cutting off Kaifeng's Jewish community from other Jews, the community was already in decline. The tolerance and prosperity that had made China such a pleasant haven was taking its toll and, as happened elsewhere, the community began to assimilate into the surrounding culture. The region's declining prosperity also contributed to the Jewish community's woes.

By the time twelve new Torah scrolls were written in the seventeenth century, the scrolls were filled with hundreds of errors. When the last rabbi passed away in the early 1800s, there was no one to replace him. Although the community treated its Torah manuscripts with respect, by the mid-1800s there was no one left who could read them.

While the latter Jews of Kaifeng might not have been able to read their *haggados*, contemporary scholars have poured over the texts, hoping to discover clues about the community's religious practices. Although the *haggados* date from a relatively late period in the community's history—one is from the 1600s and the other dates to the 1700s—scholars have found some surprises. For instance, there are several references to the Rambam's *Mishneh Torah*. Since the Rambam lived a few centuries after the first Jews arrived in China, it's thought that medieval merchants from Yemen later joined the original Persian community.

Another interesting detail is the inclusion of the *piyut* (liturgical poem) *Ata Ga'alta* by Rabbi Saadia Gaon, which is written in Hebrew with a Judeo-Persian translation. On the other hand, none of the traditional songs that appear at the end of Ashkenazi *haggados* are included. Since those songs date from the medieval period, their absence gives further credence to the community's Persian origins.

Fook-Kong Wong, a scholar from Hong Kong and the author of *The Haggadah of the Kaifeng Jews* (Brill, 2011), along with Dalia Yasharpour, was able to glean other insights thanks to his knowledge of the Chinese language. For instance, he told *Mishpacha Magazine*, via email, "They have written a Chinese word (a negative particle) next to the first word of each Hallel psalm. Dalia (the coauthor of our book) and I are not exactly sure what they mean, but it must be important because they are reproduced in exactly the same place in both manuscripts. Personally, I think it means that they'd stopped reading the Hallel at some point in time."

Wong first became familiar with the Kaifeng Jews during a conference he attended in Kaifeng in 2002. He was intrigued enough by what he learned to make the community's two surviving *haggados* the focus of his research during his sabbatical year.

He adds, "I am sure that regardless of how imperfectly they observed the Passover, it must have been observed for quite a while after the present form of the manuscript came about. Both *haggadot* have been taken apart and dried [Ed. Kaifeng experienced severe flooding several times during its history], after which fuzzy words were written over to make them legible. This painstaking work would not be necessary if they'd just kept the manuscripts in a closet somewhere."

Where are the *haggados* today?

Not in Kaifeng. Although there are still about 1000 - 2000 Kaifeng Jews living in that city, they would have to travel halfway around the world to see what remains from their once illustrious heritage. In the 1850s poverty forced the community to sell many of its manuscripts to a British missionary society. More were sold in the following years. Today, the *haggados* are in Cincinnati, part of Hebrew Union College's Klau Library Collection. The rest of the community's treasures are preserved in libraries and museums in Europe and North America—a paper trail leading west, replacing the Silk Road that first brought Jews to China.

—July 2018

FOOD FOR THOUGHT

Welcome Back, Challah!

An old adage says that absence makes the heart grow fonder, and afer Passover who isn't longing for that first delicious bite of challah! Yet most people would be surprised to learn that challah as we know it is a relative newcomer to the Shabbos table.

Ask Jewish women for one word that expresses Shabbos and many would probably cast their vote for challah — the out-of-this-world bread that is as full of symbolic meaning as it is delicious. Yet if we could time travel back seven hundred years or so and take a peek at the freshly baked loaves hidden under the cloth cover, most of us would be surprised by what was there. Instead of the fluffy braided loaves that we are familiar with, the typical bread for Shabbos would have been round and flat. What's more, back then the bread wasn't even called challah!

Challah Undercover

The Hebrew word "challah" is mentioned several times in the Torah. For instance, in *Shemos* (Exodus) 29:2 the *pasuk* (verse) mentions an offering of unleavened cakes (*challos matzos*) made from fine wheat flour. Later on, in *Bamidbar* (Numbers) 15:20, we read:

Of the first of your dough you shall set aside a cake (challah) *as an offering; as the offering of the threshing-floor, so you shall set it aside.*

That is the source of separating "challah" from dough. But nowhere does the Torah tell us to eat "challah" on Shabbos. True, in

Shabbos 117b Rabi Abba tells us that on Shabbos a person is obligated to recite *Hamotzi*, the blessing over bread, over two loaves of bread, in commemoration of the double portion of *mon* (mannah). However, the word *kikarim* is used for "loaves" and not *challos*. Even the Rambam speaks of two *kikarim* in his *Mishneh Torah*, Laws of Blessings 7:4, when he mentions the two loaves we place on the table for Shabbos and Yom Tov.

According to Gil Marks, author of *Encyclopedia of Jewish Food*, both Sephardim and Ashkenazim used flatbread for their Shabbos loaves until the fifteenth century. To honor Shabbos and differentiate the loaves from weekday bread, during the early medieval period it became customary to use white flour for Shabbos—although the Persian community continued to prefer whole-wheat flour to white. Some Sephardic communities would also sprinkle sesame or some other type of seed over the round loaves, an allusion to the *mon* that fell in the form of coriander seeds.

But whether the loaves were made from whole-wheat or white flour, or had sesame seeds or were plain, one thing they were not was "challah."

A New Twist

We have to wait until the late 1400s to find Shabbos loaves being described as "challah" in a *sefer*. That book was *Leket Yosher*, written by Rav Yosef ben Moshe, who was from Bavaria. Rav Yosef was a *talmid* of Rav Yisrael Isserlein, a leading *halachic* authority of his time, and in his *sefer* Rav Yosef records the statements, customs and daily conduct of his teacher. One passage describes some of Rav Isserlein's Shabbos customs. If you find the quote below a bit confusing, you're in good company; elsewhere, Rav Yosef admits that his writing skills leave something to be desired. Even so, he gives a fascinating glimpse into some of the Ashkenazic customs of his time:

I recall that every Erev Shabbos they would make him three thin challos, kneaded with eggs and oil and a little bit of water. At night, he would put the mid-sized challah in the middle of his table, which was square, on a cloth in the center of the table. Under the challah was a large uncut loaf, even though it [the large uncut loaf] was made of black bread, rather than on a small roll of white bread called zeml. *In the morning, the large challah and a large loaf were put on the table, like at night. For the third meal, he used the small challah and a whole loaf.*

What has caught the eye of Jewish food historians is that even though the fancier *zeml* roll was known to Rav Isserlein, he seems to have spurned it for a challah that was both thin in size and ordinary in taste. Some posit that although *zeml* might have been tastier, it was a type of bread that was eaten throughout the week—at least by those who could afford to eat white-flour bread instead of the more common black bread—and Rav Isserlein wanted a bread that was baked especially for Shabbos for his challah.

Later, Rav Yosef mentions that these challos were also called *kuchen*, giving us another clue for what this bread was like. Although today the word *kuchen* is used for cake or some other sweet dessert, in the past the word was used to describe thin round bread that was baked in a pan over a fire, using a little oil. Since that method was similar to the one used to bake the challah offerings mentioned in the Torah, it's thought that this was why *kuchen* was used for *lechem mishneh* (the second loaf) on Shabbos and Yom Tov.

According to Mordechai Kosover, author of *Yidishe Maykholim (Food and Beverages: A Study in the History of Culture and Linguistics),* although during the week *kuchen* might be pan baked using butter, for Shabbos, when the bread had to be parve, it was pan baked using just *schmaltz.* That led a nineteenth-century midwife and author named Malka Berlant to complain in her book *Di Gliklekhe Muter (The Happy Mother)* that these *schmaltz*-laden loaves were "harmful even for a healthy person."

At some point during the 1400s, braided breads using the best available white flour become popular in Germany, perhaps because braiding the dough helps to keep the bread fresh a bit longer. These breads, known as *berchisbrod*, started to make an appearance on the Shabbos table, possibly because the German word *bercht* (braid) sounds very similar to the Hebrew word *brochos* (blessings). In Southern Germany, this type of challah became known as *barches* or *berches.*

These challos apparently had wings, in addition to braids, because in the next century we see challah baking really take off as a culinary art.

Do You Speak Challah?

Braided loaves soon became popular in Alsace and parts of Hungary, where braided loaves sprinkled with poppy seeds were known as *barhesz* or *szombati kalács*. It took a little longer for the new look and lingo to reach Eastern Europe. As late as the mid-1500s Rav Moses Isserles, the Rema, referred to the Shabbos loaves as *lachamim* in his gloss on the *Shulchan Aruch*. However, by the 1600s both the braids and the term *khale* were widely used in Poland and other parts of Eastern Europe.

Of course, there continued to be innovations and variations. While the three-strand braid was the easiest to make, six-strand braids were also popular; two loaves with six strands apiece symbolized the twelve showbreads on display in the *Beis Hamikdash* (Holy Temple). Another allusion to the showbread was a loaf that had two rows with six bumps apiece.

The ingredients used to make the dough also became more varied. In some places eggs were added, as well as a pinch of saffron, to give the dough a yellow color that symbolized the color of cooked *mon*. After sugar became more affordable in Eastern Europe, this too was added to the dough, because when *mon* was pounded into cakes it tasted like honey.

Since many Sephardic *halachic* authorities argued that a dough enriched by a significant quantity of eggs and sweetener made the resulting product more like cake than bread—and therefore inappropriate for the recitation of *Hamotzi*—the Sephardim kept their challos simple.

Jews from Germany also had a recipe for a simpler challah, called *vasser challah* (water bread), that contained no eggs or oil. Yet if it was short on ingredients, *vasser challah* still had symbolic meaning. A strip of dough that ran down the length of the oblong loaf symbolized both the ascent to Heaven and the letter *vav*, which has the numerical value of six. Put two such loaves together and you once again have an allusion to the 12 loaves of showbread.

In Lithuania and Latvia, the braided loaves were called *kitke*; even today people living in South Africa will refer to their Shabbos loaves as *kitke*, because their *bubbes* and *zeides* mainly hailed from Lithuania and brought the term with them. Poland also made a linguistic contribution, calling the loaves *koilitch* or *keylitch* or something similar.

Early German immigrants to the United States brought their customs with them, and for a while the Shabbos loaves were still known as *barches*. But after Jewish immigrants from Eastern Europe began pouring into America during the early 1900s, "chollah," "chalah" and our own "challah" eventually won the day. In Israel, as well, the term most commonly heard is "challah," although the Israeli loaf is generally not as sweet as its American cousin, since Israelis love to start the Shabbos meal with lots of savory appetizers.

A Last Morsel

As we've become more aware of the health benefits of whole wheat flour—as well as spelt and other non-wheat grains—many Jewish women have gone back to the baking pan, so to speak, and opted to exchange white flour for something healthier, even on Shabbos.

The Malbin might not have approved. In his commentary on *parshas Beshalach*, he states that white flour is the best way to honor Shabbos; while the *mon* that fell throughout the week looked like bits of crystal, on *Erev Shabbos* it was white, symbolizing mercy and kindness. Hence, the preference for white flour.

Rav Pinchas of Koretz, however, stresses that it is the woman's intention while baking her challah that is important. In *Imrei Pinchas, Shabbos,* he discusses what exactly *Midrash Bereishis Rabbah 60* means when it says there was blessing in the dough of Sarah Imanu. Since Avraham Avinu was a wealthy man who could afford to give Sarah all the flour she needed, the blessing wasn't about quantity. Instead, argues the Imrei Pinchas, the blessing must have referred to the quality of her loaves—they were sweet-smelling, delightful to look at, and tasted delicious. He therefore advises women to be happy while baking, so that our challah will be pleasing like those of Sarah Imanu. If, *chas veshalom*, a woman is angry instead, her challah will come out of the oven charred and misshapen.

* * *

A Key to the Gates of Heaven

On the first Shabbos after Passover, many people have the custom to bake "Schlissel (Key) Challah." The earliest mention of the custom is in *Imrei Pinchas* (#298), a *sefer* written by Rav Pinchas Shapiro of Koritz, a follower of the Baal Shem Tov. In the *sefer Ohev Yisrael*, Rav Avraham Yehoshua Heschel, the Apter Rav, calls Schlissel Challah "an ancient custom."

The custom is also mentioned in *Ta'amei Minhagim* and other chassidic *sefarim*, although how to make the special challah varies. While the Apter Rav says to first knead the dough with a key and then form the dough into the shape of a key, another custom is to make an imprint of a key on top of the dough. A third variation calls for placing a key-shaped piece of dough on top of the loaf before baking.

The main reason given for the custom, says the Imrei Pinchas, has to do with the fact that the Gates of Heaven that were opened during Passover remain open until Pesach Sheni; the key therefore reminds us to pray with especial concentration during these days. The Apter Rav adds a few more explanations: While the Gates of Heaven were open throughout Passover, now that the holiday is over we must reopen them with our observance of Shabbos. Also, after Bnei Yisrael (the Children of Israel) entered the Land of Canaan, they continued to eat *mon* until they brought the *Omer* offering on the second day of Passover, after which the *mon* stopped falling and they had to eat food that was grown in Eretz Yisrael — with all the effort and worry that such work implies. The key on the challah is therefore a symbolic reminder of our prayer to Hashem to open the gates of sustenance for us, just as He opened the gates of sustenance for the People of Israel during the days of Yehoshua.

Today, there are some rabbis who object to the custom. Some object to the use of any *segulah* (spiritual remedy or amulet), while others claim that the practice of impressing a key into the top of the dough has its origins in a non-Jewish custom.

For those who do practice the custom, just about everyone is in agreement about one thing: Choose your key carefully, if you plan to place an actual key inside the dough. Today, many keys are made partially from plastic, which can melt in the oven. Car keys — or any keys with computer chips embedded in them — like intensive heat about as much as they like being doused with water, which is to say not at all. Therefore, use a key that's entirely metal, and be sure to warn your family and guests beforehand to bite carefully. You don't want anyone to break a tooth and transfer the blessing for a good livelihood to the dentist.

—July 2015

"King" Kugel

We greet the Shabbos Queen with a royal feast that includes, of course, a kugel. What are the origins of this quintessentially Jewish dish and why is it considered by many to possess rich spiritual powers? We begin our story in, of all places, the cholent pot.

If we were to be invited to a Shabbos evening meal of some 700 years ago, we would probably see some familiar sights: fish, soup, and chicken or meat. One thing we would not see is the dish that has pride of place on many a Shabbos table: kugel. For that, we would have to wait until Shabbos day — and even then we might not recognize the funny-looking food being dished out of the cholent (stew) pot.

The reason for the confusion is that it took a few centuries, as well as several technological advancements, for kugel to assume its present form. So let's follow the noodle trail back to where some people say the kugel's story began: the humble dumpling.

Pot Luck

According to chef and food historian Gil Marks, author of *Encyclopedia of Jewish Food*, our Jewish kugel actually has its origins in China, where the dumpling was a favorite food more than 1,300 years ago. These ancient dumplings were made from flour and stuffed with vegetables. We know, because during the 1970s a few of them were discovered in a tomb that dated back to the Tang Dynasty.

Chinese dumplings traveled west along the Silk Road, a famous trade route that connected China with the Middle East, Africa and

—most importantly for our story — Europe. Both Italian and German cooks adopted the dumpling and made it their own. While the ancient Chinese would have cooked their dumplings in a bronze pot, German housewives living during the Middle Ages used a ceramic pot that was round in shape, like a ball. These pots, which were placed directly in the fire, had their own name: *kugeltopf*. The word *"topf"* means a "jar" or "pot." As for *"kugel,"* that was the German word for "ball" back in medieval days.

For Shabbos, the lady of the house wouldn't put the *kugeltopf* directly in the fire; instead she placed the pot inside the larger pot she used for her cholent. The surrounding steam had a transformational effect upon the doughy batter: instead of a dumpling, what came out of the pot on Shabbos morning was a pudding, which was served along with the cholent. With time, at least in Eastern Europe, this pudding began to be called by the word that referred to its round shape: kugel.

By the sixteenth century, kugels were getting fancier. In some places sautéed onions were added to the batter, in other places apples or other fruits. It depended on what was available locally and local tastes, whether people liked their puddings sweet or savory. Another popular addition was sugar, which became more widely available during the 1700s and led to the creation of sweet kugels. The potato kugel couldn't be invented until potatoes gained widespread acceptance in Europe, which didn't happen until the 1800s, and by then Jewish housewives were already experimenting with using noodles and farfel, and even rice, in place of the traditional doughy batter.

Squaring the Circle

Although ovens have been around for thousands of years, the majority of medieval homes didn't have one. Instead, most foods were stewed in a pot hung over the open fire blazing away in the fireplace, which also served to heat the room. When a woman wished to bake bread, she'd prepare the dough at home and then take the dough to her local baker, who would bake the bread in his oven for a small fee. Before Shabbos, Jewish women would take their cholent pots to the baker as well, and the pots would stay in the baker's oven until Shabbos morning, when each family would retrieve their own pot and take it home.

It was only in the mid-1800s that homes began to be equipped with cast-iron stoves that had both burners on top and compartments for ovens. But as we know, Jewish traditions are hard to change. When Lady Judith Montefiore wrote her cookbook *The Jewish Manual* in 1846 (it was the first kosher cookbook written in English), her kugel recipe still called for the dish to be steamed in the cholent pot.

The date when the kugel first leaped out of the cholent pot and into the oven seems to be a mystery. But make the leap it did, and today a kugel is usually prepared in a square pan that is placed in the oven to bake.

But whether it is round in shape or square, the kugel is as popular today as it was hundreds of years ago. One reason, of course, is its delicious taste. Another reason has to do with economics. During times of austerity, when money for meat or chicken is scarce — which was most of the time for the majority of Eastern European Jews — the starchy, stomach-filling kugel ensures that no one leaves the Shabbos table hungry.

For some Jews, though, the kugel's continued popularity has a much loftier reason.

Kugel *Segulah*

Stories about the chassidim's appreciation of a kugel's spiritual qualities have been around almost as long as there have been chassidim. The Baal HaTanya, for example, once humorously commented that a Jew who eats kugel on Shabbos can achieve the same spiritual heights which are achieved on Rosh Hashanah during the blowing of the shofar. When someone challenged that statement and inquired why we don't do away with the shofar blowing and just eat kugel instead, the Baal HaTanya had a ready reply: That's exactly what we do when Rosh Hashanah falls on Shabbos; we don't blow shofar, but we do eat kugel! (*Shemuos Vesippurim*, vol. 2, page 156.)

Of course, kugel isn't the only dish that has spiritual significance for the chassidim. Just about every traditional dish on the Shabbos menu has been given a mystical meaning. But kugel is in a class of its own, and it is said that once Rabbi Menachem Mendel of Riminov and Rabbi Naftali of Ropshitz spent three hours discussing the spiritual secrets of the Shabbos kugel. During the 1800s it even generated a heated discussion amongst several chassidic rebbes, with some arguing that potato kugel was the ideal and others insisting that noodle (*lokshen*) kugel was the one that had the greatest spiritual powers.

Lokshen, of course, is a well-known *segulah* (spiritual remedy or protection) for *parnassa* (livelihood), which is why many people add noodles to the chicken soup on Shabbos night. For those who don't know why they do this, Rabbi Pinchas of Koretz explains that the tradition comes from *Pesachim* 118a, which says: "Earning a livelihood is difficult (*kashin*)." Since *lokshen* sounds like *lo kashin* (not difficult), when we eat *lokshen* we are in fact praying to Hashem that He will provide us with a "not difficult," or easy, livelihood (*Imrei Pinchas* 25).

Perhaps this is why Rabbi Yaakov Yitzchak of Peshischa, the Yid Hakodesh, resolved the above argument by declaring, "*Lokshen* kugel is the principal kugel, while potato kugel is just another Shabbos food."

Yet it wasn't just the chassidim who considered kugel to be the "king" of Shabbos foods. Several Yiddish folk sayings also convey the deep connection between the Jewish people and this favorite dish, which even non-Jews recognize as being a uniquely Jewish food. "Shabbos without kugel is like a bird without wings" is how one unknown Jew with a poetical bent expressed it, while someone more cynical once said about a Jew trying to pass himself off as a non-Jew, "You can see the kugel on his face."

Even the German poet Heinrich Heine, who sadly did become an apostate, had this to say, after eating some kugel on Shabbos at the home of a Jewish friend, "It was with a guilty conscience that I ate this holy national dish, which has done more to preserve Judaism than all three issues of the *Zeitschrift* [a magazine put out by a group of nonobservant Jews who wished to "preserve" Judaism by making it more German]."

It was a pity that Heine never ate any of the kugel prepared by the Yid Hakodesh, who once said that any child who ate some of his kugel would never go on the path of falsehood. But should someone stray and then sincerely wish to repent, the kugel can help;

according to the Chozeh of Lublin the thing to do is to serve the kugel by turning it over, so that the soft part is facing up and the hard part facing down, thereby turning harsh judgment to mercy (*Sichoson shel Avdei Avos*, vol. 2, pp. 270, 283).

* * *

The *Shalom Bayis* Kugel

Why do some people have the *minhag* (custom) of eating kugel before the Shabbos day meal? The reason dates back to the days of Rabbi Israel, the Kozhnitzer Maggid.

It once happened that a Jewish couple came to the Kozhnitzer Maggid and said they wanted to divorce. Why? The husband explained that he wanted to eat his Shabbos kugel before the meal, when he still had a good appetite. The wife countered that she had never heard of such thing; in her family, kugel was always eaten as part of the main course. Because they could see no way to resolve the conflict, they decided that divorce was the only option.

The Maggid's wife, who had overheard the conversation, disagreed. She suggested the wife make two kugels, one for after the morning Kiddush and one for the main meal. The husband and wife were delighted with this suggestion and they happily returned home.

When the Kozhnitzer Maggid saw what had happened, he declared, "If eating kugel after Kiddush can bring about *shalom bayis* (marital harmony), I want my children to do this, too."

The Maggid's family took on the *minhag*, and from there the custom spread. So did the name, which is why many people refer to the kugel after Kiddush as the "*Shalom Bayis* Kugel."

* * *

Who Put the *"Yerushalmi"* In *Yerushalmi* Kugel?

A Kiddush in Jerusalem wouldn't be complete without a *Yerushalmi* (Jerusalem) Kugel, but who brought this typically Ashkenazic dish to the Land of Israel?

Some attribute the *"aliyah"* of this kugal that is both sweet and peppery to the followers of the Maggid of Mezeritch, chassidim who settled in the Land of Israel in the 1700s. Others insist that it was followers of the Vilna Gaon, who also arrived during the 18th century, who introduced the kugel to Jerusalem. Fortunately, there is one thing that everyone can agree on: this kugel that successfully makes peace between opposites such as sugar and pepper is definitely a taste of the World to Come.

−2013

Sweet vs. Spicy: The Great Gefilte Debate

Do you like your gefilte fish sweet or peppery? Do you add a little paprika to just about everything you cook? Not so long ago, the spices a Jewish woman used didn't just add flavor — they announced where she and her family were from.

"Tell me what you eat and I will tell you what you are," wrote French epicure Jean Anthelme Brillat-Savarin. While he probably didn't have gefilte fish in mind when he penned those words a few hundred years ago, it was this Shabbos favorite that once proudly announced an Ashkenazic family's roots. If you liked it sugary sweet, you were from Poland or Russia. If you poured on the pepper you were from Lithuania.

What caused this divergence in taste? Sometimes it was the price of the spice — and sometimes it reflected an outlook on life.

On the Sugar Trail

Food historians like to point out that behind any traditional dish lies one important thing: the availability of the ingredients required to make it. Thus, even though our ancestors have been eating latkes (fried pancakes) for thousands of years, they ate potato latkes only after the New World was discovered and potatoes were brought to Europe. Fish was plentiful in many parts of Europe, thanks to the many rivers flowing through the continent and the surrounding seas. But what was added to the fish pot to give the fish flavor depended upon what was available locally.

While it's tempting to think the sweet gefilte fish enjoyed by Polish Jews goes back to when Jews first arrived there in the tenth century, adding sugar only came about when sugar became widely available in the early 19th century. Before that sugar was a luxury item that only the rich could afford.

What brought about the change? In the beginning, the world's sugar came from sugarcane, which was first cultivated in South Asia (e. g., India) and Southeast Asia (e. g., New Guinea and China). While the Ancient World knew about sugar, it was mainly used for medicinal purposes and not to flavor food. During the Medieval period, "sweet salt" was imported to Europe, along with other exotic spices, such as nutmeg, cloves, ginger and pepper, but it remained expensive. Prices only fell with the discovery that sugarcane could be successfully planted in New World territories such as Brazil and the Caribbean islands. This greater availability led to greater affordability, which led in turn to 18th-century Western Europe's sugar craze, where sugar was added to beverages such as tea, coffee and cocoa, as well as jams and cakes.

While the British continued to enjoy an abundance of sugar, by the early 1800s the French were experiencing a sugar shortage. The cause was the Napoleonic Wars, which pitted France against Britain. In what can only be described as a bitter blow to the French, the British blocked Caribbean exports to France, including sugar. Napoleon, never one to give up without a fight, responded to the British blockade by banning sugar imports in 1813. But he knew better than to tell the French people, "Let them eat sugarless cake!" Instead, he encouraged the development of a new manufacturing process: refining sugar beet roots to make sugar.

Rooting for Beets

While both France and Germany became major producers of sugar made from sugar beets during the 1800s, Eastern Europeans weren't entirely left out in the cold. The world's first sugar beet factory opened in 1801 in Silesia, which was then part of Prussia and shared a border with Poland. A few decades later, in 1838 to be exact, Poland opened its very first factory, a beet sugar refinery established by Herman Epstein.

Epstein's factory was small—he was a banker who only "dabbled" in owning factories—but from that small beginning came an industry that remained almost exclusively Jewish until the First World War, when much of Poland's industrial infrastructure was damaged. The sugar industry was primarily in Jewish hands in Ukraine as well, where the Brodsky family alone controlled 25 percent of overall Russian sugar output until World War I. Jews were also heavily involved in Belorussia's sugar industry.

With sugar readily available, and with sugar refining being primarily a Jewish business, it must have seemed almost like a *mitzvah* (commandment) to add sugar to just about everything. Sweet challah? Why not? Sweet noodle kugels? Of course! Sweet and sour stuffed cabbage? How did we ever eat cabbage before?

As for sweet gefilte fish, the question became not whether to add sugar, but how much sugar to add. The fish became so sweet that people needed something to counterbalance all that sugar. Thus, chrain—made from grated horseradish and beet juice—became a frequent accompaniment to the Friday night meal's first course.

Pass the Pepper, Please

While Galician, Romanian and Hungarian Jews also developed a sweet tooth, there was one Jewish stronghold that remained impervious to sugar's charms: Lithuania. Lithuanian Jews preferred their food savory, rather than sweet, and they became known for their peppery gefilte fish and kugels. Although pepper, like many other spices, had been an expensive delicacy in the Ancient and Medieval worlds, in the 1700s the monopoly on importing pepper crumbled and the spice became affordable to even people of just average means.

Lithuanian Jews also liked sour foods, such as iced beet soup with lemon, onions and sour cream, sorrel soup with lemon and sour cream, and fermented pickled cabbage. This great divide in culinary tastes became the stuff of folklore. To the warmhearted, sugar-loving Polisher Jew or Galician, the peppery Litvak lacked true *Yiddisher ta'am,* or authentic Jewish flavor. To the analytical, unemotional Litvak, a love of sweet foods was as suspect as the new sect that had taken root in Poland and Ukraine: Chassidism. Later, scholars of Eastern European Jewry would dub this dispute "the gefilte fish line," an imaginary line that represents no national border, but does accurately reflect the differences between Litvaks and many other Eastern European Jews.

Paint the Food Red

Just as Polish Jews had to wait until the arrival of sugar beet refineries to discover they had a sweet tooth, so too did Hungarian Jews have to wait for the arrival of red bell peppers and chili peppers from the New World to discover that a generous sprinkling of paprika makes just about everything taste better. In the words of Gyula Vegh, director of the Szeged Paprika Museum, in southern Hungary, "We believe Columbus's mission was a success because he came back to Europe with a marvelous spice. He discovered America on the way."

At first the exotic pepper plants were used mainly for ornamental purposes by wealthy noblemen who cultivated them in their gardens. Later, the spice produced from their pods was used as a cure for fever; indeed, in the 1930s Hungarian scientist Albert Szent-Györgyi discovered that paprika is loaded with vitamin C.

It was the Turks who introduced pepper plants to Ottoman Hungary, which they ruled from 1541 to 1699. According to Gil Marks, author of *The Encyclopedia of Jewish Food*, after the Turks left, they left behind the many red pepper plants they had cultivated. Since it was much cheaper to use the paprika from locally grown red pepper plants than to import peppercorns and make black pepper, paprika became the spice of choice.

Paprika—which is the diminutive form of the Slavic word for pepper, *papar*—was made from either bell peppers, chili peppers, or a combination of the two. Originally, all paprika was hot and spicy. But in the 1920s a planter living in Szeged—the capital of Hungarian paprika—found one plant that produced a sweeter fruit. He grafted it onto other plants and sweet paprika was born.

Ironically, because paprika was so widely available, at first upper-class Hungarians refused to use it. The spice used to season the hearty goulash that the peasants ate was much too plebian for supposedly refined tastes. Eventually, though, they couldn't resist those paprika-seasoned goulashes, and paprika became the national spice. Hungary's Jews also embraced the spice, and chicken paprikash became a Shabbos favorite.

Easy Does It

While it was Germany, or Ashkenaz, that gave Eastern European Jews their name, when most people think of "authentic" Ashkenazic cuisine, it's usually not German-Jewish food that comes to mind. With the exception of a dollop of spicy mustard on a frankfurter, German food is rarely overly sweet or spicy. Instead, the seasonings of choice are the gentler parsley, thyme, chives, nutmeg, caraway and the like. When black pepper was used, it was used in small amounts.

But while German-Jewish food may be more subtly spiced, its dishes do find a prominent place on the Jewish table. Take gefilte fish, for instance. Although the great debate about how to season the fish took place in Lithuania and Poland, there wouldn't have been a debate if Franco-German cooks hadn't invented the dish in the late 1300s. Then there are comfort foods such as schnitzel and knodel (dumplings). Finally, the German-Jewish predilection for pickling vegetables and preserving meats — sauerkraut on that kosher hot dog, anyone, or a corned beef sandwich on rye? — helped kosher deli food find an honored place on the American culinary map.

Indeed, it was in the United States that Polish, Lithuanian, Hungarian and German cuisine jumped into the melting pot and emerged as something called "Jewish cooking." It's therefore not unusual today to plan Shabbos meals that include sweet gefilte fish followed by chicken paprikash for dinner, with cholent accompanied by schnitzel and a peppery kugel for lunch.

As for a nosh, there was never a disagreement about that! No matter what dialect of Yiddish was spoken, a glass of tea or cup of coffee and a tempting piece of cake was always a welcome treat.

—September 2015

Courtly and Kosher:
Dinner with Lady Judith Montefiore

Lady Judith Montefiore, one of the richest women of her era, was known for her kind heart and advocacy on behalf of the Jewish people. But few people know that she was also the anonymous "Lady" who authored the first Jewish cookbook to be published in the English language. This cookbook, along with her diaries, gives us a fascinating insight into kosher dining during England's Regency era – an era that was famous for its scrumptious food and elegant dinner parties.

In 1846 the planet Neptune was discovered, the Potato Famine was raging in Ireland, the Liberty Bell cracked, the sewing machine was patented, and the United States went to war with Mexico. It was also the year when an anonymous English "Lady" published the first kosher cookbook in the English language: *The Jewish Manual, or Practical Information in Jewish & Modern Cookery with a Collection of Valuable Recipes & Hints Relating to the Toilette.*

For almost a century the identity of the person who wrote *The Jewish Manual* was a mystery. Then in the year 1983 some Jewish researchers, who were of course searching for something else entirely, came across an article from an October 1862 issue of England's *The Jewish Chronicle*, which discussed a *Yom Kippur* sermon by Britain's then chief rabbi, Rabbi Dr. Nathan Marcus Adler. Rabbi Adler suggested that a fitting memorial to Lady Judith Montefiore, who had recently passed away, would be to set up a fund to defray the dowry costs of a Jewish girl "who has distinguished herself by her unstained moral character." Preference would be given to Jewish girls who had been trained to serve as Jewish cooks, since Lady Judith "wrote a book for Jewish cookery, or at least assisted in its composition."

But if the mystery of the cookbook's author has been solved, the solution creates yet another question: Why would Lady Montefiore—who was a fabulously wealthy woman and presumably had a house full of servants—write a cookbook? Although the lady of the house was expected to supervise the menu and the household accounts, what could someone like Judith Montefiore know or care about the finer details of boiling and braising?

The answer may be found in the age when she lived, a time of great change for England and an era of unprecedented wealth and opulence due to the Industrial Revolution, which created a new class in class-conscious Britain—well-to-do manufacturers, merchants, and financiers (such as her husband, Sir Moses Montefiore). All this created an opportunity for the country's Jews to climb up the social ladder. But that climb had its dangers. The more open society often led to assimilation, and since dining out was practically the national pastime during the nineteenth century, the first entry into "fashionable" non-Jewish circles was usually at the non-kosher dinner table.

The Jewish home wasn't immune to the influences of the "street" either. As Lady Montefiore laments in the Editor's Preface to her cookbook, wealthy Jewish girls were no longer being instructed in the domestic arts: "The various acquirements, which in the present day are deemed essential to female education, rarely leave much time or inclination for the humble study of household affairs; and it not unfrequently happens, that the mistress of a family understands little more concerning the dinner table over which she presides, than the graceful arrangement of the flowers which adorn it; thus she is incompetent to direct her servant, upon whose inferior judgment and taste she is obliged to depend."

The Jewish Manual was therefore an attempt to "guide the young Jewish housekeeper in the luxury and economy of 'The Table,' on which so much of the pleasure of social intercourse depends"—i.e., teach the young woman some useful culinary tricks—and show that one could keep kosher and still eat well!

When Do We Eat?

The remainder of the evening we passed in reading and walking, and at ten o'clock our friend came according to appointment to supper, which consisted of a roast duck, green peas, potatoes, and a boiled gooseberry pudding, and an excellent bottle of red port. We passed till twelve o'clock in conversation at which we took leave of our friend, and after returning thanks to God, retired to rest. —Diary of Lady Montefiore

In an age when diversions and entertainments were less plentiful, dinner was often a person's main social event and therefore the eagerly awaited highlight of the day. So what time was dinner served?

At the beginning of the nineteenth century dinner was usually eaten sometime between two and three o'clock in the afternoon. The early hour allowed people to take advantage of natural sunlight to light the dining area. (Candles were expensive!) It also enabled people who lived in the country to return safely home before nightfall, when the roads lit only by moonlight became dangerous. By the end of the first decade, though, fashionable London was sitting down to the dinner table at around eight o'clock at night (the price of candles wasn't a concern for the very rich) and the middle class slowly followed suit, with dinner being served sometime between four and six o'clock. Of course, Jewish families would eat their evening Shabbos meal after nightfall, regardless of the fashions of the times, and so for at least one night of the week they would eat their meal by the glow of candlelight.

In Lady Montefiore's personal diary, which she began on her wedding day—June 10, 1812—she often mentions who she dined with and what she ate. She also discloses that she much preferred small dinner parties where the guests were family members and close friends. But as the wife of Sir Moses Montefiore she would be expected to entertain on a more lavish scale. What might she have served at one of her dinners?

Since one's table was considered to be a symbol of a person's wealth, the answer can be summed up in one word: lots!

The meal always began with soup, and an etiquette guidebook of the time, *True Politeness: A Handbook of Etiquette for Ladies*, advises to never refuse it. "If you do not eat it," writes the author, "you can toy with it until it is followed by fish. ... Soup must be eaten from the side, not the point of the spoon; and in eating it, be careful not to make a noise, by strongly inhaling the breath: this habit is excessively vulgar; you cannot eat too quietly."

The first course also included fish, which was followed by several meat and vegetable dishes. In fact, anywhere from five to 25 different dishes were served at this course, depending upon the wealth and rank of the hosts. The serving dishes were placed in the middle of the dining table and passed round to the guests, and since there was so much food a guest wasn't expected to sample every dish. And that was just the first course; after it was cleared away there was more to come.

The second course was much like the first, but without the soup. Various meat and fowl dishes were served, which were usually accompanied by several savory and sweet side dishes. While the main part of the meal would end here for most people, the very wealthy might serve ten courses or more on special occasions. For instance, at the coronation banquet for King George IV in the year 1820, the dinner menu for the 300 invited guests included 20 first courses, 22 main courses, 31 desserts, and approximately 1,000 different side dishes.

After the main courses were concluded, the tablecloth was removed and dessert was served. The dessert course served at the dining room table was usually a light repast of pastries, fruit, nuts, and ices. For those who were still hungry, after dinner the group withdrew to the "withdrawing" (or drawing) room, where tea and coffee were served accompanied by more cakes and other desserts.

If the guests lingered until late in the evening, a cold buffet supper (also referred to as "the tea board") would be brought out. This meal might include cold meats, more savories, more desserts and, of course, more tea. The removal of the tea board was a polite way for hosts to signal that it was time for their guests to go home.

What Do We Eat?

We ordered dinner to be ready at four o'clock ... which consisted of boiled soles and peas, and beef-steaks and potatoes, ale and a pint of wine. — Diary of Lady Montefiore

The number of dishes served at even a small family dinner shows that nineteenth-century Englishmen had a wider variety of foods available to them than we might suppose. A middle-class family could afford to eat beef or mutton at least once a day. Vegetables such as carrots, peas, turnips, and onions were in plentiful supply, as were potatoes, which were once considered to be poisonous but had become a staple of the English diet.

Since this was the period when Britannia was beginning her rule of the Seven Seas, new and exciting spices such as nutmeg, cardamom, saffron, ginger, and cloves were being added to dishes, along with pepper, which had been a delicacy a few centuries earlier. Beverages such as tea, coffee, and chocolate had also become affordable, as well as the sugar needed to sweeten them.

However, preserving food was still a problem and the fish and meat that appeared on the table would rarely meet the standard of freshness that we're accustomed to today. And since a recipe for a single cake or pudding might call for a dozen eggs, the cholesterol level of the average person must have been extraordinarily high.

But Is It Kosher?

In addition to a fondness for eggs, cooks of that era loved to lavish all sorts of dishes with thick sauces made from cream and butter (perhaps to disguise the taste of the less-than-fresh fish and meat). Those sauces obviously posed a problem for the Jewish hostess who kept a kosher kitchen. Lady Montefiore's cookbook addresses the issue by providing alternative recipes for things like "A Fish Sauce Without Butter," a "Mushroom Sauce" that leaves out the cream, and a "Sauce Without Butter for a Boiled Pudding" (boiled puddings, which could be either savory or sweet, were a popular accompaniment to meat dishes).

The cookbook also gives us a glimpse into the uphill struggle that people like Lady Montefiore faced when it came to convincing their fellow Jews that one could maintain a kosher kitchen and serve all the most up-to-date dishes. Under the entry for Veloute and Bechamel, two popular sauces of the time, she writes:

"These preparations are so frequently mentioned in modern cookery, that we shall give the receipts for them, although they are not appropriate for the Jewish kitchen. Veloute is a fine white sauce, made by reducing a certain quantity of well-flavoured consomme or stock, over a charcoal fire, and mixing it with boiling cream, stirring it carefully till it thickens.

"Bechamel is another sort of fine white stock, thickened with cream, there is more flavouring in this than the former, the stock is made of veal, with some of the smoked meats used in English kitchens, butter, mace, onion, mushrooms, bay leaf, nutmeg, and a little salt. An excellent substitute for these sauces can in Jewish kitchens be made in the following way:

"Take some veal broth flavored with smoked beef, and the above named seasonings, then beat up two or three yolks of eggs, with a little of the stock and a spoonful of potatoe flour, stir this into the broth, until it thickens, it will not be quite as white, but will be excellent."

An even greater challenge was to find a palatable substitute for the dish that was all the rage in the early decades of the nineteenth century: Turtle Soup.

Perhaps future generations will look back on our generation's current craze for sushi and scratch their heads, just as we can only wonder about the English madness for Turtle Soup. But the fact remains that no dinner party could be considered first rate without this exotic dish. Turtles had to be imported from the Cayman Islands, located in the Caribbean, and so the soup was very expensive to make—a detail that probably contributed a great deal to its popularity since during the Regency period aristocratic hostesses vied to outdo one another to show off their wealth.

Of course, the cost didn't matter to the hostess who kept kosher since turtles, no matter where they come from, are *treif* (not kosher). So what could the Jewish hostess do? Actually, the kosher-keeping hostess was in the same boat as middle-class non-Jewish women who couldn't afford the real thing. Therefore, a recipe for Mock Turtle Soup was developed which used a calf's head instead of turtle to give the soup its rich distinctive flavor.

Lady Montefiore included this modified version in her cookbook, thereby ensuring that her contemporaries could give a dinner party that was both unquestionably fashionable and one hundred percent kosher.

—December 2010

SHYLOCK, FAGIN & CO.

Shakespeare on Trial

Shylock, the world's most despised moneylender, is once again sharpening his knife in a new production of The Merchant of Venice *that is playing in New York City's Central Park. Do we need this, during a summer when the Jewish people have enough problems on their plate? Or can a case be made for the Bard of Avon and his troubling play?*

The lights come up on a darkened stage, revealing a courtroom. Standing in the prisoner's dock is a gentleman, about 50 years of age, balding, sporting a thin mustache, and wearing a doublet.

> **Lawyer:** Your name, please?
> **Gentleman:** William Shakespeare.
> **Lawyer:** Your profession?
> **Shakespeare:** Playwright.
> **Lawyer:** Are you the author of a play called *The Merchant of Venice*?
> **Shakespeare:** I say so. But there are those who claim my plays were really written by Christopher Marlowe, or the Earl of Oxford, or a few others.

The Crowd seated in the gallery laughs appreciatively. The Judge pounds his gavel and calls for order.

> **Lawyer:** Assuming that you are the author, as most educated people do believe today, why did you write this play?
> **Shakespeare:** To make people laugh. It's a comedy.

Shakespeare removes a bright red wig and a big false red nose from his doublet, puts them on, and makes a face at the Crowd, which roars with laughter. The Judge pounds furiously with his gavel, until the courtroom is silent.

Lawyer: So you think it's funny that your character, Shylock, has become the world's symbol for the supposedly heartless, villainous Jew? You admit that your play is anti-Semitic and that you, Mr. Shakespeare, are an anti-Semite?

Shakespeare stares at the Lawyer, stunned. Then he relaxes and turns to the Crowd and says:

Shakespeare: Gentlemen, what would you have me do? Laugh at my losses? Ignore my disgrace? Hath not a Playwright eyes? Hath not a Playwright hands, organs, dimensions, senses, affections, passions? If another author writes a play that's a hit, shall I not copy it? If another theatre's audience is tickled by a Jew, shall I not tickle my audience, too? The way to box office success my rivals taught me, and all I did was better their instruction.

Blackout.

All the World's a Courtroom

William Shakespeare, the Elizabethan poet and dramatist, is considered by most people to be the greatest playwright of all time. Although it's true that not everything he wrote was a masterpiece — his career spanned about a quarter of a century and he wrote at least 37 plays, 154 sonnets, and two narrative poems — at his worst the Bard of Avon, as he is often called, is still equal to, if not better than, his contemporaries. At his most problematic, he is more entertaining and thought-provoking than the vast majority of dramatists who have set pen to page.

And therein lies the rub. Because the same Shakespeare who gave the world the brooding Hamlet and the tragic King Lear also gave the world a Jew named Shylock — and this portrayal of the Jew as an *uber* usurer who won't stop even at murder to take his revenge still haunts us, Jew and non-Jew alike.

And therein lies another rub. Because even though the plot of *The Merchant of Venice* is a shaky structure cobbled together from several ill-fitting sources, the play is still one of Shakespeare's most popular. Every year "Shylock, a Jew" makes his ghastly appearance in classrooms around the globe. Every year some actor somewhere is sharpening his knife, on stage, in preparation for receiving his "pound of flesh."

This summer one of those stages is located in New York City's Central Park, where the New York Shakespeare Festival has mounted a new production of the play starring the Hollywood actor Al Pacino in the role of Shylock. Mr. Pacino, who visited a chassidic shul in Boro Park as part of his preparation for the role, has received generally glowing reviews.

But do we need this "praise"? In a summer where the world is demanding an international investigation into Israel's conduct during the Gaza-bound flotilla raid, and where a United States court has sentenced Sholom Rubashkin to a 27-year prison term that even many non-Jewish lawyers and law professors believe is too severe, do we really need to see the spectacle of another Jew—albeit a literary figure—hauled before a court and demonized?

Should we not, instead, insist upon an international investigation into the harm inflicted upon the Jewish people by Mr. William Shakespeare? And, if he is found guilty, should we not insist upon a stiff prison sentence, preferably in solitary confinement, for his play *The Merchant of Venice* and the play's villain, Shylock?

I interviewed a few expert witnesses, to see if the Jewish people have a case.

"A Merry Sport" or Deadly Seriously?

For those who missed reading the play, here's a brief synopsis: Antonio, the merchant of Venice that is referred to in the play's title, wants to lend 3,000 ducats to his friend Bassanio, who needs the money to make a "*shidduch*" with a wealthy Venetian heiress named Portia. Since Antonio's own money is tied up in merchandise that is at sea, he borrows the money from Shylock, a Jewish moneylender. In "merry sport," Shylock makes a strange deal: if Antonio defaults on the loan, Shylock will receive one pound of Antonio's flesh as payment, instead.

Meanwhile Shylock's daughter, Jessica, elopes with a non-Jew. When news arrives that Antonio's ships have been lost at sea, an angry Shylock demands his payment and his revenge upon the Christian world. Shylock takes his case to court, but he loses. As punishment he is forced to convert to Christianity and forfeit his money. The play ends "happily" with the news that Antonio's ships have arrived safely at port.

The Merchant of Venice was written sometime between the years 1595-1598. England's Jews were expelled from that country in 1290, some 300 years before the play was written. They only returned to England in the mid-1600s, about 40 years after Shakespeare's death. A community of crypto-Jews was living in London while Shakespeare was busy writing his plays, but it's not known if he had any contact with them. So what kind of knowledge could Shakespeare have had of Jews?

He would have known about older works of English literature, which invariably cast their Jewish characters in a negative light. England was the home of early blood libels, for instance, which were kept alive in a variety of "histories" and popular ballads. And a vilified Judas character made frequent appearances on the medieval stage. Portrayed in a ridiculous, grotesque manner, he was garbed in a costume that became the standard for Jewish characters down to Shakespeare's day: a fiery red wig and beard, and a long nose of the same color.

The playwright also most likely heard about Jews living in other countries. English diplomats and merchants would have brought back news of wealthy Jewish businessmen living in the Ottoman Empire, as well as the Portuguese *anusim* (crypto-Jews) based in the Netherlands, who dominated the spice trade. In fact, many English literature scholars believe that the Jewish villain of Christopher Marlowe's play *The Jew of Malta*, which was produced a few years before *The Merchant of Venice*, was based upon Don Yosef Nasi, the wealthy and powerful nephew of one of Portugal's most famous crypto-Jews, Dona Gracia.

Englishmen of Shakespeare's day also would have been riveted by a sensational trial that took place in 1594 involving a New Christian originally from Portugal, Dr. Rodrigo Lopez, who was accused of plotting to poison Queen Elizabeth I. During his trial, his judges referred to him as "that vile Jew." When he stood on the executioner's block and protested that he was innocent of the charges, as well as a true Christian, the crowd jeered.

It was into this poisoned atmosphere that Shylock first saw the light of day. What made Shakespeare write the play? Was Shakespeare, an astute businessman, just cashing in on the Jew-hating craze that had swept London thanks to the Lopez trial and the runaway success of *The Jew of Malta*? Or was he an anti-Semite, eager to do his bit to help fan the flames of anti-Jewish sentiment? Or was he actually appalled by the frenzy and so he wrote a play that would show the world a different kind of Jew — a Jew who was human, like Christians, and, to borrow a line from *King Lear*, "more sinned against than sinning"?

We call the first witness, Victoria Buckley.

The Turks Are Coming!

Victoria Buckley is Associate Tutor and DPhil Researcher at the University of Sussex, England, where her area of research is Shakespeare and Jacobean politics and culture. During our initial correspondence, where I raised the question of Shakespeare's possible anti-Semitism, she pointed out an important and sometimes overlooked detail in discussions of the play: for the English Christian audience of Shakespeare's era, any "other" was viewed with distrust. In a follow-up email, she expanded upon this point.

Victoria Buckley: During Shakespeare's lifetime, knowledge about the world beyond England exploded, due to trade, exploration, immigration, and colonisation. But with this knowledge came anxiety. Unfamiliar cultures and people had to somehow be assimilated into the English psyche, while at the same time England had to protect her sense of national identity and security. "Others" — Moroccans, Turks, Moors, Indians, Egyptians, the Irish, Jews, Gypsies — were suspicious, alluring, frightening, evil, heathen, exotic. And this push and pull, this attraction and revulsion, was contested and negotiated on Shakespeare's stage.

But can it be said that the Jews were in a special category, which is perhaps why Shylock is forced to convert to Christianity at the end of the play?

Victoria Buckley: Most depictions of Jews on the London stage at this time might be viewed as "negative," but Jews weren't necessarily treated differently from any other minority. Indeed their status was often interchangeable with that of the Moor or Turk. An excellent example of this is found in Robert Daborne's *Christian Turned Turk* (1612). Daborne parodies the Jew Benwash, but his treatment of him does not fundamentally differ from his treatment of the Turks.

Theatregoers in Elizabethan England came from all walks of life. The job of any London playwright, therefore, was to cater to as wide a taste (and education) as possible. Shylock's conversion to Christianity might be seen as a simple plot denouement at the end of the play; he converts from the "other" to a Christian; the loose ends are tied up, and everybody is happy.

This ending would have suited the groundlings heckling in the pit whose knowledge of Jews might perhaps have been limited to the scandal and gossip circulating in the aftermath of the recent Lopez trial. But if we read *The Merchant of Venice* as a more complex and critical play, then it could be argued that Shylock's conversion is *ironic*; his subjugation at the hands of Antonio and the Venetians throughout the play serves to highlight the contrast between stereotypical negative notions of the Jew, and the perceived "mercy" and "generosity" of the Christian. These supposed differences run throughout the play, and yet it is in the character of Shylock, not Antonio, that we see the essence of purity and truth.

If the actor playing Shylock was wearing a bright red wig and a long red nose, would an Elizabethan audience have been able to look past this grotesque disguise and see this essence of purity and truth?

Victoria Buckley: That's a very good question. It's true that, to an extent, any stereotypical costumes or props on Shakespeare's stage would have made it much harder for him to portray Shylock with any degree of sympathy. But it's worth bearing in mind that the irony in the play can in fact be *highlighted* by the use of stereotypical props or apparel. Shylock may appear to some a seemingly ridiculous figure on the stage at first glance. But as the plot weaves its way towards the climax, it seems clear to me that Shakespeare is exploring and critiquing anti-Semitic prejudice through the character of Shylock.

So you would say that Shakespeare wasn't anti-Semitic?

Victoria Buckley: Opinion continues to differ on the issue of whether Shakespeare and *The Merchant of Venice* are anti-Semitic in nature. One of the problems of course is that of applying contemporary notions of anti-Semitism to early modern thinking. Certainly there were those in Shakespeare's London who would have been suspicious and hostile to Jews. But there was as much a lack of toleration between Protestants and Catholics and indeed Puritans, in some sectors of society, as there was towards minorities.

My own opinion is that far from being anti-Semitic, Shakespeare was in fact challenging prejudice in *The Merchant of Venice*. He takes the fear of "others," in this case, Jews, as his starting point, but utilises this to present a world in which corruption is rife within *all* communities. The world of *The Merchant of Venice* is certainly dark, but that darkness does not emanate from Shylock. It emanates from the play's themes: the rise of capitalism and the greed of the merchant class. Ultimately the play is less about the concept of the "other," and much more about the corrupting influence of hard-bitten commerce.

"Which is the merchant here? and which the Jew?"

As Victoria Buckley has pointed out, the picture that Shakespeare painted of Venice, which had been an important center of trade and commerce since the Middle Ages, was not a pretty one. Why might Shakespeare have decided to explore the dark underside of the glittering Venetian economy?

England during the Elizabethan era was just starting to make the transition from a feudal, land-based economy to a commercial one. In a highly controversial move, moneylending became legal in England in the mid-1500s. Therefore, just as the average Englishman had a distrust of the Turk or the Moor, he also had a distrust of the new class of home-grown merchants who were springing up on England's shores.

British critic John Gross, author of *Shylock: A Legend and Its Legacy*, notes that Shakespeare's villainous moneylender could have just as easily been a Christian. But in an era where the word "usurer" was synonymous with the word "Jew," was it really possible to cast a Christian in such an ignoble role? Wasn't Shakespeare already pushing the envelope, so to speak, by casting a Christian in the role of a merchant, a profession that also had Jewish connotations?

According to Jennifer Rich, a faculty member of Hofstra University, in an article titled *The Merchant Formerly Known as Jew*, one of the tasks of the play is to make the profession of merchant "kosher" by stripping away any association with Jews. The "knife" that is used to perform this delicate operation is none other than Shylock. In this reading of the play, when the Jewish Shylock is forced to convert to Christianity, it has less to do with religious dogma than a need to pave the way for a new and improved merchant/moneylender — as embodied by the Christian Antonio.

Anti- or Anti-Anti-Semitic?

While arguments about the "other" and England's transition from a feudal to a capitalistic economy might make for a fascinating classroom discussion, there's no escaping the fact that Shakespeare meant for the play to be performed—and in performance Shylock's Jewishness can't be avoided. Although Shylock appears in only five of the play's scenes, he is referred to as a "Jew" some 60 times. The word is not used as a compliment.

Yet after two centuries of actors playing Shylock as either a villain or a buffoon, in 1814 an English actor by the name of Edmund Kean decided to exchange the red wig for a black one, the slovenly caftan for more contemporary garb, and present his Shylock as a persecuted martyr who tries to take his revenge only because of the circumstances that have been forced upon him by Venice's Christian society. What caused the change?

Jews began to return to England in the mid-1600s. They didn't have full rights, but England was hospitable enough to allow for a rather rapid assimilation. One of the byproducts of that assimilation

was that London Jews of the 1800s became avid—and vocal—
theatergoers, who weren't afraid to express their disapproval of a
play that cast Jews in an unflattering light. For instance, a riot broke
out in 1802 when Jewish members of the audience took offense at a
Jewish reference in a play called *Family Quarrels*, while an 1818
revival of *The Jew of Malta* so enraged Jewish theatergoers that they
boycotted London theatres for the rest of the season.

Was worry about the box office receipts the only reason why
productions of *The Merchant of Venice* began to present Shylock in a
sympathetic light? Probably not. But a generally sympathetic
portrayal of Shylock continued into the 1900s, and even famous
actors of the Yiddish stage tackled the role.

Today, after the Holocaust, that trend continues. As their
predecessors did before them, modern-day directors will often add
scenes in an attempt to make the play more palatable to their
audiences. For instance, in a 1970 National Theatre production,
Kaddish is sung offstage in the final scene, an audio hint that this
Shylock has committed suicide rather than convert to Christianity.
The production currently playing in New York's Central Park gives
Shylock a different fate. The director has added a scene that shows
Shylock being baptized—and defiantly putting his yarmulke back
on his head after the dunking.

Do such rewrites, which are usually well received by critics and
audiences alike, provide convincing evidence that Shakespeare's
play is sympathetic to Jews? Or are they merely band-aides
designed to protect overly sensitive members of the audience from
the play's anti-Semitic sting?

We posed the question to Anthony Julius, deputy chairman of
the British law firm Mishcon de Reya. Mr. Julius is perhaps best
known in the Jewish community for his successful representation of
historian Deborah Lipstadt in a libel action brought against her by
Holocaust denier David Irving. Julius is also the author of *Trials of
the Diaspora: A History of Anti-Semitism in England* (Oxford University
Press), which includes a discussion of how Jews have been
represented in English literature.

In his book, he quotes a nineteenth-century American who
asked, "How many thousands of Christians have been prejudiced
against the whole tribe of Israel by Shakespeare's Shylock, though

they have never seen a Jew?"   In our telephone conversation, he reveals his own thoughts about the matter.

Anthony Julius: I think Shylock has been an affliction for the Jews for 400 years. The term "to be a Shylock" is still in contemporary usage. Shylock represents a character-prism from which actual Jews still struggle to escape.

So would you say that The Merchant of Venice *is an anti-Semitic play?*

Anthony Julius: It's both anti-Semitic and anti-anti-Semitic. It has an aspect that's hostile to Jews, and it has an aspect that's hostile toward hostility toward Jews. Most productions of the play don't show both these dynamics. They either emphasize the anti-Semitic aspects or try to turn Shylock into a sympathetic character. I prefer to recognize that Shakespeare holds the two aspects in tension.

In equal tension?

Anthony Julius: I think the play is more anti-Semitic than anti-anti-Semitic.

Can we therefore infer that Shakespeare was anti-Semitic?

Anthony Julius: You don't go to a work of literature to find out where is the author's heart. You can't infer through any particular reading of the literature what Shakespeare thought. History has portrayed Shakespeare as a secret Catholic and a staunch Protestant, as a Republican and as a Monarchist. He embraces all those totalities.

If Shylock is still an affliction for the Jews, should we want to ban the play?

Anthony Julius: I'm absolutely against censorship. It's right that we should expose ourselves to the play. It allows a discussion to take place. But the play has got to be taught in the right way. The play will always be with us. You can't wish it away.

Dark, Very Dark

There is at least one Jewish literary critic and ardent Shakespeare admirer who disagrees with the notion that *Merchant* is both anti- and anti-anti-Semitic: Harold Bloom, who has taught at Yale University for more than half a century. In his book *Shakespeare and the Invention of the Human*, he writes: "One would have to be blind, deaf, and dumb not to recognize that Shakespeare's grand, equivocal comedy *The Merchant of Venice* is nevertheless a profoundly anti-Semitic work."

Indeed, there's no question that when the Nazis looked into the play, they saw it as the perfect vehicle for disseminating fear and loathing of Jews to the German people. In the 1930s alone there were some 50 productions.

But even though Mr. Bloom has gone on record as saying it would have been better for the Jewish people if Shakespeare had never written the play, he doesn't go so far as to accuse the Bard of being anti-Semitic. Instead, he wonders "if Shylock did not cause Shakespeare more discomfort than we now apprehend."

So it appears that Mr. Shakespeare, if not his play, is not guilty of our charges. But in the spirit of rewriting the play's ending, I'd like to add a revisionist final scene of my own. Because even though the history of the Jewish people might be tragic, we are not a tragic people. And so in my production Shylock doesn't submit to baptism, nor does he take his life with his own hand. When Shylock leaves the Venetian courtroom, he boards a ship bound for Turkey. There he is welcomed by Dona Gracia and Don Yosef Nasi, who help him rebuild his life, both materially and spiritually. A repentant Jessica joins him, and All's Well That Ends Well. But that's already a different story.

* * *

Was the Contract Valid?

During the past 100 years or so, there have been a few attempts to analyze the contract made between Antonio and Shylock to see if it was a binding contract according to Jewish law. One of those who provided an analysis was Rabbi Shlomo Yosef Zevin, a founder of the *Encyclopedia Talmudica*. But after analyzing the various legal issues, Rav Zevin came to a surprising conclusion:

"The power of life that resides in the body of a human being is not his own—it does not belong to this person, that is the crucial point. ...When one sells or gives or mortgages the flesh of his own body in order that it be cut up for someone else, this resembles one who sells an object that is not his own. Hashem (God) gave life to a person in order that he uses it. It was never given to him to do with it whatever he wishes. The right to take this life back is given only to the One who gave it in the first place—Hashem."

Rabbi Zevin based this concept on many sources, among them the Rambam, the *Shulchan Aruch Choshen Mishpat* 420.21, and *Shulchan Aruch Harav* Vol.5 *Hilchos Nizkei Guf Venefesh* 4.

Therefore, according to Rabbi Zevin, the contract signed between Antonio and Shylock is invalid for the simple reason that Antonio never had the right to offer the flesh of his own body as collateral to be used in case of delay in repaying the loan.

—June 2010

Old Clo'!

Two hundred years ago any person living in London – including a young writer named Charles Dickens – could have told you the city was filled with Jews who spoke with funny accents and wore funny clothes. So today why is it that almost no one knows there were Ashkenazic Jews living in London during the Regency era? When the Netanya branch of the Association of Americans & Canadians in Israel (AACI) asked me to speak about Regency London's Jews, I jumped at the chance to see if this mystery could be solved.

I have to admit that the topic of London's Jewish community during the Regency era is a topic that is very dear to my heart. And it's not just because I'm the author of the Jewish Regency Mystery Series, which is about Regency London's Ashkenazic Jewish community. Rather, it has to do with the fact that during the course of my marketing of these books to the public, I discovered an amazing thing: most people don't know very much about this chapter in Jewish history — and what people think they do know is generally wrong.

Why do I say this? The reason is because whenever I say my mystery series is about the Ashkenazic community — Jews who came to England from places like Germany, Holland, and Central and Eastern Europe — I invariably receive a reprimand that there were no Ashkenazic Jews living in England during the early years of the nineteenth century; or if there were, they were very few in number.

In those days, I am told, the Jewish community consisted mainly of Sephardic Jews, the Jews from Spain and Portugal.

And yet by the end of the 1700s, when there were some 15,000-18,000 Jews living in England, only about 12 percent of them were Sephardim. The others were Ashkenazim.

Why do most people know so little about the Ashkenazic Jews of this time?

First, a Little History

Although Jews may have lived in Britain during Roman times, the first recorded evidence of a Jewish presence in England isn't until 1066, when some Jews arrived there along with William the Conqueror. The Jews weren't allowed to stay very long, for in 1290 they were expelled from England by King Edward I.

Today we know that during the Tudor and Elizabethan eras, there were communities of *anusim* living in England—these were Jews from Spain and Portugal who had converted to Christianity but still practiced Judaism secretly. But it wasn't until the mid-1600s that Jews were allowed back in England and allowed to live there openly as Jews.

As many of us will recall, a Sephardic rabbi from Amsterdam named Menasseh ben Israel came to England in 1655 to petition Oliver Cromwell to officially allow the Jews to return. Although official permission wasn't granted, unofficially Jews were permitted to live in England a year later, in 1656.

Some of these new English Jews were actually former *anusim* already living in England. They were joined by small groups of Sephardic Jews from Spain, Portugal and Holland, and by the late 1600s, the Sephardic community had grown to about 400 souls. They established a synagogue on Creechurch Lane, which later moved to Bevis Marks, to the site where the famous Bevis Marks Synagogue still stands until today.

What most of us won't recall, because apparently it's rarely mentioned, is that Ashkenazic Jews came to England, too. It's not clear when exactly the first groups began to arrive, but according to the Anglo-Jewish historian Cecil Roth we can find in the burial records from that Sephardic synagogue on Creechurch Lane the names of a few Ashkenazic Jews as early as the 1670s. The reason, of course, why there would have been Ashkenazic Jews praying at a Sephardic synagogue is that the Jewish community was still too small to support two congregations, two cemeteries, and other institutions needed for a fully functioning community.

Another population misconception is that during these early years of the Anglo-Jewish community, every Sephardic Jew was a wealthy merchant, and every Ashkenazic Jew was a poor *schlepper* in need of communal assistance.

That wasn't 100 percent true. One Ashkenazic Jew that we know a fair amount about is Benjamin Levi, a Jew from Hamburg, who arrived in England in about 1669. At that time, Hamburg was home to many wealthy Jewish gem merchants, one of which was Benjamin's father. Benjamin apparently did pretty well in England, because in 1697 he was one of only 12 Jews licensed to work as a broker at the Royal Exchange. He was also an original subscriber to the Bank of England when that institution was established in 1694.

There were other Ashkenazic Jews who came to England at this time with a little capital and did well. But there were also enough poor Ashkenazic Jews flowing into England that the Sephardic Jews—who were, by and large, wealthy merchants and traders—got nervous. In the 1670s they began to pay for the return passage back to the European Continent for some of these Jews to get rid of them, so they wouldn't become a burden on the community.

But by about 1690, there were enough Azhkenzaic Jews living in London, which is where most of the Jews lived, for them to form their own *kehillah* (community). Their first synagogue, which later became the Great Synagogue, consisted of just a few rooms in Duke's Place, located in London's East End. The community acquired land for a cemetery in about 1697. The Sephardim moved their synagogue to Bevis Marks in 1701. Therefore, by the start of the 18th century, both communities had a solid foundation for building a *kehillah*.

There's obviously much more that can be said about these early years after the Readmission. But since it's not our topic, interested readers can turn to Cecil Roth's very thorough *The History of the Great Synagogue*, which is available online, at no charge, as part of the Susser Archive.

The Regency Era

In 1690, the total Jewish population in England was only about 400 souls. By 1734, that number had jumped to about 6,000 Jews, most of whom were Ashkenazim. And by the late 1700s, the Jewish population had soared to somewhere between 15,000-18,000 souls.

Obviously this dramatic increase didn't happen only due to natural growth. Jews were pouring into England and, again, they were mainly Ashkenazim. Many of them were poor Jews who were fleeing from the harsh political and economic conditions that were prevalent on the European Continent at that time. However, these new arrivals quickly discovered that the streets of London were not paved with gold. Indeed, according to the reckoning of one person living at the time, there were only about 50 members of the entire Ashkenazic community who could be considered well off. The rest were poor.

But even though the poor were mainly Ashkenazic Jews, by the late 1700s poverty had also become a problem for the Sephardic community. According to the secretary of the Bevis Marks synagogue, at least half of the Sephardic community was also poor.

If everybody was so poor, why did Jews keep coming to England? We have to keep in mind that despite the poverty, conditions in England were much better for Jews than on the Continent. For instance, even though new immigrants tended to congregate around Duke's Place, in London's East End, where the synagogues were located, there was no official ghetto where they had to live. And there was no organized government-sponsored violence against the Jewish community, although individual incidents did occur.

On the other hand, Jews, like Catholics and other religious minorities living in England, could not become a citizen of England with full political rights. There were also all sorts of economic restrictions for foreign-born residents of England that were in addition to the political restrictions. For instance, a foreign-born person couldn't buy property or engage in the lucrative trade with the colonies that was making so many people rich. There were also special taxes that a foreign-born resident had to pay. The only way for a foreign-born Jew to get around some of these economic restrictions was to purchase what was called a royal letter of patent, which allowed him to become something called a free denizen. Needless to say, someone already had to be pretty wealthy to be able to afford to do this.

Those who weren't wealthy had to settle for a more humble occupation. While some Jews who had a few skills were able to become skilled craftsmen or open a shop, many of the new arrivals had to start at the bottom of the economic ladder, which meant becoming an Old Clothes Man — that archetypal figure who roamed the streets of London during this time.

Anything to Sell?

If we could go back to Regency London, we wouldn't hear people shouting into their cell phones. But in the morning, at least, we would hear lots of shouting in the streets. We'd hear the potato seller shouting out about his fresh potatoes, and the fish seller announcing he had mackerel to sell, and the tinker, banging on his frying pan, inquiring if the lady of the house had anything to mend. And we'd hear the cry of the Old Clothes Man, who bought used clothing and often bartered cheap trinkets in return.

The Jewish Old Clothes Man was a ubiquitous sight in Regency England. The reason was that both the Sephardic and the Ashkenazic communities saw this "profession" as a way to give poor new arrivals to England an opportunity to make a living. Being a peddler didn't require much skill or capital, so the *kehillah* would give the newcomer a little pack of cheap goods, or old clothes, and in this way set the person up in business. Some of the new immigrants received a "sales territory" in London, while others were sent to places outside of London, where they eventually formed the nucleus of England's "out of town" Jewish communities.

These people worked long hours, often from sunup to sundown. Their rounds might be in the poorest parts of town or the wealthiest, because in the days when everything was recycled, rather than thrown away, due to the high cost of goods, everyone—rich and poor, alike—had something they no longer wanted, but which was something that someone else wanted to buy.

Therefore, even though the Old Clothes Man himself might have been at the bottom of the economic heap, the "rag trade" as a whole was a huge business. In the late afternoon thousands of people would gather at the Old Clothes Exchange, located near Rosemary Lane, and there they would buy and sell, doing thousands of pounds of business every day as the goods collected in the morning changed hands and were resold, sometimes several times within the same day.

Whereas much of the business was 100 percent above board, there was one rule that gave the profession an unsavory reputation, which was this: you never asked where the goods came from. For instance, a buyer never asked the seller for his name or for the name or address of where the seller had acquired the goods. It therefore was conceivable that stolen goods got mixed in with the things that were legally obtained, and that a person could unknowingly buy a stolen object, which he would then resell later.

The Inspiration for Fagin?

London was a study in contrasts during this period. On the one hand, there was a small group of fabulously wealthy aristocrats and financiers and the like, and on the other hand there was a very large group of people who were very poor. In those days before government assistance programs and, we should add, an organized police force, which only came about in 1829, many poor people turned to crime as a way to survive. Others, however, saw crime as a way to make a pretty good living, and one of the people in this second category was one of the most famous criminals of the period, a Jewish man named Ikey Solomon.

Solomon was born in 1785 in London's East End, on Gravel Lane. He started out as a petty thief, got caught and was sent to jail. When he got out he decided there had to be a better way to do business. He therefore opened a shop near Petticoat Lane, which was either a jewelry shop or pawn shop, it's not exactly clear, and the shop was his cover for receiving stolen goods from a group of thieves who did the dirty work for him. He was arrested several times, but somehow always managed to escape both deportation and hanging—the usual sentences for his type of crime—until 1827, when he was caught red-handed with these stolen goods: 6 watches, 3½ yards of woollen cloth, 17 shawls, 12 pieces of Valentia cloth, lace, bobbinet (a kind of imitation lace), caps and other articles.

Now, perhaps this doesn't sound like much of a haul to us. But we have to remember that in those days, salaries for the working classes were a pittance and things like clothing and food were a small fortune. For instance, an experienced laborer would have had to work a full week to purchase the wool needed to make a suit of clothes; finding someone to sew it, the buttons, etc., would have been extra. Therefore, if you were a relatively poor person and someone broke into your house and stole your jacket—or even your shirt or your nightcap—it could be a real tragedy.

Ikey Solomon's haul in 1827 therefore was worth something. But he eluded transport once again, through a daring escape, and he fled, all the way to the United States. He was eventually captured in 1829, and when he was brought to the Old Bailey courthouse for trial in 1830, he was found guilty of two of the eight charges of receiving stolen goods, and sentenced to transportation for 14 years, to an island south of Australia called Tasmania.

If Ikey Solomon's story is remembered today, it has to do with the fact that some people think he was the inspiration for Fagin, the Jewish villain in *Oliver Twist*, a novel written by Charles Dickens. In his day, Solomon was considered to be the biggest receiver of stolen goods in London, and his trial was a sensation. The trial was written about in all the newspapers, and many people say that Dickens, who was a budding author and journalist at the time, must have read about it or even might have been seated in the gallery at the Old Bailey, listening to the proceedings. At any rate, seven years later, Dickens did write *Oliver Twist* and the villain of that novel was a Jewish receiver of stolen goods, who is considered to be the second-most offensive Jewish character in English literature, Shakespeare's Shylock being the first.

However, there are a few problems with this theory. For one, Ikey Solomon was a fairly wealthy man, who dressed as a gentleman. He also had a wife and children. And even though he did employ a group of thieves, there is no evidence from the historical record—and his name does appear in newspaper accounts and the records of the Old Bailey criminal court—that these thieves were children.

So besides their common profession, it would seem that the only connection between Solomon and Fagin is the fact that they are both Jewish. And, indeed, Dickens, who had extensive knowledge of the darker side of London crime and street life, said that he had made Fagin Jewish because "it unfortunately was true, of the time to which the story refers, that that class of criminal almost invariably was a Jew."

But was it?

The Dark Side of Regency London

As most of us know, Dickens, who was born in 1812, had a rather harrowing childhood. After his father was sentenced to debtors' prison, he had to work in a boot-blacking factory. He later made the comment that as a child he had a great fear that the only opportunity that awaited him was to enter a life of crime, to be, in his own words, "a little robber or a little vagabond."

That fear was not entirely the result of an overly active imagination. Just as a wealthy person living in Regency England was able to enjoy a lavish and luxurious lifestyle, a very poor person lived in a world that can only be described as hellish. Very poor people often lived in decrepit buildings called Flash Houses, where there might be as many as 400 people crowded into one rat-infested building. Children who were either orphaned or abandoned by their parents or had run away from home had only two "careers" open to them: if they were boys, they were trained to be pickpockets and the like, and if they were girls they were forced to become prostitutes.

Of course, Charles Dickens did escape that fate. He didn't end up in a Flash House. But even when he became a successful novelist, he continued to be fascinated by crime and in his books can be found bank thefts, forgery, embezzlement and even grave robbing.

A criminal, therefore, is not unique in the Dickens canon; there are many criminals. But unlike Dickens's other criminals, who might be scheming and greedy and hypocritical but are still recognizably human, Fagin is cut from a different cloth; he belongs to an earlier, almost mythic time. In the words of author Edgar Rosenberg, in his book *From Shylock to Svengali: Jewish Stereotypes in English Fiction*, in *Oliver Twist* Dickens has pitted the angelic Christian choir boy against a serpent named Fagin; it's the golden prince of the fairy tale against the child-eating ogre.

But to accomplish that, Dickens didn't have to have a Jewish criminal. There were plenty of pickpockets and receivers of stolen goods who were not Jewish. What is more, according to some historians who have made a thorough research of the London crime statistics of the 1830s, there is no evidence that Jews controlled gangs of child pickpockets. So why did Dickens make Fagin not only Jewish, but grotesquely Jewish?

Was This the Real Inspiration for Fagin?

What's fascinating — or some might say infuriating — about being a historian is that just when you think you have developed a perfect theory, someone comes along with a new piece of evidence and destroys the whole thing. And that is what has happened with theories about Dickens's source of inspiration for Fagin.

In 2011, Rose Wild, an archive editor for *The Times* of London, discovered a *Times* article from January 14, 1834 that described the plight of a young English runaway. He was taken to the London lair of a father and son duo, who were the organizers of a group of young thieves.

So far it sounds like the plot of *Oliver Twist*, but here's the catch: the father, a 60-year-old man named Henry Murphy, who was also known as "Old Henry, the Child Stealer," wasn't Jewish. He and his 13-year-old son were black. They were members of the small black community that was also a part of Regency London — and according to historian S. I. Martin it's very possible that Murphy and his son were the inspirations for Fagin and the Artful Dodger.

Why then, when Charles Dickens sat down to write *Oliver Twist*, didn't he make his villain a black person? Well, we can't go back and ask him, but we do know that he was an outspoken champion of Abolitionists, who rightfully wanted to put a stop to the African slave trade that was going on across the ocean in the United States. Britain did, indeed, abolish slavery in its own colonies in the same year that the *Times* article was written. Therefore, at a time when sympathy for the blacks was very strong, Dickens might not have wanted to dampen that sympathy by portraying a black person in a negative light.

Instead, he turned to a group for whom a prejudiced view was more acceptable in British society, and by doing so his name will be forever linked with one of the most damaging, anti-Semitic literary creations in history, that of Fagin the Jew.

The Heavy Load of History

But Dickens was not being totally anti-Semitic when he made his comment that most receivers of stolen goods were Jews. Jews were engaged in this business, as well as breaking into houses, pickpocketing, counterfeiting money, and other crimes. And if in his creation of the character Fagin he was no better than his times, he wasn't much worse. For the Christian Englishman, the Old Clothes Man—the Jew most people were familiar with—wasn't just an unsavory character found amongst other unsavory characters on London's streets, or even just a figure of fun with his Yiddish accent; he was also a very real bogey man. In the pack he had slung on his back, he wasn't just carrying old clothes— he was also carrying, symbolically, the memory of the old blood libel stories.

Ironically, when British author Maria Edgeworth wanted to break out of the mold of stereotypical Jewish characters and write a book that had a positive image of the Jew in it, which she did in her novel written in 1817, a book called *Harrington,* she begins the novel by telling how her hero was terrorized as a child by his maid. This maid told him stories about how Jewish Old Clothes Men would snatch him up and put him in their bag and carry him off, if he didn't behave. Here's a short excerpt from an early scene in the novel:

Above all others, there was one story--horrible! most horrible! — which she used to tell at midnight, about a Jew who lived in Paris in a dark alley, and who professed to sell pork pies; but it was found out at last that the pies were not pork — they were made of the flesh of little children. His wife used to stand at the door of her den to watch for little children, and, as they were passing, would tempt them in with cakes and sweetmeats. There was a trap-door in the cellar, and the children were dragged down; and — Oh! how my blood ran cold when we came to the terrible trap-door. Were there, I asked, such things in London now?

Oh, yes! In dark narrow lanes there were Jews now living, and watching always for such little children as me; I should take care they did not catch me, whenever I was walking in the streets; and Fowler (that was my maid's name) added, "There was no knowing what they might do with me."

Harrington continues with the hero discovering that many of the prejudices he grew up with were unfounded. But the novel was only partially successful in its goal of creating sympathetic Jewish characters, mainly because its author, Maria Edgeworth, was no Charles Dickens. But she does deserve credit for writing the first English novel that has in it a full-length portrait of a sympathetic Jew. Indeed, during this time period — when the American and French Revolutions were still fresh in people's minds — there were calls from some members of England's political and intellectual elite to give the country's minorities, including the Jews, full political rights.

Although full emancipation for the Jews didn't occur until the Victorian era, the Jews of England were not entirely friendless during the Regency period. Therefore, from time to time we do see other sympathetic Jewish characters popping up in English literature, such as Rebecca in Sir Walter Scott's *Ivanhoe*. Unfortunately, though, these Jewish heroes and heroines are not as compelling as the Jewish villains who continued to turn up in novels and plays, and so the negative stereotype continued to live on.

As for Dickens, he did show some remorse. While *Oliver Twist* was being serialized in his magazine, the Jewish communities in both Britain and the United States made a loud protest, which he heard. And so whereas in the first two-thirds of the novel Fagin is often referred to as "Fagin the Jew" or just "the Jew," in the later chapters he is referred to as "Fagin" and the Jewish reference is mostly dropped.

Anything to Buy?

Although the Old Clothes Man might have been the most visible Jewish figure in Regency London, the Jewish community was certainly more diversified. Fabulously wealthy Jewish financiers such as Nathan Mayer Rothschild, Sir Moses Montefiore, and the Goldsmid brothers were active during this time. This was also the era when the Sephardic prize fighter Daniel Mendoza became the Champion of England, and Jewish actors and singers appeared regularly on the London stage. And, of course, there were the ordinary Jews—the greengrocers and clockmakers and tea dealers—who added another stitch to the fabric of Regency London life.

Why, then, do so many historical accounts of England's Jews give this era just a passing glance—treating it as a sort of unimportant passageway between the Readmission of the Jews in the mid-1600s and Jewish Emancipation in the mid-1800s?

One reason could be because early Anglo-Jewish historians, such as the founders of the influential Jewish Historical Society of England, tended to concentrate on the positive contributions that Anglo Jewry had made to British life. Since the majority of the Jews of the Regency period didn't make much of a contribution to British political life and culture—they were mostly businessmen, large and small—these Jewish historians weren't interested in them. Even though later historians such as Todd M. Endelman, who wrote the influential *The Jews of Georgian England 1714-1830: Tradition and Change in a Liberal Society* (Ann Arbor Paperbacks), have written extensively about this period, it seems that their findings haven't trickled down to the common Jewish person, who is still convinced there were no Ashkenazic Jews living in England until the arrival of Eastern European Jews in the late 1800s.

Another reason for the neglect might be due to the fact that there weren't any contemporary Jewish novelists or journalists who wrote about Regency England's Jews. There was no Jewish Jane Austen or Charles Dickens to write about the hopes and challenges of the Jews at that time. What was written by non-Jewish writers was either ugly in its perpetuation of the negative stereotype or was "too good to be true," and there's nothing in between to draw us into the era.

All we have is the Old Clothes Man, who began his sojourn in England as an honest worker but somewhere along the way got kidnapped and transformed into a grotesque caricature called Fagin. No wonder, then, that most Jews prefer to quickly turn the page.

—January 2013

THE HOLOCAUST

Forgotten Heroine

Truus Wijsmuller isn't a name most people have heard of, but this unknown savior – who fearlessly bargained with Adolf Eichmann and put in motion the Kindertransports – rescued thousands of Jewish children from Europe. Now, two Dutch women, a Jewish researcher and a filmmaker, want to make sure her memory lives on.

Vienna, December 1938. A 42-year-old woman from the Netherlands named Geertruida Wijsmuller arrives at the Central Office for Jewish Emigration and asks to speak with the man in charge. At first, she is rebuffed Nazi Lieutenant Adolf Eichmann is a busy man. But Geertruida – or Truus, as she is called by her friends – is not afraid of powerful people.

Eichmann finally grants her an interview, which begins with him saying, "I'm not accustomed to dealing with women."

"I'm sorry, sir, but I left my husband at home," Truus replies. "You'll have to deal with me."

Truus, in fact, has a deal for Eichmann: The Nazis want to make Austria Judenfrei, and in 1938 the goal is not to kill all the Jews but to force them to emigrate from Nazi-controlled lands – after stripping them of all their wealth and property. Truus will help Eichmann do the first part. She will arrange for Jewish children to be transported to England.

Eichmann regards her with disdain. Who is this woman who thinks she can whisk people out of Vienna with a snap of the fingers? He knows—it's his job to know—the logistics work involved: arranging trains and boats, not to mention the paperwork.

"You can have 600 children," he tells her, treating the matter as a joke. Because there is a caveat. He will give her only five days to get the children out of Austria.

He is certain she will fail.

On December 11, a *New York Times* headline announces: "630 Children Quit Vienna."

Truus Who?

The above scene might sound like it came out of a Hollywood movie, but it didn't – at least not yet. Unlike better-known Holocaust rescuers, no movie has been made about Truus Wijsmuller, even though she saved the lives of thousands of Jewish children. In fact, until recently there was very little information available in English about the life of Mrs. Wijsmuller, who passed away in 1978.

"No one knows who she is," comments Miriam Keesing, who has spent the past six years researching the history of Jewish children who entered the Netherlands as unaccompanied refugees during the late 1930s. "But she was really remarkable, and she should get a lot more recognition."

"She saved thousands of children—and the generations that came after," adds Pamela Sturhoofd, a Dutch filmmaker who is making a documentary, *Truus' Children*, about Mrs. Wijsmuller and the children she saved. "What she accomplished can be compared to Oskar Schindler."

But mention the name Truus Wijsmuller, and you'll probably get blank stares. So, who was this nearly forgotten heroine?

Truus Wijsmuller was born in 1896 in Alkmaar, a picturesque Dutch town famous for its cheese market. Her father, Jacob Meijer, owned a pharmacy, while her mother, Hendrika, was a dressmaker. They also temporarily took in Austrian children seeking refuge during the First World War. Later, Truus would recall that it was her parents who taught her to help needy people, no matter the color of their skin or their religion.

After attending trade school for a few years, Truus found employment in a bank in Amsterdam, where she met her future husband, banker Johannes "Joop" Wijsmuller. They married in 1923. She and Joop were crazy about children, and Truus quit her job in the hope she would soon become a mother.

It was not to be. Truus was devastated when she learned she could never have children, but when her physician suggested she channel her love for children into doing volunteer social work, she took his advice.

After Adolf Hitler came to power in Germany in the early 1930s and began his persecution of German Jews, Truus had plenty to do. She worked with the Jewish Refugee Committee (JRC) and the Committee for Special Jewish Interests, and later the Netherlands Children's Refugee Committee, to help relocate German Jewish children.

When Germany annexed Austria and parts of former Czechoslovakia known as the Sudetenland in 1938, the situation for Jews became increasingly desperate in these places too. Then came Kristallnacht, the two-day rampage on November 9-10, where hundreds of synagogues and Jewish businesses and homes were destroyed.

It was obvious to Truus that more needed to be done to get Jewish children out of Nazi-controlled lands — and it had to be done fast.

Heartbreaking Goodbye

Kristallnacht shocked the world — and was an embarrassment for British Prime Minister Neville Chamberlain. Chamberlain had assured Parliament in September 1938 that the just-signed Munich Agreement, which gave Germany the Sudetenland, would grant Britain "peace with honor."

The British government had previously refused to allow 10,000 Jewish children to enter what was then British-controlled Palestine. But due to the efforts of Jewish activists and sympathetic non-Jewish citizens, after Kristallnacht pressure was put on the British government to let Jewish children come to England instead.

Parliament passed a bill on November 21 with the following provisos: An unspecified number of children under the age of 17 from Germany, Austria and the Sudetenland would be allowed to enter Great Britain on a temporary travel visa. Parents or guardians could not accompany the children, whose care and education would be paid for by British citizens who guaranteed to sponsor the children. When the "crisis would be over" — war hadn't yet been declared and it was assumed the "crisis" would be over in a few months — the children were expected to leave England and return to their families, again at the expense of the people who had sponsored them.

The first Kindertransport, as the rescue operation was dubbed, arrived in Harwich, England, on December 2. On board were 200 Jewish orphans from Berlin whose orphanage had been destroyed during Kristallnacht. The second transport to arrive was the one from Vienna, organized by Truus Wijsmuller.

While British activists such as Helen Bentwich and Dennis Cohn prepared for the children's arrival in England, it was up to Truus and other activists on the Continent to figure out the logistics for getting the children out of Europe. The already-complicated task was made even more complex after Germany refused to let the children sail from German ports. The Kindertransports that left Austria therefore traveled through Germany via Cologne, crossed the border into the Netherlands and continued up to Hoek van Holland, a Dutch port, where a boat-train took the children across the North Sea to England.

A *New York Times* correspondent described the scene at the first Kindertransport that left Vienna: "Mothers and relatives were not permitted to enter the station. They held what may have been their last meeting with the children in near-by hotels. … The emotional stress of parting was too much for some of them. One mother died of a heart attack after kissing her 5-year-old child good-bye … Seven mothers fainted as the children marched to the train."

The children weren't allowed to leave the sealed cabins, but when the train reached a station on the Netherlands's side of the border, Truus arranged for a "welcoming committee" of Dutch women to greet it. The women passed milk and chocolate through the windows to the children, and then the train continued on its journey.

The Danger Was Obvious

Nearly 10,000 children were rescued and taken to England on Kindertransports, which were forced to stop when war broke out on September 1, 1939. As many people and organizations were involved with arranging the transports, the credit for saving these children doesn't belong to Truus alone. But she personally organized 74 transports and saved thousands of lives—including that of Dr. Joseph Eisinger.

Today, Dr. Eisinger is professor emeritus in the Department of Structural and Chemical Biology at Mount Sinai School of Medicine in New York. The recipient of two Guggenheim fellowships, he is also the author of *Flight and Refuge: Reminiscences of a Motley Youth*, which recounts his wartime experiences.

Dr. Eisinger, who was born in Vienna to a middle-class family, relates that he left Vienna on a Kindertransport in March 1939, when he was 15 years old. "A lot of people wonder how parents could send their children away," he comments. "But the danger was so obvious that there was no hesitation. They did it to save us."

He recalls that there were lots of Gestapo and SS men at the Vienna train station. Once on board the train, he says he had mixed feelings.

"On one hand, leaving my parents was hard. But I was excited about going to England, which was an exotic place. You must understand—nobody knew there would be war or that there would be a Holocaust. It was true the Jews were gradually being deprived of their livelihoods. But it was inconceivable to me that anything really terrible was going to happen."

His older sister was already in London, where she worked as an au pair for a Sephardic family. This family had told the Kindertransport organizers that they would sponsor Josef as well, but when the boy arrived at London's Liverpool Street Station, where sponsors were supposed to pick up the children, there was no one to meet him.

As the hall emptied out, an official told Josef that he would have to return to Germany, if he didn't have a sponsor to sign the necessary papers. Then a young man entered, took a seat next to Josef, and asked Josef to point to his suitcase. "He grabbed it and we both ran out of the hall and into a waiting car," Dr. Eisinger recounts. "Everyone ran after the car, but it was too late."

The "kidnapping" scheme had actually been planned by the family, who were willing to help bring Josef to England, but had no intention of being his sponsor and giving him a home. "I had a joyous reunion with my sister at their home," says Dr. Eisinger. "But the father told me this was all he was going to do for me. I couldn't stay with them. So I became an illegal alien."

Despite that inauspicious beginning, the end of Dr. Eisinger's story is happier than most. Not only did he and his sister survive the war, but his parents managed to escape to British Mandate Palestine right before war broke out.

"I never met Mrs. Wijsmuller," he says. "She was involved behind the scenes and I only heard about her later. She was a remarkable lady."

Holed Up in Holland

Although organized Kindertransports ended when Britain entered World War II, that didn't mean Truus's work also came to an end. There were about 2,000 Jewish children who entered Holland after Kristallnacht as unaccompanied refugees, but only about 700 of them were able to obtain one of the coveted places on a Kindertransport, because most of the transports didn't originate in Holland. The rest were trapped there after Germany invaded the country.

One of them was a German Jewish boy named Uli Herzberg, who was taken in by Miriam Keesing's grandparents. Miriam learned about the existence of the boy while she was going through the papers of her father, Leo Keesing. She wanted to know what happened to Uli after her grandparents emigrated to Cuba in 1942. What she discovered was that Uli, who didn't leave with the Keesing family, was later deported and murdered at the Sobibor concentration camp.

But this wasn't the end of the story for Miriam. It was the beginning of a research project — and a life's mission: She wanted to find out what happened to every single one of these 2,000 children.

"If I had realized how much work was involved, I probably wouldn't have started it," Miriam admits in a conversation from her home in the Netherlands. Her initial visits to the Netherlands Institute for War Documentation (NIOD) were disappointing:

Although she found a few memoirs and documents, she didn't come up with anything that answered all her questions. If she wanted answers, she realized, she'd have to write her own book.

The book has yet to be completed and published, but there is an incredible amount of valuable information on her website, www.dokin.nl. Dokin is a Dutch acronym for *Duitse Oorlogskinderen In Nederland* (German War Children in the Netherlands).

Although about a third of the children who entered Holland were eventually deported and murdered, Miriam decided she would try to meet the survivors, now in their 80s or 90s – those who had left Holland on a Kindertransport, escaped to freedom some other way, or spent the war in hiding in the Netherlands. Using her own funds, she flew to the United States, Israel and Germany to interview those who were still living.

Why did she put in all this effort?

"It's important that somebody writes this story," she says. "For me it's been very meaningful. I've found letters written by parents who were later killed, and I've sent these letters to the children. The children I've been in contact with have told me how important it is to fill in the pieces of the puzzle."

She found 50 of these missing pieces in the files of the Dutch Red Cross, when she discovered the names of about 50 children who were killed in the camps yet had never appeared on any list of victims. "Children can't just disappear," she says. "This is what's kept me going."

It was while she was researching the fate of these 2,000 refugee children that Miriam Keesing first ran across the name Truus Wijsmuller.

"I hadn't heard about her beforehand, and I was surprised. She was a real hero. She got so much done, she traveled extensively — and in those days a woman traveling alone wasn't done. I don't believe I would have had the courage to do what she did. When you read about her meeting with Eichmann, you can say, 'Yeah, so she talked to this Eichmann guy.' Or you can say, 'Wow!'

"I'm sure there were times when she was afraid. But I believe she was led by what she thought had to be done, what was right. She realized much earlier than most people that the Jews were in mortal danger and she didn't let her fear stop her."

The Last Transport

It was while doing her research that Miriam ran across mention of one of Truus's most daring rescue attempts.

Although the Netherlands was a neutral country, Germany invaded it on May 10, 1940, and the Dutch government surrendered five days later. By then, Truus had rescued 66 children who had been staying at the Burgerweeshuis, a municipal orphanage in Amsterdam which had been turned into a hostel for refugee children. It was the last transport that left the country.

Joseph Helmreich was one of the children on that last transport. Born in Cologne in 1927, only he and his brother were able to escape to the Netherlands, where they were given shelter at the Burgerweeshuis. Although one sister and his mother did survive the war, the rest of his family was murdered in concentration camps.

"We didn't know where our parents were," he explains. "No one knew what was going on. But Mrs. Wijsmuller (who the children fondly called "Auntie Truus") would come to visit every day, sometimes with her husband. She arranged everything. She was concerned about our welfare. There was a public pool nearby and she even arranged for us to learn how to swim."

Mr. Helmreich and his brother were among the few children who came from Torah-observant homes. Although the food served at the hostel was kosher, in his 12-year-old mind, he remembers it being terrible. Every day for lunch they were served tomato soup, and the kids joked that they could turn the bowl upside down and the soup would stay inside.

But the days of gravity-defying tomato soup came to an abrupt end when the children were told to pack their suitcases and board a waiting bus.

"We knew the Germans had invaded," he says. "The streets of Amsterdam were eerie. We looked out the window of our bus — we were boys, you know, and we were interested — and the streets were deserted. There were no cars or trams. Nothing. No one wanted to go out. We arrived at the dock at dusk and that was also eerie."

When they got to Ijmuiden, a port near Amsterdam, they saw a squadron of a dozen British soldiers with machine guns. "They had come to show solidarity with the Dutch, which we thought was very funny," he recalls. "After all, what could they do?"

After the children and other passengers were on their boat, a freighter called Bodegraven, they found out.

"All of a sudden we heard a plane, a German diving bomber. The plane had a glass nose and was flying so low we could see the soldier lying in the nose with a machine gun aimed at us! He started shooting, but no one was hit, *baruch Hashem*. Then the British squadron that we thought was so useless started shooting back and the plane flew away. It was a big miracle."

Because it was wartime, at first England didn't want to let the boat dock -- they didn't want to take in German citizens – but after five days the British relented and the freighter docked at Liverpool. Eventually, Joseph was allowed to go to Gateshead and learn in yeshivah there. After the war, he moved to the United States, where he married and raised a family.

"It was incredible what Mrs. Wijsmuller did," he comments. But because he was a child at the time, he couldn't know even half the story.

Truus was in France when the Germans invaded the Netherlands; she had brought a very young Jewish child to France's border with Spain and the child was eventually brought to the Dutch Caribbean. She rushed back to Amsterdam when she heard the news, although it took her three days to get there.

Her first stop was the Burgerweeshuis to talk with the children. On May 14, she received permission from the garrison commander of Amsterdam to take the children to Ijmuiden. She also learned that Dr. David Cohen, chairman of the JRC, had gotten word from The Hague that a boat would be waiting for them. After her meeting with the garrison commander, she commandeered five buses for the journey to Ijmuiden.

Even with permission from the garrison commander, Truus and her children were stopped at numerous roadblocks. Using her connections, she managed to speak with a high-up official of the Dutch navy, who gave her permission to continue.

The boat set sail just hours before the Netherlands surrendered to Germany. Truus stood on the dock, waving goodbye to the children.

Never Give Up

During the war, Truus joined a resistance group and continued her rescue work. She smuggled Jews into Spain and Switzerland and medicine into occupied France, until she was arrested by the Gestapo in May 1941. Although this time she was released due to lack of evidence, the group asked her to stop her smuggling activities, lest she endanger the lives of the other members.

Instead, she sent food packages to Westerbork, Bergen-Belson, Theresienstadt and other camps and prisons. When she found out that a group of 50 young children interned at Westerbork were going to be sent to Auschwitz, Truus persuaded the officials that they weren't Jewish children, but rather the Aryan offspring of German soldiers and Dutch women. The ruse worked and the children were sent to Theresienstadt instead. When the first train from Theresienstadt arrived in Maastricht after the war, Truus was at the train station to meet the children. All 50 of them had survived.

After the war, Truus became a member of the Amsterdam city council and fought to advance the rights of the disabled. In 1966 Yad Vashem honored her as one of the "Righteous Among the Nations." But after her death, her many accomplishments began to be forgotten, perhaps because she had no descendants.

"This is such an important part of our history," comments filmmaker Pamela Sturhoofd, whose father had to go into hiding during the war. "This is why we said we had to make this documentary."

Her film production company, Special Eyes, which she founded along with Jessica van Tijn, began work two years ago. Since then they've interviewed 19 "children" who were saved by Truus, including Dr. Eisinger and Mr. Helmreich. (You can see a preview at www.truus-children.com.)

"One way to make a documentary is to take your camera and just begin filming," she comments. "But we've also invested a lot of time in doing research."

Thanks to that research, she can verify Mr. Helmreich's account of what happened on board the freighter. She found the same story recounted in newspapers gathering dust in Liverpool's archives.

"When people are old, you have to ask if what they are saying is really the truth or a fantasy," Sturhoofd comments, echoing a concern that all Holocaust researchers must confront. "But the people we interviewed had very good memories, and their recollections of Truus were very similar. They all mentioned that she was very kind and had a lot of charisma, but she was also very determined and could be tough. Even though these children have never spoken with one another, they're telling the same story."

Sturhoofd hopes the 90-minute documentary will be released in November or December 2019. So far, she has about 80 percent of the needed funding, and she's confident the rest will come through. She comments that people get excited when they hear about Truus's story — and even after two years of intensive research and flying around the world to interview the children, she hasn't lost her enthusiasm, or her admiration for Mrs. Wijsmuller. In fact, she plans to begin work on a filmscript after she completes the documentary, so Truus Wijsmuller will finally get her Hollywood movie.

"Truus could have said, 'I did enough.' But she didn't. She pretended to be part of the Dutch Red Cross, so she could take Jewish children into France. When the Netherlands told her that she couldn't do this anymore — the letters are in the archives — Truus pleaded. When they still refused, she went to the Red Cross in Belgium and they said okay -- she could pretend to be working for them instead.

"She was always trying to find solutions. And she was persistent. She never, never gave up."

— April 2019

Tunnel to Life

They faced a certain death, so they dug an escape route in the dead of night to flee to life.

For decades, the escape tunnel at Ponar, Lithuania had largely been the stuff of legend. In the thick of the Second World War, Jewish members of a forced-labor brigade had supposedly dug the tunnel using spoons, screwdrivers, and even their bare hands. They were members of the so-called Burning Brigade, dozens of Jews assigned to the cruel and grisly task of exhuming and burning the bodies of more than 70,000 Jews who had been executed at Ponar, outside Vilna, by the Nazis.

But did the tunnel really exist? Did the desperate members of the Burning Brigade really elude their Nazi tormentors by crawling to freedom on that last night of Passover in April 1944?

In 2016, an international team of archeologists came to Ponar to find out. Armed with up-to-date, alphabet-soup-sounding equipment such as GPR and ERT, they began the laborious process of testing the soil, searching for telltale inconsistencies that might signal the tunnel's presence below the earth.

Suddenly, a ghostly figure appeared amidst the trees, an elderly woman who seemed to know exactly what these archeologists were looking for.

"I was a partisan in 1944," she told them. "I was the one who received the escapees. The Germans had radioed that they were looking for them and they'd give a reward to anyone who found them. So we went out to look for them.

"After three days we found them — they were in two groups — and brought them to the partisan camp. No one could stand next to them because they smelled of death. Until today, I can still smell them. The first thing we did was burn their clothes. But even their skin smelled of rotting bodies."

The Road to Ponar

"Many roads lead to Ponar, but no road leads back," wrote Yiddish author Shmerke Kaczerginski in 1943. His lyrics for the song *"Shtiler, Shtiler"* ("Quiet, Quiet"), composed by Aleksander Volkoviski, was written in memory of the mass murders committed at Ponar and became one of the Holocaust's best-known songs.

Kaczerginski and Volkoviski were both born and raised in Vilna and witnessed the destruction of the city's Jewish *kehillah*, a community that could trace its roots back to the Middle Ages. One of the Jewish world's most important centers for Torah study since the sixteenth century, as well as the home of the Vilna Gaon, Vilna was affectionately known as the Jerusalem of Lithuania. Its famous *Shulhoyf* (synagogue courtyard) housed not only the Great Synagogue, but also twelve other synagogues, the offices of communal institutions such as the *beis din* (Jewish court of law) and *chevrah kaddishe* (burial society), a bathhouse and *mikvah* (ritual bath), kosher meat stalls, a library, and even a prison. Vilna was 40 percent Jewish before the war, and in addition to the *Shulhoyf* there were more than 100 synagogues, as well as many *yeshivos*, serving the city's pre-war population of approximately 70,000 Jews.

After the Nazis occupied Vilna in July 1941, German troops, aided by their Lithuanian counterparts, began to transport Jewish men to the Ponar forest, located about six miles south of the city, and shoot them. In September 1941, the Germans liquidated a ghetto they had established in Vilna for those who couldn't work, and these Jews were taken to Ponar and executed as well. By the end of 1941, more than 40,000 Jewish men, women, and children had been murdered there.

Before the war, Ponar had been the site of a holiday resort. But the forested area was also the site of almost a dozen 20-foot-deep pits dug by the Red Army to store fuel tanks for a nearby airfield. When the Germans took over, they turned these ready-made pits into mass graves. Eyewitnesses have described the victims' final hour: After the Jews were transported to Ponar, they were forced to undress and then blindfolded with a piece of cloth ripped from their clothing. Walking single file, with one hand on the shoulder or arm of the person before them, they were led to a pit in groups of 10 or 20 and shot. After the bodies fell into the pit, a thin layer of sand was shoveled over them. Then the next group was led to the pit and murdered.

The Nazis continued to use Ponar as a killing field during the following year. When the large ghetto in Vilna was liquidated in September 1943, many of the Jews were brought to Ponar and murdered. Tens of thousands of Poles and Soviet prisoners of war were also murdered there. But by the end of 1943 the tide was turning. With Soviet troops advancing, the Germans decided to cover up what they had done. But how does one destroy the silent testimony of nearly 100,000 victims of Nazi atrocities?

The Burning Brigade

"The Germans decided to burn the bodies that were buried there," explains Dr. Jon Seligman, director of the Israel Antiquities Authority's Excavations, Surveys & Research Department and a member of the international team that went to Ponar in 2016.

Despite his having been interviewed many times about Ponar, his calm professional demeanor can't quite hide the emotions being stirred up by having to recall yet again what happened in that *gehinnom* (hell). While his grandparents left Lithuania for South Africa before the war, many members of his extended family remained. "Knowing that my grandfather's siblings and their families had been murdered at Ponar, I wasn't enthusiastic about working there," he admits.

But he does feel a need to speak about what happened there, and so he continues, "They brought to Ponar Jews who were captured in Vilna after the liquidation of the main ghetto—76 men and four women. The women were there to cook. Most of them were Jews who had lived in Vilna or the surrounding areas, but some were Red

Army soldiers who had been taken prisoner and who were suspected of being Jewish.

"They had to dig up the bodies, which the Germans, in their methodical way, counted one by one. The bodies were piled up on pyres and burnt. There were usually 1,000 bodies on the pyre, and the burning would take a number of days. The ashes and bones were then ground up and mixed with sand, which was distributed throughout the forest. That was the process."

The Jews assigned to this gruesome task became known to historians as the Burning Brigade. They lived at the site, "home" being one of the already emptied execution pits. A ladder was let down in the morning, so they could climb out of the pit and begin their work; at night, after all the prisoners had returned to the pit, the ladder was removed. In addition, their legs were shackled, making it impossible to climb out of the pit and escape during the night.

The kitchen was also in the pit, and unlike many others who worked in Nazi slave labor camps, the members of the Burning Brigade were well fed. They were also supplied with alcohol and cigarettes. The reason for the generous rations was simple: the Germans wanted the work done quickly, and they knew the prisoners would work faster on a full stomach.

Yet the group had no illusions about what would happen to them after they finished their work in the pits. They knew too much. Therefore, they would be executed and burned too.

"They decided to build a tunnel to escape," says Seligman. "They didn't have tools, so they used things like spoons. Because the soil there is very sandy, they were able to dig."

They were fortunate in that one of the group, Yuli Farber, had been an engineer in the Red Army. He designed the tunnel, including the wood scaffolding used to support it so it wouldn't cave in. Because the lack of air was a problem, they had to keep changing the team that was digging inside—one person dug, while the other removed the dirt from the tunnel—a process that went on throughout the night. Lack of light was yet another obstacle. They had candles, but they kept going out.

"One of the prisoners, Yitzchak Dugin, was an electrician by trade," Seligman continues. "He was the electrician for the whole camp. There was lighting in the kitchen. He managed to get hold of pieces of wire and, connecting them to the wires in the kitchen, was able to bring light into the tunnel."

The group's objective was to dig a tunnel from their pit to the adjacent one, which had already been emptied. From there they planned to make a run for the barbed wire fence that surrounded the camp. On the last night of Passover, April 15, 1944, they were ready to put their plan into action.

"They divided themselves into groups," Seligman explains. "The order of who left first was determined by how much effort the person had put into digging the tunnel. Once they were inside the tunnel, they filed off their chains. Then they went running toward the fence, but somebody stepped on something that made a sound and the Germans opened fire in all directions. Of the 80 people who were supposed to go through the tunnel—and we're not sure how many actually managed to do it—we think only 12 or 15 made it outside the camp. Only 11 survived the war."

The Smell of Death

Most of those who escaped went to fight with the partisans, whose hideout was in the forest. After the war, most of the survivors went to Eretz Yisrael, although one, Shlomo Gol, eventually settled in Florida, and Yuli Farber went to live in Moscow. The children of some of the survivors were recently interviewed for a documentary about the Ponar escape tunnel produced by NOVA, a science television program, which was broadcast on PBS in the spring of 2017.

Chana Amir, daughter of survivor Motke Zeidel, said that what she remembers the most about her father was that he was always washing his hands. She recalls her father telling her, "We were stinking from the smell of the bodies. And we ate with the hands that we worked with on the bodies, like we were like animals."

But Zeidel, who was the youngest member of the Burning Brigade and who was number five in line to escape, had also used his hands to dig away the sand, when there was no spoon or other utensil available. "After a whole day of burning the bodies, he went into the tunnel to dig," says Amir.

Zalman Matzkin, another member of the Burning Brigade, had the harrowing experience of discovering his dead wife's body among the corpses he had to dig up and burn. His son, Chaim Matzkin, thinks his father might have seen the bodies of his two children as well.

The elder Matzkin told his son about Ponar and the family he had had before the war when Chaim Matzkin was in high school, telling the teenager, "You need to know." Thus, Chaim learned about how his father, along with the others, was first ordered to chop down trees in the forest — without being told why. It was only after the Germans ordered them to exhume the bodies and burn them on the pyres constructed from the logs they had previously cut down that the prisoners, realizing they would be murdered in the end too, began to desperately make plans to escape.

After discussing several alternatives, it was decided that their best chance lay with digging a tunnel out of their pit. Not everybody was happy with the idea. "They didn't think that it would succeed," says Chaim Matzkin, recalling his father's words. "But there was a smaller number of people who decided that was the only way. And he said the more they dug, the more people joined."

The elder Matzkin recalled using his spoon and plate to dig. Others mention also using a screwdriver or whatever small implement they could find. But time was running out. Soon there would be no one left to burn, except themselves.

"They were looking for the darkest night," says Matzkin. "And the darkest night was on the seventh day of Pesach." Having decided that this would be the day of their escape, they waited for sundown. Although none of them was religious, one of them knew some prayers, "… so they prayed together with him."

But just seconds later the Germans started shooting. "There was light like mid-day. … There was so much light they didn't know where to run."

Zalman Matzkin was shot in the leg. But like Motke Zeidel, he was able to make his way to the partisans.

How did the prisoners manage to dig a tunnel for more than three months without the Germans noticing anything amiss? For one thing, what did they do with the dirt they removed?

According to Avraham Gol, his father, Shlomo Gol, was the liaison between the prisoners and the Germans. Shlomo Gol asked the Germans for lumber to place around the walls of the pit where the prisoners lived to make the pit more livable. The Germans agreed. The prisoners left a separation between the original walls and the new ones that was large enough for them to dump the dirt they had removed from the tunnel.

When Avraham learned about his father's leadership role during the war, he says he was surprised. The father he knew was a withdrawn man, saddened not only by what he had experienced at Ponar, but also by memories of an entire world that was lost. Shlomo Gol could recall the *Yomim Noraim* (High Holidays) at Vilna's Great Synagogue, when, he said, people would be standing outside, circling the synagogue, and praying in unison with those seated inside. "He said it was some sight to behold," says Avraham. "My father felt that it was completely lost. He said the Germans seemed to destroy it completely."

Out of the Ashes

Seligman's work in Lithuania has its roots in a 2013 trip, when he and his father visited places associated with their family. "We're from the *shtetlach*, not the big city," he explains. "We visited places located in the triangle that is now Belarus, Latvia, and Lithuania. We also visited Vilna, of course, and I saw they were doing investigative work on the Great Synagogue, which had been partially destroyed by the Germans and demolished by the Soviets. I made contact with Dr. Zenonas Baubonis, the Lithuanian archeologist in charge of the work, and I told him this sounded like it could be a great opportunity to do a joint project. We obviously have an interest because of the past of the place, and the Lithuanians have an interest because they're the present custodians of the site."

Seligman returned to Vilna in 2015, this time not as a tourist but as an archeologist. Along with Baubonis and Professor Richard Freund of the University of Hartford, Seligman used Ground Penetrating Radar (GPR) to better understand the underground space of the synagogue, as a preliminary to doing more excavations. Because an elementary school stands on about 60 percent of what once were the Great Synagogue and *Shulhoyf*, they couldn't just take out shovels and dig.

"GPR sends radio waves into ground," Seligman explains. "When it hits an object, the wave bounces back like any other radar and then you can read the signal—which requires interpretation.

The interpretation of the signal requires professionals, and even then it's a matter of speculation of what it all means."

While they were exploring the underground remains, the team was contacted by the Vilna Gaon Jewish State Museum, which maintains a small museum at Ponar. In 2004 Lithuanian archeologists had done work in the pit that housed the Burning Brigade and discovered an entrance to … somewhere. But the archeologists couldn't find the rest of the tunnel. And so the doubts about the tunnel's existence persisted. Perhaps a new team of archeologists would have more luck.

Seligman and the rest of the archeological team chose to work with non-invasive equipment, rather than shovels and picks, to preserve the sanctity of the site. They therefore came equipped with their GPR sensors, along with another relatively new technology, Electrical Resistivity Tomography, or ERT.

"Basically. all the techniques we used come from ones developed for mineral and oil companies, because that's where the money is and the equipment is very expensive," says Seligman. "In the pictures it looks like the team members are wearing ordinary backpacks, but each one of them has $200,000 worth of equipment inside.

"The idea of ERT is to put electrodes into the ground, in a line, and pass electricity through the electrodes, which then go into the ground. This judges the resistivity of the soil—in other words, where there is resistance to the electrical current. You're looking for differences in the composition of the soil; for example, differences in humidity."

And find differences, they did. According to Seligman, when the ERT results of the Ponar pit that housed the escapees were fed into their computer program, "The tunnel came up immediately. It was very, very clear because the consistency of the soil within the tunnel was different from the background. The soil had been disturbed and so it was different."

Moving their equipment from place to place, they could map out the entire path of the 100-foot-long tunnel.

"It was very exciting," Seligman recalls. "It was every emotional as well."

The *New York Times* agreed, proclaiming the story the scientific discovery of the year. "I think it got this attention for two reasons," says Seligman. "First, it's an amazing human story. Second was the utilization of scientific techniques and seeing how they produce results. If we had discovered a tunnel used by a badger, for instance, no one would have been excited. But because of the nature of the story, it generated a lot of interest."

That interest helped Seligman locate Chana Amir, who left a comment on an online article about the tunnel and later introduced him to the families of some of the other survivors. "Having contact with the families gave faces to the story—not only the faces of the escapees but also the children, grandchildren, and great-grandchildren who wouldn't be alive if not for the escape. It made the story very human."

The Road Back

While Seligman returned to Vilna this summer to continue work at the Great Synagogue, he says there isn't yet a decision about excavating the escape tunnel at Ponar. "That's the decision of the custodians of the site, the Vilna Gaon Jewish Museum," he says.

There was a tragic ending to the Ponar story, he adds. "After the escape, the Germans brought other Jews to finish the work. It made a difference for the 11 who survived the war, but it didn't stop what the Germans were doing."

Whatever his feelings about possibly excavating a site that evokes so many strong emotions, Seligman seems happy to have played a part in vindicating the testimony of the survivors of the Burning Brigade. And when he pulls up a photo on his computer screen of the Burning Brigade at work—the only one in existence, to our knowledge—he points to a man in the photo like he's a long-lost friend.

"The stories of the escapees tended to repeat themselves," he comments. "'I was found in the ghetto. I was taken to prison. Then I was taken to the camp.' But the story of this person, Avraham Blaser, is unusual. He escaped from Ponar twice."

Blaser first arrived at Ponar as a Jew about to be executed. But even though he was shot, he wasn't killed. He managed to crawl out of the pit and he returned to the Vilna ghetto, where his wife and child remained. Since he was officially dead, he no longer had the all-important work permit that often meant the difference between life and starving to death. But somehow the resourceful Blaser managed. And when the ghetto was being liquidated, he managed to hide his family with a non-Jewish friend living in Vilna. Then for some reason Blaser returned to the ghetto, where he was captured and brought to Ponar a second time, this time as one of the Burning Brigade.

"Blaser was one of the escapees," says Seligman, "but he didn't stay in the forest with the partisans. He went back to Vilna, and he was very much a cat with nine lives—on the way he stepped on a mine that didn't explode—and found his wife and child. They all managed to survive the war. They went to Israel in 1950, where they had one more child. He passed away in 1953."

Who shall live and who shall die? It may be months before Rosh Hashanah, but you can feel the question hovering in the air.

"And you wonder," as Avraham Gol remarked about his father and his friends, the other escapees from Ponar, " … after what they had gone through, how could they even think that there would be some kind of normalcy left for them?"

But rebuild their lives they did, a testimony to the inextinguishable spark that burns within every Jewish soul.

—July 2017

The Last Witnesses

Father Patrick Desbois is on a mission to record eyewitness testimony about every Holocaust-era mass grave site in Eastern Europe. But what began 16 years ago as a straightforward effort to document Nazi war crimes has taken on a new urgency. Not only is the generation that lived through the Holocaust passing away, Holocaust denial is on the rise, entrapping many young Jews who know distressingly little about their history and heritage. Can anything help rescue today's young Jews from this new narrative of lies?

Some people turn to religion to escape from reality. Father Patrick Desbois, a Catholic priest from France, isn't one of them. For the past 15 years, he has been doggedly documenting a reality that many would like to forget or deny: the Holocaust. His goal is to document every single incident that occurred in what he calls the "Holocaust by Bullets," the killing of Jews and Roma (Gypsies) by Nazi death squads.

To date, he has visited more than 2,000 cities and villages in Eastern Europe and interviewed some 5,800 non-Jews who witnessed the slaughter. Along the way, he has founded a nonprofit research organization dedicated to preserving and disseminating his findings, Yahad In-Unum — the Hebrew and Latin phrase means "Together, in One"; written an award-winning book; been featured on television news programs such as *60 Minutes*; and been honored with a slew of humanitarian awards.

But even though he is approaching the age when many people retire, he shows no signs of slowing down or resting on his laurels. He is too haunted by yet another fear: death. Most of the people who witnessed the crimes have either already passed away or are now in their nineties. With more than a million killings still waiting to be documented, he is, literally, in a race against time.

The summer of 2018 therefore found him once again on the road, as he continued his search for the last witnesses — the frail nonagenarians who still remember, the only ones left who are able to testify about the tragic events they saw with their own eyes.

FatherDesbois usually travels with a team of researchers, translators, and cameramen, who help him record the lengthy interviews he conducts in the field. These filmed interviews form the basis of Yahad's Archives and Research Center (CERRESE), which can be accessed by academics conducting Holocaust-related research. But for two days in July he joined a tour to Ukraine and Poland organized by Heritage Retreats, a *kiruv* organization founded 19 years ago by Rabbi Mordechai Kreitenberg, which *Mishpacha Magazine* was invited to join as well.

While the goal of Heritage Retreats is to introduce assimilated young Jews to intensive Torah learning and open their eyes to their rich Jewish heritage, Rabbi Kreitenberg saw in Father Desbois's work yet another way to wake up the *pintele Yid* (Jewish spark) in their slumbering souls.

"Our current privileged status in North America has weakened our collective memory, but Father Desbois's work has a message that's compelling for all sorts of Jews," says Rabbi Kreitenberg. "If a Catholic priest has dedicated his life to uncovering truths about the Holocaust, shouldn't we care about our Jewish heritage and history too?"

Unquiet in the Ukraine

"I knew people were being killed. I heard shooting. But I didn't see it. It was happening behind the wall. I did see three young men who were hanging from a balcony. - Lydia, Lviv

The first witness we meet is Lydia. (Yahad doesn't publicize the last names of the people who agree to be interviewed.) Still vivacious at

90, Lydia doesn't live in Lviv anymore. But she lived near the city's Jewish ghetto during the war, and she agreed to return to Lviv to share her memories. A Ukrainian member of the Yahad team, Olga, translates for us.

Lydia tells us that before the war there were many Jews who lived on her street—craftsmen, doctors, and lawyers. That changed when the Germans arrived in the summer of 1941 and the ghetto was established. Because she and her family lived near the ghetto, the teenager had a front-row seat, so to speak, to the new reality imposed upon her former neighbors.

"I saw Jews leave the ghetto to go to the workshops where they made shoes and clothes. The Jews wore a star. They were young and middle-aged men. People could hear them from far away, because they wore wooden shoes which clattered on the cobblestones."

I try to imagine the sound of those clattering shoes in the early morning hours. It isn't easy. Lviv, at least in its historic center, is a picture-perfect city. The buildings, painted in delicate hues of cream, pink and yellow, exude an old-world charm, as do the quaint cobblestone streets. The immaculate city squares are filled with people enjoying a mid-day meal in an outdoor café or simply soaking up the sun.

"Pictures about the Holocaust are in black and white, but I always say the Jews were killed in color," comments Father Desbois, putting into words the dissonance that at least some of us are feeling on this first day of our trip. How do we reconcile this sunny, colorful city with the black and white photographs from the summer of 1941, when Lviv was the scene of several horrific pogroms where more than 4,000 Jews were savagely humiliated and killed? And how do we respond to Lydia, who saw but … did what?

Father Desbois mentions that unlike the Soviets, who usually did their dirty work at night, the Germans committed genocide in broad daylight. They wanted the local populace to see. This tactic was used to intimidate some people into silence and obedience, but in Lviv some of the inhabitants welcomed the Nazis with open arms. To understand why, we need to review the history of this area.

Lviv had been a center of Torah and Jewish commerce since medieval times. Along with periods of stability and prosperity, there were times of persecution and economic hardship. But the first decades of the 20th century were especially tumultuous and grim.

In 1914 the city, which was then part of the Austro-Hungarian Empire and called Lemberg, was conquered by the Russian Army, only to be retaken by the Austrians in 1915, and then captured by the Poles in 1918. Under the Poles, the city was called Lvov. However, Ukrainian nationalists claimed the city as well. Tensions between the Poles and Ukrainians grew and, as usual, the Jews were caught in the crossfire. When pogroms erupted in 1917 and 1918, more than 100 Jews were killed and hundreds more were wounded.

During the interwar years, Lvov became one of Poland's most important Jewish centers, but more bad times were on the way. The city became part of Soviet Ukraine in 1939, and the Ukrainians living in Lviv (the Ukrainian name) were no fans of the Soviets. They were particularly bitter about the Great Famine of 1932 - 33, the Holodomor, when millions of their fellow Ukrainians, who had come under Soviet rule after World War I, died of starvation.

According to some historians, the Great Famine was deliberately caused by Soviet economic policy, which explains why Ukrainians welcomed the Nazis when the Germans occupied Lviv in 1941; believing they were victims of a Soviet attempt at genocide, they saw the Germans as liberators from the Soviets. When Germans accused Lviv's Jews of having collaborated with the Soviets, some Ukrainians expressed their fury in the pogroms that killed thousands of Jews.

And what of Lydia and her family? Did they see the brutal beatings and other atrocities? What did they say when the Jews were herded into the hastily erected ghetto? Did they do anything to help their former neighbors? How did they feel about the Nazis?

Our group of about 20 Torah-observant Jews from the United States and Israel—most are children of Holocaust survivors—are eager to ask Lydia these questions and more. But Father Desbois quickly silences us.

"Either you want to investigate and find out the truth about the crime, or you want to tell her she is a bad person," he tells us, explaining that if you make a witness feel bad, they won't talk.

"And you cannot ask someone who lived under the Soviet Union how they feel," he adds, referring to the fact that Ukraine only gained its independence in 1991, after the dissolution of the USSR. "You can ask only factual questions. Where were you? What did you see? It's like you are a policeman at the scene of the crime.

You don't ask the witness, 'How did you feel when you saw the person being shot?' You ask only about facts."

We therefore hold our tongues and listen to the rest of Lydia's story. Her memories of going to Belzec to buy food: "The train station wasn't far from the Belzec concentration camp. I could smell the odor of burning bodies." The glimpse she got of the last day of the Lviv ghetto, when she heard shooting and saw three bodies hanging from a balcony.

We thank her, and Lydia leaves.

I don't think it's my imagination, a certain sense of letdown in the group. Despite Father Desbois's admonishment, and even though we realize it's no small thing for a 90-year-old woman to travel to speak with us, I think we were expecting something more — tears, perhaps, maybe even the words "I'm sorry."

"My question is not, is someone guilty or not guilty," Father Desbois insists. "Violence was already a way of life for the Ukrainians. Stalin killed a lot of people. The problem is to save the memory of the dead. There were 2.4 million Jews living in Ukraine when the Nazis invaded. More than 220,000 people were killed in just this region. There are mass graves everywhere. But no one comes to say Kaddish. In the Ukraine, I would say that 75 percent of the graves have been reopened — people are looking for gold teeth, jewelry. The people know the Jews aren't coming back."

A Walk in the Forest

"I saw trucks arrive. I saw soldiers dig here. They were here a week, maybe more. I was five or six years old. A child could go everywhere." – Iossyp, Lysynychi Forest

Some of Lviv's Jews died in the ghetto. Others were murdered at Belzec or sent to the nearby Janowska slave labor camp to die there from hunger, disease, or exhaustion. Or they were transported by truck to the Lysynychi Forest, our next destination, where they were shot.

After we leave the comfort of our air-conditioned bus and enter the wooded area on foot, we are greeted by a blast of hot and humid air and a swarm of mosquitos. Along the way we pass by an elderly man, who doesn't greet us. He just stares as we continue deeper into the forest.

When we reach a certain point, Father Desbois tells us to stop. We have arrived. But where are we? There is no monument, no signpost to give us a clue.

He points to a clearing, a small area where the ground is a bit higher. It is a mass grave, he tells us — one of about 29 that he and his team have located since they began coming to this place around 10 years ago. According to German and Soviet archives, between 46,000 and 92,000 people were shot and buried here. Most of them are Jews, but there are some Italian soldiers, prisoners of war, who are buried here too.

It's up to Father Desbois to tell us the story of this place, because the witnesses he was able to locate and interview have since died. One of them, Adolf, was a teenager at the time. From a perch in a tree, he saw the graves being dug. Afterward, he saw trucks filled with Jews arrive.

Pointing to the top of a hill, where a narrow path leading downward can still be seen, Father Desbois relates what he heard from Adolf. "Most of the Jews came from the Janowska labor camp or the ghetto, and so they weren't very healthy. There were wooden boxes so people could undress and put their clothes in the boxes. Then the Jews were forced to run down the hill to the mass graves, where they were shot."

The shooting was done by the *Einsatzgruppen*, German killing squads. It's estimated that in the Ukraine alone there were some 2,000 mass shootings. The most infamous occurred at Babi Yar, where practically all of Kiev's Jewish population — some 33,000 souls — were shot and killed over a two-day period in September 1941.

But the mass shootings were only half the story. When the Germans realized they were losing the war and would probably be tried by an international court for their crimes, they rushed to destroy the evidence, using Jewish slave laborers to open the burial pits and burn the bodies. The code name for the large-scale campaign, which lasted from June 1942 until late 1944, was Aktion 1005.

"It was terrible for the Jews who had to burn the bodies," says Father Desbois, who located three Jews who were forced to do the work in this forest. One was Leon Weliczker Wells, who moved to New Jersey after the war and wrote an account of his experiences, *The Janowska Road*. Father Desbois, recalling what Wells told him in their interview, says, "The commander would say to them every day, 'Are you happy?' And they had to say they were happy and joke and sing. Anytime someone was tired or not happy, he was shot. Afterward, most of the Jews who did the burnings were killed."

After the Soviets arrived, they went to the various sites and opened the mass graves. They documented their findings — there is a copy at the United States Holocaust Memorial Museum in Washington, DC, and another copy at Yad Vashem in Jerusalem — but the report is millions of pages long and some of it is handwritten. One of the things Father Desbois would like to do is have the entire report, as well as the German archives, translated into English, to make the archives more widely available to future Holocaust historians. They would also like to translate into English the thousands of eyewitness testimonies that Yahad has filmed. He estimates this translation work would cost about $500,000. Although the organization has received funding from dozens of American and European foundations, including the Azrieli, Cummings, and Rothschild Foundations, and has an "American Friends" fundraising arm, to date the focus has been on funding Yahad's work in the field as they document the testimony of the witnesses. Translation of the material archived in their Research Center is the important and necessary next step.

Part of the reason why no one knows exactly how many people were buried in this forest — or other places — is because the German and Russian archives don't always agree, or they're incomplete. Yahad doesn't open the graves they find, out of respect for Jewish law. They also don't use ground-penetrating radar, which is not against *halacha* (Jewish law), but which is very expensive. They do record the location of the graves, so other historians will be able to find them, and an interactive map of their findings is on the Yahad website. But the main work of the Yahad team is to try to fill in the gaps by interviewing the locals. Of course, not everyone is willing to talk, and no one witness can provide a complete picture of what happened.

"You must crisscross from the testimony to the archives," Father Desbois explains. "You cannot ask a survivor what happened in a Gestapo meeting, because he was not there." He adds that they use a lot of material from survivors, in addition to the testimony of non-Jews, to document what happened. But it is the testimony from non-Jewish witnesses that he feels is the stronger ammunition in his fight against Holocaust deniers. "If it is only Jews who talk about the Holocaust, people will say it is Jewish propaganda."

And when he says "people," he isn't talking about just a few cranks.

According to a survey conducted last April for the Claims Conference, which negotiates reparations on behalf of survivors and provides them with social services, 41 percent of Millennials (young Americans in their 20s and 30s) believe that only two million or fewer Jews were killed during the Holocaust. Approximately 66 percent of these young people couldn't name a single concentration camp or ghetto. Not even Auschwitz.

And it gets worse.

A 2014 study conducted by the Anti-Defamation League, which interviewed more than 53,000 people in 100 countries, discovered that only a third of the people interviewed believe the Holocaust has been described accurately in historical accounts, with some of the doubters believing the number of deaths has been greatly exaggerated and others claiming the Holocaust is a myth. The study also found that people under 65, regardless of their religious affiliation, were more likely to believe that facts about the Holocaust have been distorted.

The decline in knowledge about the Holocaust can be attributed, at least in part, to the passage of time. For most young people, World War II is the story of their "great-grandpa," in the words of Father Desbois; it isn't relevant to their lives.

The increase in the number of people casting doubt on the historical record, on the other hand, can be traced to the work of Holocaust deniers, who have successfully used the internet and social media to disseminate false information

To help combat this growing trend of Holocaust denial and distortion, and create a new generation of Holocaust scholars, Father Desbois teaches a course at Georgetown University's Center for Jewish Civilization about the forensic study of the Holocaust.

Forensics is a discipline that collects and identifies physical remnants to draw conclusions about the "who, what, when, and where" of a crime. He and the Yahad staff also offer field courses where American and European students can meet with witnesses, as we are doing on our trip, and see some of the killing sites with their own eyes.

We retrace our steps and return to the entrance of the forest. The elderly man is still there. Apparently, he has been waiting for us. He begins to speak, in Ukrainian. Fortunately, Olga is still with us to translate.

Iossyp tells us that his family arrived at a nearby village after the war, when there was a population exchange between the Poles and Ukrainians. He saw the Soviet soldiers come in their trucks and open the graves. He was only five or six years old at the time.

He seems relieved to have shared this memory of long ago. We don't ask how often he comes to the forest, or what he thinks about when he is there. We are beginning to think like Father Desbois and his team of forensic detectives — this is one more small piece of evidence to add to the gigantic jigsaw puzzle called the Holocaust, one more voice declaring the crimes really did happen.

Remember the Children

"What I witnessed with the children was near the road, where the trucks were stopping. The trucks were opened, and the children started to fall down. They were falling on heads. They were falling on arms. They were all shouting and crying." – Zygmunt, Zbylitowska Gora

On the second day of the trip, we meet with two witnesses at the mass grave site near Zbylitowska Gora, a Polish village near Tarnow, a city which was home to 25,000 Jews before the war. Michal Chojak, Yahad's deputy research director, serves as our translator.

Jan, the first witness, says he was forced to become part of the Baudienst labor force when he was 20. According to Father Desbois, the Nazi policy of forcing the locals to work for them is one reason the Poles don't feel guilt. They feel they were just a tool, not the perpetrators of war crimes.

Jan spent only one day working at this killing site. Along with the other members of his team, he had to drag already dead bodies to a mass grave and assist with the killing of a truck full of Jews who were still alive. He didn't personally witness the slaughter of Tarnow's children. But a friend saw it and described to him how the Germans grabbed the children and smashed them against trees, before throwing their now lifeless bodies into the pit.

At the age of 95, Jan is frail and walks with a cane. But as he speaks, his face becomes animated and his words, even in translation, become more urgent. It's clear there is something more he wants to say, something more he wants us to hear.

He describes a scene he witnessed when the Jews of Tarnow were being deported. His job was to search the now-deserted homes for valuables. Anything of value had to be given to the Germans, who shipped the items back to Germany. The locals got what the Germans didn't want. While he was transferring the valuables to a warehouse, he passed a building where he heard some Jews screaming.

"I heard people asking for water," he tells us. "They were suffocating inside. There was a well nearby. I decided to bring a bucket of water to the people. At that moment there was an S.S. who saw me. He kicked me, and he told me that if I do it one more time he will shoot me."

After Jan leaves, Father Desbois explains, "You must know that in Ukraine every German commander was free to do as he pleased. He had a general order to kill Jews, but he could shoot them, suffocate them, or kill them with knives. He didn't have to explain how he did it. That is why we have filmed 5,800 witnesses. Because after these witnesses are gone, there will be no trace of the crimes."

The second witness, Zygmunt, was seven years old when he saw a truck filled with Jewish children pull up to this field, which was near his family's farm. After telling us about the way most of the children tumbled out of the truck, he adds, "I don't know what happened with one child, but he couldn't walk. A German took him by the leg and started to drag him in the direction of the pit. At that time there was a kind of barrier that led to the field, and this German took this child and smashed his head on the barrier. The child was maybe nine or ten."

Ever dispassionate, Father Desbois comments, "What was not resolved for me as an investigator, when I first heard testimony about this site, was how you could make children stand still and not move. You cannot put children near a mass grave and say, 'Stand still, while I shoot you.' The children will try to run away."

The testimonies we have just heard resolve that question. But it raises another: How can he remain so unmoved by the stories he hears?

As it turns out, his unemotional "just the facts" veneer is not the entire story. His commitment to locating Jewish mass graves — not a usual occupation for a Catholic priest — has its source in the very strong emotional connection he still has to his now deceased grandfather, Claudius Desbois, who was a French prisoner of war during World War II. The elder Desbois was incarcerated in a prison in Rava Ruska, a Ukrainian town located near the border with Poland.

"I knew nothing about the Holocaust until I was 13," Father Desbois explains. "No one talked. My grandfather only said that although conditions in his camp were bad, it was worse outside."

As a youngster, Father Desbois would wonder what could be worse than being a prisoner, with little to eat or drink. Later he realized his grandfather must have been referring to the Jews. "I am certain he saw what was going on — outside the camp they shot 15,000 Jews."

In 2002 he traveled to Rava Ruska to see the place where his grandfather had been imprisoned. When he realized there was nothing to commemorate the spot where the Jews had been murdered, he was determined to rectify the situation. How did that turn into a 15-year odyssey that has taken him all over Eastern Europe?

"I don't know," he says. Then he adds, "I still feel the presence of my grandpa."

From Generation to Generation

Father Desbois's work has won him many accolades and honors, including the Légion d'honneur (France's highest honor), the Humanitarian Award by the U.S. Holocaust Memorial Museum, and the National Jewish Book Award for his 2008 book *Holocaust by*

Bullets, an account of his search for the mass graves of Eastern Europe.

Naturally, he has his critics as well. Historian Omer Bartev, for example, a professor of European history and German studies at Brown University who is considered an expert on genocide, has criticized Father Desbois for being too accepting of his witnesses' testimony, especially when it comes to absolving them of guilt. In reply, others make the same point that Father Desbois made to us: once you start blaming people, they shut up.

Indeed, the Catholic priest's recurring criticism about the Jewish people's lack of interest in visiting and setting up memorials at Ukraine's mass grave sites has made more than a few members of our group uneasy.

In truth, his criticism isn't 100 percent accurate. Ohalei Zadikim, Lo Tishkach European Jewish Cemeteries Initiative, and the Association of Jewish Organizations and Communities (VAAD) Ukraine are three examples of Jewish organizations working to find and preserve Jewish cemeteries and mass graves.

Yet there is no escaping the fact that of the many Jews who come to Ukraine to daven at the graves of *tzaddikim* (righteous people) such as the Baal Shem Tov or Rebbe Nachman of Breslov, very few will hike out to the fields where the mass graves are located and say Kaddish. As for the hundreds of mass graves filled with ordinary and nameless Jews scattered across Ukraine and other Eastern European countries, they are mainly untended and forgotten, unless a family with a connection to the site has put up a marker.

To learn why more Jews don't visit Ukraine, I turn to Rabbi Aubrey Hersh, a protege of renowned British historian Sir Martin Gilbert, who has been invited by Heritage Retreats to provide a Torah and historical perspective to our group. In addition to being senior lecturer and projects director at London's JLE, a social and educational center for young Jews, Rabbi Hersh has taken 150 heritage tours to Europe.

"If people are traveling to Eastern Europe with the intention of seeing firsthand the places where the Holocaust happened, it is very important to incorporate Ukraine into the itinerary," Rabbi Hersh comments. "The difference between Ukraine and Poland is that for most people Poland is about the larger, more mechanized, more impersonal factories of death, where the numbers are staggering but the process was somewhat at arm's length. In Ukraine, as in Lithuania and Latvia, the killings were face to face. The Jews found their end in the very places where they had lived. But there are a number of difficulties which exist—technical and historical."

While there are a few Ukrainian cities where Yiddishkeit is thriving, such as Kiev, Odessa and Zhitomir, in general, the tourism infrastructure isn't as well developed in Ukraine as in Poland. This means the logistics of a kosher tour are harder to organize, and a trip can cost significantly more. An even larger problem is what Rabbi Hersh calls "the absence of a narrative." The mass graves are scattered across the countryside. Even if a group were to make the effort to visit some of the sites, in most places there is nothing to see, other than an empty field or forest clearing.

"You often don't know in any great depth the particular narrative of the village where the killings took place," he says. "Unlike the *Sifrei Zikaron* (Books of Remberance) that exist for large towns, you won't find anything specific for the smaller ones. Father Desbois's work gives a broader picture, but not all of it is available in English. All this makes it much more demanding to create a trip."

Later in our trip, when we are having dinner in Krakow, at the site of Sarah Schenirer's Bais Yaakov Seminary, Rabbi Hersh will address an even larger question: Whether it's Poland or Ukraine, why are we visiting places where our people suffered and were destroyed? Why come here?

"I came to Poland once with Rav Moshe Shapira *ztz"l*, whose grandparents were killed in Lithuania in a mass grave," says Rabbi Hersh, who explains that Rav Shapira was visibly distressed when they arrived at Auschwitz-Birkenau and was unable to bring himself to enter the camps. Later, when he was asked to give a *shiur* (Torah lecture), Rav Shapira said he wasn't in a frame of mind where he felt he could teach. "But he did give us one thought. Basically, he posed the question I just asked: What are we doing here? What do we hope to achieve?

"He said there is a *pasuk* (verse) in *sefer Devarim* (Deuteronomy) which tells us about how we merit the *geulah* (Redemption)—how we merit Eretz Yisrael and the Beis Hamikdash. It says that it's not as a result of your righteousness and your straight path that Hakadosh Baruch Hu is disinheriting the non-Jews of Eretz Canaan and giving it to you. It's because of what they have done to you.

"So we have to be "*mishtayech*" — we have to be linked to what has occurred to our people — in order for us to say to Hakadosh Baruch Hu, '*Higiyah zman*. Bring us the *geulah*.' That is a reason to come to these places, to understand how deep the *galus* (Exile) is, how much suffering we have been through, whether that *galus* happened directly to our ancestors or whether it happened thousands of years ago. We have an individual destiny and a national destiny. The route can be circuitous, depending on the choices we make as a nation, but our national destiny gets us from A to B to Mashiach."

Gathering the Missing Links

At a roundtable discussion, Father Desbois brings up a few topics that are on his mind: the new Holocaust law in Poland ("It will have a bad effect. We see that more people who don't like the Jews feel freer to say it."); the situation in Europe, where Jews are once again being killed because they're Jews ("The enemies of the Jews don't sleep. I would say that 80 percent of the planet has a positive memory of Hitler."); the one million mass grave sites that still need to be investigated.

"I'm the old guy, but my team is young," he says, cracking a rare smile. Then he quickly becomes serious again. "A third of my students at Georgetown University are secular Jews and even they are beginning to doubt the scale of the Holocaust," he says. "Because they know nothing.

"We need to prepare the new generation — teach a new generation how to investigate for themselves. The new generation won't meet survivors or witnesses. There will only be memory and history."

Yahad has several educational initiatives in the United States and Europe, including college and teacher-training courses, traveling exhibitions, and a website with an interactive map showing the sites of mass graves. There are, of course, many other Holocaust studies programs. But the nagging question remains: Who will be the guardians of Holocaust memory and history?

While we'd like to think it will be serious scholars in search of the truth, Dr. Manfred Gersentfeld, emeritus chairman of the Jerusalem Center for Public Affairs, wrote back in 2007 about the ways Holocaust memory is being distorted. He listed 11 of them, including: Holocaust Equivalence, which today we are seeing in countries like Ukraine, where some have made an equivalence between the Nazi brutality toward the Jews and the Soviet brutality toward Ukrainians; Holocaust Deflection, like the right-wing nationalists in Poland who insist Poles were also the victims of Nazi aggression and therefore shouldn't be blamed for the crimes they themselves committed; Holocaust Trivialization, where the word "Nazi" is used to describe any politician or authority figure you don't like and "genocide" becomes a catch-all description of any act of aggression; and Holocaust Inversion, which has been taken up by a small but noisy group of American Millennials belonging to student groups like If Not Now, who claim that Israelis are the new Nazis and they are committing genocide against the Palestinians.

"We should have *hakores hatov* (gratitude) for the work Father Desbois is doing," comments Rabbi Mordechai Kreitenberg, who has seen with his own eyes the toll that ignorance and apathy has taken on young Jews. "But preserving the memory of the Holocaust is only one aspect of the war we Jews are presently fighting. We have broader concerns. We have to ensure the future of *klal Yisrael* as well."

Rabbi Kreitenberg is himself the child of Holocaust survivors. Pictures of some members of his father's family arriving at Birkenau — only his father and one uncle survived — are hanging on the walls of the Auschwitz-Birkenau museum. They also hang in Rabbi Kreitenberg's office.

"I grew up in Los Angeles," he says. "About 95 percent of the kids in my high school were Jewish. When I went back for my 10th year reunion, I looked around the room and saw that no one cared that they were born Jewish or realized what a gift they had been given. My response, as an observant Jew and the son of Holocaust survivors, has been to be involved in Jewish education, specifically focusing on the unaffiliated. We have to save this generation of assimilated Jews from self-imposed obliteration."

Heritage Retreats, the organization founded by Rabbi Kreitenberg in 2000, combines an outdoor camping and hiking experience at one of America's gorgeous national parks with an intensive Torah learning program led by leading rabbis. While the retreats may be only one week, Rabbi Kreitenberg says the impact is very often long-lasting. Many of the young people go on to learn in in *yeshivos* in Israel and the United States.

"One young man was recently offered a six-figure job at Amazon, but he deferred it to learn in yeshivah for a year," says Rabbi Kreitenberg, who adds that many of the earlier participants of the program are today very involved in their respective Torah-observant communities.

Five years ago, he added an annual trip to Poland. "I'm always searching for tools to engage young people to explore their identity," he says. "Possibly, as a result, they will let Hashem and Torah into their lives. I saw Poland as one of those tools."

Many of the young professionals who sign up for the Poland trip have already done a Birthright trip to Israel. What does a trip to Poland add?

Rabbi Kreitenberg explains that unlike our tour with Father Desbois, which focused on the historical aspects of the Holocaust, the tour for these young people is geared toward seeing the heroic nature and perseverance of the Jewish people and the vibrancy of Jewish life in prewar Europe.

"Many have told me afterward that the trip to Poland awakened their Jewish pride—they saw how we have prevailed as a people, getting from the Holocaust to where we are today. Because of the political situation in Israel, the picture has become blurred and doesn't have the same impact.

"We live in a world that is so out of focus," he adds. "This generation has pretty much grown up with a silver spoon in their mouth. When there is so much material comfort and almost no adversity, they can lose perspective. So when you take people to a concentration camp or a mass grave, it makes them stop and think about what's important. It creates a call to action. I've had a number of people say they never valued having a Jewish family, or even having kids, but after being in Poland they have a new appreciation of the value of life. It's the same with keeping *mitzvos* (Torah commandments). When they learn about how our people kept the *mitzvos* while under such duress, it makes them realize, 'I should keep them too.'"

When asked how he would respond to Father Desbois's charges that the Jewish people aren't doing enough to preserve the memory of the mass graves, Rabbi Kreitenberg replies, "Father Desbois's message that we must not forget the dead is meaningful, but his way of remembering is different from ours. His idea is about the sanctity of the place, what transpired.

"But the education I received from my *rebbeim* (Torah teachers) has to do with the sanctity of the person and the growth that is supposed to take place. Our response is that our remembrance of how these people died has to translate into how we are going to live our life differently.

"I once heard a *shiur* from Rav Moshe Shapira during the Intifada about how we all had to do something. I walked up to him after the *shiur* and asked, 'What should I do?' And he said, 'If I tell you what to do, it's worthless.'

"You have to figure it out on your own. When I think about the sacrifices my parents and their families made during the Holocaust because they were Jewish, I know I have to do something. So for me, it's my *kiruv* organization. For others, it might be making a better Shabbos, or becoming a better parent, or having a stronger commitment to *ahavas Yisrael* (love for the Jewish people). But the Holocaust requires a response from all of us. It requires us to breathe new life into ourselves."

—July 2018

Choose Life!

For some of us, Poland is the last place we'd choose to spend our summer vacation. But as I recently discovered, it's davka *within that valley of death that we can learn some important lessons about life.*

"I would never go to Poland!"

I don't say anything. I know that my friend has really called to wish me a safe trip. Really. But somehow those other words slipped out instead.

My next-door neighbor, who also really means to wish me a safe trip, enlarges upon the topic. "My son wanted to go on one of those trips to Poland and I told him, 'Absolutely not! You'd be stepping on the ashes of your great-grandfather!'"

I understand their feelings, because I feel the same way. So why am I going to Poland? Is it just because I've been invited to accompany a Bais Yaakov tour of Poland by Nesivos Tours, an organization that has been bringing groups of yeshivah boys and seminary girls to Eastern Europe for more than a decade? The invitation certainly influenced my decision. What tipped the scales, though, was a promise made by the wife of Nesivos founder Rabbi Yehuda Fried.

"The tour isn't just about death," Mrs. Fried told me. "It's also about life."

Life? In Poland? This I had to see.

Serve Hashem with Gladness

And so that it is how I found myself standing in the middle of what had once been the Warsaw Ghetto, surrounded by more than 50 Bais Yaakov graduates (Bais Yaakov is a school system for Torah-observant girls). The girls, who come from the United States, Canada, and England, have just finished their seminary year in Israel. In another week they will be returning to home and "real life," as they call it. For the moment, though, our attention is focused on the red brick wall that stands before us. Our Polish tour guide, Tomasz Kuberczyk, explains that this is one of the few remaining sections of a wall that sealed off the ghetto from the rest of Warsaw, which had been one-third Jewish before the war.

The Warsaw Ghetto was the largest Jewish ghetto in German-occupied Poland. Most of the ghetto was destroyed in May 1943, after the unsuccessful Jewish uprising. At its peak, the ghetto was "home" to about 400,000 Jews. Approximately 300,000 of them were sent to the gas chambers at Treblinka in 1942. Another 100,000 Jews died inside the ghetto from sickness and starvation.

Later in the day we will go to the Warsaw Jewish Cemetery, where we will see the *kever achim* – common grave – where many of those unknown Jews who died within the ghetto's walls are buried. At this moment, we can only try to visualize what the ghetto must have been like in the early 1940s, when the ghetto was filled not only with sickness and misery but also with secret synagogues and *yeshivos* and other signs of traditional Jewish life. It's not an easy task, and not just because of the faceless blocks of buildings that were built upon the ruins of the ghetto after the war.

"It's empty," comments Mrs. Sarah Waldshein, as she looks around.

Mrs. Waldshein is the daughter of Rabbi Meir Wunder, the rabbi who leads our trip. Rabbi Wunder – who is an historian and the author of *Meori Galicia*, a six-volume encyclopedia of Galician Torah Sages – has the ability to keep a busload of kids fascinated with his seemingly endless store of stories about Poland's *tzaddikim* (righteous people). But right now I am struck by his daughter's ability to accurately sum up the paradox of Poland in those two brief words.

Poland – which was a home to Jews for almost 1,000 years and which had a population of 3,000,000 Jews before the Second World

War—is today an empty vessel. Highway signs may still point the way to Lublin, Krakow, Chelm, and dozens of others place that loom large in our religious and cultural history, but the *shuls* (synagogues) in those places—if they're still standing—are mostly silent. Homes that were once filled with the aroma of *challahs* baking in the oven are now occupied by non-Jews. Streets that were once playgrounds for little Jewish boys, who raced down them with their *peyos* (sidelocks) flying, are empty of Jewish children. The only place where one can get a sense of what Jewish life was once like is the cemetery. There, at least in the old Warsaw cemetery, the gravestones proudly announce that here rests a Levy or a *talmid chacham* (Torah scholar). Others tell us that this is the final resting place for a *tzenuah* (modest) wife and mother who lit Shabbos *licht* (candles) and gave *tzedakah* (charity) with an open hand.

Yet it is within this emptiness that I discover my first reason for making a trip to Poland. Methods for transmitting the Holocaust have changed drastically during the past sixty years. In the 1960s and the 1970s, the emphasis was on the six million *kedoshim* (martyrs), as a group. By the 1990s the emphasis had shifted to the individual narrative. The goal was to put a human face on what had become an impersonal and incomprehensible number. Both approaches have their positive points. Neither approach, though, gives the complete picture.

But standing in the middle of Warsaw—and every other Polish town that once had a sizeable Jewish population—does. The lack of Jewish life in a country that once teemed with Jewish life is so palpable that it practically slaps you on the face. And when standing in the middle of Warsaw with a group of Bais Yaakov girls whose grandparents and great-grandparents either came from Poland or were sent to concentration camps in Poland, the personal aspect of the tragedy also comes alive. Each girl has her own story to tell. In the Nozyk Synagogue, which is the only synagogue in Warsaw that survived the war, we hear the first one.

That story is introduced by Devorah Frankiel, whose father, Dr. Hershel Frankiel, and his parents and aunt were hidden by a Polish family. A member of that family, Stanislaw Wrobel, is already waiting for us as we take our seats inside the renovated shul.

Through an interpreter, Stanislaw explains that he was only 18 years old when he and his elderly parents agreed to hide the

Frankiels. After unsuccessfully trying to hide the family in the attic and cellar of their one-room farmhouse, Stanislaw turned to a shed that stood next to their barn. There he dug a pit about eight feet wide, eight feet long, and 30 inches deep, and this became the Frankiels hiding place for the next two years.

Soldiers from the Gestapo eventually showed up at the Wrobels' front door. They didn't find the pit, but the Wrobels were terrified and Stanislaw's parents wanted the Frankiels to leave. At this point in his story Stanislaw, who is now an elderly man, breaks down. Tearfully, he describes how the Frankiels begged him to let them remain. He couldn't say no.

The fact that both the Frankiels and Wrobrels survived the war was a miracle. But I can't imagine how anyone could survive living in a pit for two years, and so after the trip I telephone Dr. Frankiel and ask about his family's emotional and physical state at the time of their liberation.

"My father was ill," he tells me. "He could barely walk. I was the least affected by it, because I was young."

But they were alive. And what Dr. Frankiel chooses to stress is not the difficulty of their situation during the war but the selfless dedication of the Wrobel family, who risked their own lives to save the lives of a Jewish family.

I, on the other hand, who get nervous if an elevator door doesn't open at the exact second it's supposed to, can't stop thinking about that pit. The darkness. The dampness. The narrowness of the space.

"Serve Hashem with gladness," a voice whispers to me. Or course, I knew that I am supposed to serve Hashem with gladness before I went on this trip—after all, this verse is one of the most famous in *Sefer Tehillim* (*Book of Psalms*) and it was a favorite of Sarah Schenirer, the founder of Bais Yaakov. But that pit puts the verse on an entirely different level. Serve Hashem with gladness because you can stand up, see the sun, breathe in fresh air.

The list can go on and on, but it's time to go to the Warsaw Jewish Cemetery, where we daven at the graves of the Netziv, Rav Chaim Brisker, and other giants of Torah. Then we travel to Ger to daven beside the graves of Gerrer Rebbes and their wives. It's been a long and full day, and the terrifying vision of the pit has receded. But as I glance at the trip's itinerary another vision, this one even more disturbing, takes its place. For tomorrow we are scheduled to go to the capital city of the Kingdom of Night: Auschwitz.

I Have Set Hashem Before Me Always

"Now I see what I missed."

The speaker is Mrs. Lillian Listhaus, currently a resident of Brooklyn, New York, formerly a resident of Auschwitz-Birkenau, Lager C. She is standing outside of the crematorium of Auschwitz I. She hasn't flinched once during our tour.

Mrs. Listhaus has come on the trip with her daughter Mrs. Sharon Landau and her granddaughter Chani Landau. Also on the trip is another mother-daughter pair, Mrs. Golda Gross and Kiki Gross of Kew Gardens Hills. The presence of these mothers gives the trip an added dimension. The presence of Mrs. Listhaus takes the trip into an entirely different universe.

During the guided tour of Auschwitz I, which was mainly used for Polish political prisoners, Mrs. Listhaus is mostly silent. But when we reach Auschwitz II, which is also known as Birkenau and which is the camp where more than one million Jews were killed, the memories begin to tumble out.

"This is where we lived," she says, pointing to the windowless wooden barracks. Then she points into the distance. "That's where the crematoriums were. You could see the smoke and the flames."

The Birkenau crematoriums were destroyed by the Nazis in January 1945, in an attempt to hide what had gone on there from the advancing Soviet troops. The original wooden barracks were not intentionally destroyed, but they slowly disintegrated over time. So what is there to see today?

A replica of a row of barracks is on display. Behind the barracks are the eerie remnants of the original wooden structures, as well as the barbed wire fences that surrounded them. The forbidding red brick entrance to the camp is also still there, along with the train tracks that carried the trains filled with Jews to the spot inside the camp where the selection took place. While Mrs. Listhhaus and I stand beside these tracks, I ask her about her family's arrival at the concentration camp.

"Three of us went one way, and three of us went the other way," she says simply, referring to her parents and a sibling who were sent straight to the gas chamber and herself and two sisters who passed the initial selection.

"Every morning before breakfast we had to stand in line," she continues. "They made us stand from 5:30 until 7:00. God forbid you slouched, or they saw that you weren't with it. They took you out of the line and sent you to the gas chamber. They just took you out."

A few days after our visit to the concentration camp, I ask Mrs. Listhaus how she had the courage to make such a trip. Her daughter, Mrs. Sharon Landau, explains that she was the one who first broached the subject. But when Mrs. Listhaus immediately said yes, Mrs. Landau warned her, "Ma, don't answer so fast. We're not talking about a trip to Aruba. We're talking about Poland. Think it over. Talk to somebody."

Mrs. Listhaus sought out a friend from shul who was also a survivor. This friend had gone back to Poland, despite her initial fears about how she would react. When she told Mrs. Listhaus that it was the most calming experience she had ever had — that it had been a relief to visit the camp where her parents had perished — Mrs. Listhaus knew that she wanted to make the trip too.

"You have no idea how I felt to go to Birkenau," Mrs. Listhaus adds. "For 60 years I never went to the *kevarim* (graves) of my parents. I could never say *tefillos* (prayers) for them. I feel like a great weight has been lifted from my heart. And the rest of the trip — these girls — I feel like I'm their grandmother."

Those aren't just empty words. During our visit to Birkenau, Mrs. Listhaus becomes everyone's honorary *bubbe*. When she describes what it was like to be in the camp, the girls flock around her to hear her every word. And when we arrive at the spot of the demolished crematorium to say *tehillim* (psalms), the elderly woman is a source of strength for all the girls who have relatives who perished in those flames.

Of course, the group has been intellectually and emotionally prepared beforehand by Rebbetzin Blimie Birnbaum, who has taught at Bnos Chava Seminary for 21 years and who is the Educational Director of Nesivos. In addition to her lectures that explain responses to the Holocaust by rabbis such as Rabbi Avigdor Miller, Rabbi Shimshon Pincus, and the Nesivos Shalom, Rebbetzin Birnbaum — whose mother was a survivor of Birkenau, and who has three grandparents who perished there—has given us inspiring examples of responses that she saw in her own home.

"Although my mother and father spoke about the *Shoah* (Holocaust) from day one," Rebbetzin Birnbaum told the girls, "I never ever heard a question. Can you imagine? Never did they question. They didn't have a need to understand. They just accepted it with such *emunah* (faith). And that gave them the strength and the mental ability to recuperate and rebuild."

The girls standing in front of the giant abyss that was the Auschwitz-Birkenau crematorium—with tears streaming down their cheeks, but prayer books firmly clutched in their hands—are the fruits of that generation's *emunah* and heroic effort to rebuild. They also have no questions. But having taken to heart the second of Sarah Schenirer's five favorite verses—I have set Hashem before me always—they do have an answer, which we say together before we take our leave of this place of suffering and death: "*Shema Yisrael, Hashem Elokeinu, Hashem Echad!*" Hear, O Israel, the Lord our God, the Lord is One!

The Beginning of Wisdom is the Fear of Hashem

Late at night we arrive at a city that is synonymous with Jewish legends and dreams: Krakow. Kazimierz, the neighborhood that is the heart of Jewish Krakow, was where the Remah, Rav Moshe Isserles, had his yeshivah and *shul* and where he wrote his famous commentary on the *Shulchan Aruch*. It was in Kazimierz that Elijah the Prophet made his nightly visits to Rabbi Noson Nota Shapira, the Megaleh Amukos. And, of course, it was in Kazimierz that a poor Jew named Isaac Jakubowicz dreamt that a buried treasure lay in Prague, only to discover that this fortune was actually buried back in Krakow and in his own home.

Kazimierz is easily covered on foot. What's more, it's one of the few places in Poland where one can still sense a glimmer of the great *kedushah* (holiness) that once permeated its streets and squares. On our first morning we visit the Remah's *shul*, and then go to the *shul's* cemetery to pray by the graves of the Remah, the Bach, the Megaleh Amukos, and the Tosafos Yom Tov. Afterward, we pay a visit to the magnificent *shul* built by Isaac Jakubowicz and see the outside of the home where the Megaleh Amukos lived. Kazimierz was also home to ordinary Jews, of course. And so during our visit we see the still busy square where Jewish butchers once slaughtered their chickens and *baalabustas* (housewives) haggled over the price of those chickens, as well as potatoes and fish.

But Krakow is a very special stop for another reason: It was here that a young woman named Sarah Schenirer dreamed a dream that would transform the entire Torah-observant world. The Bais Yaakov educational system that she created and cultivated restored Jewish pride to thousands of young girls who had been taught in Polish public schools to despise their heritage. And she engraved on their hearts another one of her favorite verses from *Sefer Tehillim*, the knowledge that wisdom—true wisdom—can only be found in the Torah and the person who has *yiras Hashem* (awe of God).

"Sarah Schenirer understood that the truth of Torah is eternal. She inspired her students to see the beauty of the world through the beauty of Torah," explains Rebbetzin Esther Elfenbein, another of the Nesivos educators on the trip and assistant principal of Me'ohr Bais Yaakov Teachers Seminary, as our bus approaches the Jewish cemetery where Sarah Schenirer is buried.

"She also taught her students to have pride in being part of a group—Bais Yaakov," Rebbetzin Elfenbein continues. "We are the bearers of that torch. We have to take the message of Sarah Schenirer and continue to bring the light of Bais Yaakov into the world."

By the time we reach Sarah Schenirer's gravestone, the gray clouds that have been following us all day decide to let loose a downpour of bone-chilling rain. The girls silently open their umbrellas and begin to pray—and pray. Even when Rabbi Wunder signals that it's time to return to the bus, they refuse to be torn away. Finally, though, we must journey to our next stop: Number 10 Stanislaw Street, where the original Bais Yaakov Teachers Seminary building is located.

Today the building is used by non-Jews, and so the girls have to be content with taking photos outside the building. In a few days, though, we will be in Lublin, where we will be able to enter another famous landmark—Yeshivas Chochmei Lublin, the yeshivah established by Rabbi Meir Shapiro.

Like Sarah Schenirer, Rabbi Shapiro and his wife had no children. But through the institutions that he established—his yeshivah and his *daf yomi* program, where one page of Talmud is learned every day, until the entire Talmud has been completed—Rabbi Shapiro merited to have students that numbered in the thousands and tens of thousands. The inspiring examples set by these two great Torah personalities will be discussed again and again during the following days. But it is Rebbetzin Birnbaum who expresses both the vision and the challenge so eloquently, during the lecture that she gives in the Yeshivas Chochmei Lublin *beis medrash* (study hall).

"See the power of the individual," she tells the girls. "See how much impact one person can have on *klal Yisrael* (the Jewish community). They had vision. They had a dream. They had drive.

"Within a few days you girls will go home. Remember what you can do. Dream. Have vision. Have drive. And remember to *daven* (pray). *Daven* to Hakodesh Baruch Hu (the Holy One, blessed be He) that He should give you the *kochos*—physical strength, spiritual strength, and *siyatta d'shayamah* (help from Heaven)—to build a beautiful home and contribute to *klal Yisrael* in your own unique way."

Teach Us to Count the Days

There is so much more to write about: the visit to Tarnow, where we saw the heartbreaking *kever achim* of the 800 children who were taken to the forest and murdered; Lansut, where we saw a magnificent *shul* that escaped being destroyed by the Nazis; the afternoon spent at the Majdanek concentration camp.

Then there was the visit to one of the most beautiful villages in Poland, Kuzmir. This is where the Modzitz chassidic dynasty began, and our visit was enhanced by the presence of a granddaughter of the Modzitzer Rebbe, who was with us on the tour. We also spent an afternoon in Tiktin, another beautifully preserved shtetl, and followed the path of the approximately 1,500 Jews who were marched into the forest on August 25, 1941 and massacred by a Nazi firing squad. There were visits to the graves of the Chozeh of Lublin and the Maharshal—and, of course, there was the unforgettable hour we spent *davening* at the grave of Rebbe Elimelech of Lizensk.

"It's an overwhelmingly rich trip," comments Mrs. Golda Gross. "And experiencing it with my daughter Kiki has been an experience that we'll be able to share for life."

In addition to being Kiki's mother and the daughter of Holocaust survivors, Mrs. Gross is the General Studies Principal of Yeshiva Ketana of Long Island. She has also taken courses in teaching the Holocaust and so I ask her about something that has been on mind throughout the entire trip—the girls' ability to not get stuck in the sadness. Was that due to their education and the preparation they received before the trip, I wonder? Or is it just a natural resilience that comes with being young?

"You can't really be prepared for Auschwitz," Mrs. Gross replies. "No matter how much you prepare for it, it's still heart-wrenching. That's why it's important to have emotional support.

"When we came to the end of our tour of Auschwitz I, and the girls were crying and saying *tehillim*, I was surprised when Rebbetzin Birnbaum said to the girls, 'Let's sing a song.' I wondered if she was trying to create something that wasn't there. But then I saw that when the girls joined in and sang with such emotion—the tears stopped. It was such a perfect transition. Putting those emotions into a song that has meaning and feeling enabled them to walk out of it. Because you can't stay there. We have to transmit the *Shoah*, but we have to be able to walk out of it and look to the future."

Mrs. Gross then adds, "We tend to think of the Nazis as animals. But they were human beings who made choices. We can't forget that. It's a very important lesson for life that we are the choices we make."

This comment transports me back to Krakow, where Rebbetzin Elfenbein, describing the very different choices that Sarah Schenirer made with her life, told the girls, "One of Sarah Schenirer's favorite *pesukim* (verses) was 'Teach us to count the days.' She wanted to make every minute important and meaningful."

The Torah of Hashem Is Perfect, It Restores the Soul

Those who have been counting the days described in this article will have noticed that one very important day is missing: Shabbos. We spend the day in Krakow. But how can one describe the feeling of *achdus* (unity) in the room where we eat the delicious Shabbos meals that have been prepared by Rav Fried and his staff—or the incredibly moving sight of more than 50 Bais Yaakov girls singing Shabbos songs in Krakow, the place where Bais Yaakov began?

Our Shabbos meals are "spiced" by inspiring Torah lectures given by Rebbetzin Birnbaum and Rebbetzin Elfenbein. Several of the girls also speak, including Rivkah Steinberg, who comments, "Our generation has a big responsibility. We'll have to transmit the stories of the *Shoah* to our children and grandchildren—who won't have the opportunity to hear them directly from survivors."

At the end of Shabbos, the girls form a circle and we all begin to dance. As I glance over at Mrs. Listhaus, I realize that I am witnessing a very special moment in Jewish history. For what Rivkah Steinberg has said is true.

Hers is the last generation that will have the privilege of walking through the valleys of death that are Auschwitz, Majdanek, and Treblinka in the presence of those who survived that *gehenom* (hell). Hers is also the last generation that will have the privilege of dancing on Motzaei Shabbos and in Poland with those who made the incredible decision, despite all they had endured, to cling to Hashem's Torah with simple faith—a decision that has enabled them, and all the generations that have come after them, to choose life.

And so I leave the final words of this story to Mrs. Listhaus, who has given the girls this parting blessing: "May you all be married by the time you're twenty-two!"

—July 2009

If you enjoyed Day Trips to Jewish History, *please let others know by leaving a review at your favorite online bookseller. Thank you!*

SELECTED BIBLIOGRAPHY

Altabe, David F., *Judeo-Spanish as a Language of Liturgy and Religious Identification*, 1981

Ben David, Nachum and Slutz, Shlomo, *Dehiya al-Kahina Malkat Afriqah*, Emunos, Tel Aviv, 1933.
Benveniste, Arthur, *500th Anniversary of the Forced Conversion of the Jews of Portugal*, 1997
Berger, Shulamith Z., *Tehines, Women's Prayers*
Bloom, Harold, *The Jewish Question: British Anti-Semitism*, 2010
Brook, Kevin Alan, *An Introduction to the History of Khazaria*, 2004

Center for Judaic Studies, Penn Libaries, *From Written to Printed Text: The Transmission of Jewish Tradition*
Chouraqui, Andre, *Between East and West: A History of the Jews of North Africa*, JPS, 1968
Cohen, Martin A.: *The Autobiography of Luis de Carvajal, the Younger* (translator), American Jewish Historical Quarterly, Vol. 55, No. 3 (March 1966)
-- *The Martyr*, JPS, 1973.
Cohn, Paul, *Sao Tome, Journey to the Abyss, Portugal's Stolen Children*, 2010

Edofolks.com. *Discovery of Benin*
Endelman, Todd M., *The Jews of Georgian England 1714-1830: Tradition and Change in a Liberal Society*, Univeristy of Michigan Press, 1979

Garfield, Richard, *A History of Sao Tome Island, 1470-1655*, 1992
Gerber, Jane S., *The Jews of Spain: A History of the Sephardic Experience*, Free Press, 1994,
Gluckel of Hameln, *The Memoirs of Gluckel of Hameln*, trans. Marvin Lowenthal, Schocken Books, 1977
Goldblatt, David, *Jewish Women of the Southwest*
Golden, Peter B., *Khazar Studies*, 1980
Golinken, David, *Solomon Schechter, Rivka Lipa and Jewish Women's Studies*, 2005
Gross, John, *Shylock: A Legend and Its Legacy*, Touchstone, 1994

Heise, Jennifer A., *Women and Medicine in the Middle Ages and Renaissance*, 2003

Heller, Rabbi Yom Tov Lipmann, *A Chronicle of Hardship and Hope*, CIS Publishers, 1991

Hull, Richard, *Jews and Judaism in African History*, Markus Wiener Publishers, 2009

Jewish Encyclopedia, 1906
Jewish History Sourcebook
Jewish Virtual Library
Jewish Women's Archive
JPS Guide to Jewish Women: Taitz, Emily; Henry, Sondra; Tallen, Cheryl, *Rivkah bat Meir Tiktiner, Sixteenth century educator, author, & scholar.*

Kay, Devra. *Seyder Tkhines: The Forgotten Book of Common Prayer for Jewish Women*, Philadelphia, 2004.

Kushner, Aviya, *Ladino Today: Is the Language of Sephardic Jews Undergoing a Revival?*

Lazar, Moshe, *Scorched Parchments and Tortured Memories: The "Jewishness" of the Anussim (Crypto-Jews)*

Levine, Yael, *Simkhes Toyre Lid le-Rivkah Tiktiner*

Liba, Moshe, *Jewish Children Slaves in Sao Tome*

Lobban, Richard, *Jews in Cape Verde and the Guinea Coast*, 1996

Longoria, Frank, *17th Century Conversos in Amsterdam*

Marcus, Jacob, *The Jew in the Medieval World: A Sourcebook*, JPS, 1938.

Marks, Gil, *Encyclopedia of Jewish Food*, Lifestyle, 2010.

Montefiore, Lady Judith, *A Jewish Manual, Or Practical Information in Jewish And Modern Cookery*, 1846

Moseley, Marcus, *Being for Myself Alone: Origins of Jewish Autobiography*

Mozeson, Isaac E., *The Word: The Dictionary That Reveals the Hebrew Source of English*, S.P.I. Books, 2001

Naggar Betty, *Old Clothes Men, 18th and 19th Centuries*

Newit, Malyn, *Formal and Informal Empire in the Portuguese Empire*, 2001

— *The Portuguese in West Africa, 1415-1670: A Documentary History* (Edited by), Cambridge Univeristy Press, 2010

Old Yishuv Court Museum
Orfali, Moshe, *The Fast of Esther in the Lore of the Marranos*, 2002

Palomino, Michael, *Jews in Brazil 02: Agriculture Settlements*, 2008

Raphael, David, *The Expulsion 1492 Chronicles*, Carmi House Press, 1992
Rich, Jennifer, *The Merchant Formerly Known as Jew: Redefining the Rhetoric of Merchantry in Shakespeare's Merchant of Venice*
Rivkah Bas Meir, *Meneket Rivkah: A Manual of Wisdom and Piety for Jewish Women,* edited by Frauke von Rohden, trans. Samuel Spinner, JPS 2009
Robinson III, Charles M., *Flour Tortillas and Other JewishLegacies of Colonial Texas*, 2001
Rogers, Jami, *Shylock and History*
Rosenberg, Edgar, *From Shylock to Svengali: Jewish Stereotypes in English Fiction*, Stanford University Press, 1960
Rosenthal, Monroe and Isaac Mozeson, *Wars of the Jews*, Hippocrene Books, NY, 1990
Roth, Cecil, *Dona Gracia and the House of Nasi,* JPS, 1977
— *A History of the Great Synagogue,* 1950
— *A History of the Marronos,* 1966
Roth, Norman, *Jewish Moneylending*, Medieval Jewish Civilization, An Encyclopedia, Routledge, 2002
Rozovsky, Lorne, *Will Ladino Rise Again?*

Santos, Richard, *Silent Heritage: The Sephardim and the Colonization of the Spanish North American Frontier, 1492-1600*, New Sepharad Press, 2000
Seigal, Eliezer, *Esther the Marrano*, 1995
Stanislawaski, Michael, *Autobiographical Jews: Essays in Jewish Self-Fashioning*, Multiculural Review, 2005

Turniansky, Chava, *Old Yiddish Language and Literature*
Wolf, Lucien, *Essays in Jewish History*, 1934

ABOUT THE AUTHOR

LIBI ASTAIRE is an award-winning author who often writes about Jewish history. In addition to her Jewish Regency Mystery Series featuring Ezra Melamed, General Well'ngone and the Earl of Gravel Lane, she is the author of *Terra Incognita,* a novel about modern-day descendants of Spain's crypto-Jews, *The Banished Heart*, a novel about Shakespeare's writing of *The Merchant of Venice*, and several volumes of chassidic tales. She lives in Jerusalem, Israel.

Also by Libi Astaire:

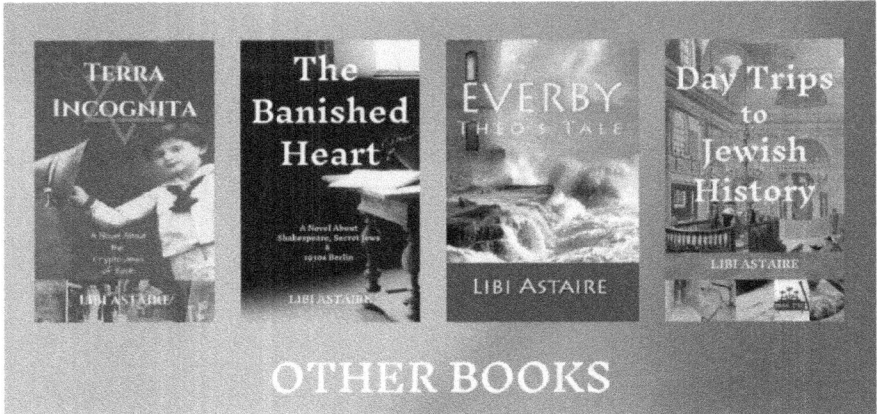

OTHER BOOKS

Terra Incognita
"Masterfully weaves deep well-developed characters with historical underpinnings that make this a must read" — Amazon.com

Sant Joan Januz. A village locked away from strangers' prying eyes. But when Vidal Bonet, a young man with big dreams, tries to turn his sleepy Catalan village into a world-class resort, he unwittingly stumbles upon a long-buried family secret that threatens to destroy everyone he loves.

The Banished Heart
"A surprisingly GREAT read" — Goodreads.com

Who controls a person's identity; a society's notion of who is noble and good – and who should be shunned and despised? For Paul Hoffmann, an aspiring Shakespearean scholar in 1930s Berlin, disturbing questions about his long-buried Jewish identity have suddenly become a matter of life and death.

Everby: Theo's Tale

"Beautiful writing, fascinating story line, lots of food for thought" – Amazon.com

When Theo—a misfit with a passion for music—is rejected from a top music school, he feels like he has nothing left to live for. His awful day gets even worse when he falls into Everby, a "Post-Catastrophe" kingdom where hope and happiness are banished in a cynical struggle for wealth and power. There he unwillingly gets caught up in court intrigue. But Theo is no storybook hero. Or so he thinks, until tragedy forces him to realize that in Everby there are only two options: Die or dare to dream again.

GET COZY WITH A FUN MYSTERY

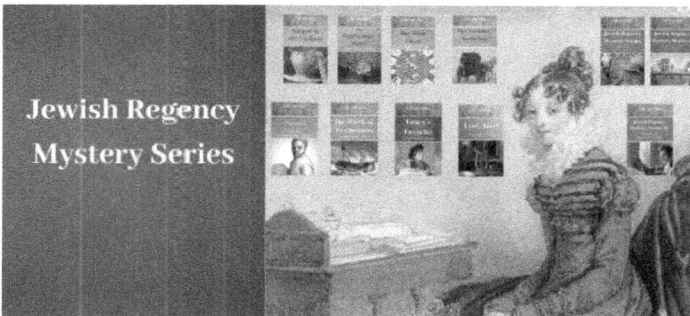

"A more unique and colorful cast of characters would be difficult to find." - Amazon.com

Mystery is rife and so is the fun when a crew of loveably quirky characters set out to solve a slew of crimes causing havoc in Regency London's Jewish community. Included in the **Jewish Regency Mystery Series** are:

Tempest in the Tea Room   *The Doppelganger's Dance*
The Moor Taker   *The Vanisher Variations*
Matzah Mia!   *The Wreck of Two Brothers*
Fancy's Favorite   *Lyre, Liar!*
Jewish Regency Mystery Stories, Vol. I, II, and III

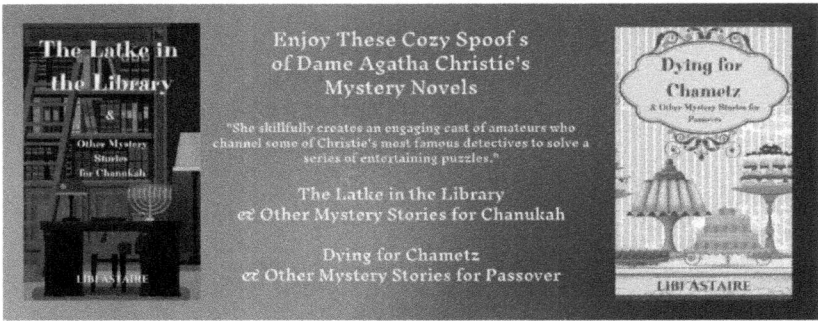
The Latke in the Library & Other Mystery Stories for Chanukah

"Fun and Clever" – Amazon.com

Oy vey! When elderly mystery writer Agatha Krinsky falls for the fifth time, her nephew Sheldon insists she move into an assisted living facility. True to form, on her first day in her new home Agatha discovers a body in the library. But the staff won't take her seriously, and even her luncheon companions — Herschel Perlow, Miss Eppel, and Ronny and Rubles Bernfeld — are more interested in talking about bodies they encountered in their earlier careers than helping Agatha solve her mystery.

Dying for Chametz & Other Mystery Stories for Passover

"An outstanding book with charming and funny characters and beautifully woven Jewish ideas" – Amazon.com

Barnet Court's connoisseurs of crime are back! Join retired Jewish detectives Herschel Perlow, Miss Janice Eppel, Ronny and Rubles Bernfeld, and author Agatha Krinsky as they tackle new mysteries to solve in this humorous, Passover-themed homage to Dame Agatha Christie.

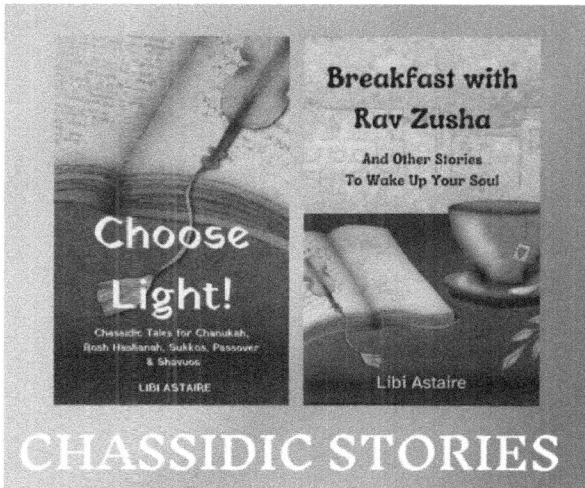
CHASSIDIC STORIES

CHOOSE LIGHT!
Chassidic Tales for Chanukah, Rosh Hashanah, Sukkos, Passover, and Shavuos

Let the Chassidic masters give you a new appreciation for the Jewish holidays, as well as insights into the Jewish people's ability to remain joyous and optimistic even during the darkest times.

BREAKFAST WITH RAV ZUSHA
And Other Stories To Wake Up Your Soul

Our Jewish Sages understood there is no such thing as an unimportant person or action. Every day we have opportunities to become better - and even extraordinary - people. With these inspiring and entertaining stories to guide you, you'll learn how to spot these opportunities too.

For more information about these and other books, visit Libi's website at libiastaire.weebly.com.

www.ingramcontent.com/pod-product-compliance
Lightning Source LLC
Chambersburg PA
CBHW030818090426
42737CB00009B/773